Your
Chinese
Horoscope
2015

Neil Somerville

What the Year of the Goat holds in store for you

Your
Chinese
Horoscope
2015

HARPER
element

HarperElement
An Imprint of HarperCollins*Publishers*
77–85 Fulham Palace Road,
Hammersmith, London W6 8JB

www.harpercollins.co.uk

and *HarperElement* are trademarks of
HarperCollins*Publishers* Ltd

Published by HarperElement 2014

1 3 5 7 9 10 8 6 4 2

A catalogue record of this book is
available from the British Library

ISBN 978-0-00-754451-6

Printed and bound in Great Britain by
Clays Ltd, St Ives plc

FSC™ is a non-profit international organisation established to promote
the responsible management of the world's forests. Products carrying the
FSC label are independently certified to assure consumers that they come
from forests that are managed to meet the social, economic and
ecological needs of present and future generations,
and other controlled sources.

Find out more about HarperCollins and the environment at
www.harpercollins.co.uk/green

About the Author

Neil Somerville is one of the leading writers in the West on Chinese horoscopes. He has been interested in Eastern forms of divination for many years and believes that much can be learned from the ancient wisdom of the East. His annual book on Chinese horoscopes has built up an international following and he is also the author of *What's Your Chinese Love Sign?* (Thorsons, 2000; HarperElement, 2013), *Chinese Success Signs* (Thorsons, 2001) and *The Answers* (Element, 2004).

Neil Somerville was born in the year of the Water Snake. His wife was born under the sign of the Monkey, his son is an Ox and daughter a Horse.

TO ROS, RICHARD AND EMILY

As we march through life,
we each have our hopes, our ambitions and our dreams.

Sometimes fate and circumstance will assist us,
sometimes we will struggle and despair,
but march we must.

For it is those who keep going,
and who keep their aspirations alive,
who stand the greatest chance of securing what they want.

March determinedly,
and your determination will, in some way, be rewarded.

Neil Somerville

Contents

Acknowledgements

In writing *Your Chinese Horoscope 2015* I am grateful for the assistance and invaluable support that those around me have given.

I would also like to acknowledge Theodora Lau's *The Handbook of Chinese Horoscopes* (Harper & Row, 1979; Arrow, 1981), which was particularly useful to me in my research.

In addition to Ms Lau's work, I commend the following books to those who wish to find out more about Chinese horoscopes: Kristyna Arcarti, *Chinese Horoscopes for Beginners* (Headway, 1995); Catherine Aubier, *Chinese Zodiac Signs* (Arrow, 1984), series of 12 books; E. A. Crawford and Teresa Kennedy, *Chinese Elemental Astrology* (Piatkus Books, 1992); Paula Delsol, *Chinese Horoscopes* (Pan, 1973); Barry Fantoni, *Barry Fantoni's Chinese Horoscopes* (Warner, 1994); Bridget Giles and the Diagram Group, *Chinese Astrology* (HarperCollins, 1996); Kwok Man-Ho, *Complete Chinese Horoscopes* (Sunburst Books, 1995); Lori Reid, *The Complete Book of Chinese Horoscopes* (Element Books, 1997); Paul Rigby and Harvey Bean, *Chinese Astrologics* (Publications Division, South China Morning Post Ltd, 1981); Ruth Q. Sun, *The Asian Animal Zodiac* (Charles E. Tuttle Company, Inc., 1996); Derek Walters, *Ming Shu* (Pagoda Books, 1987), *The Chinese Astrology Workbook* (The Aquarian Press, 1988) and *Chinese Horoscope Bible* (Godsfield Press, 2008); Suzanne White, *The New Astrology* (Pan, 1987), *The New Chinese Astrology* (Pan, 1994) and *Chinese Astrology Plain and Simple* (Eden Grove Editions, 1998).

Introduction

The origins of Chinese horoscopes have been lost in the mists of time. It is known, however, that oriental astrologers practised their art many thousands of years ago and even today Chinese astrology continues to fascinate and intrigue.

In Chinese astrology there are 12 signs named after 12 different animals. No one quite knows how the signs acquired their names, but there is one legend that offers an explanation. According to this legend, one Chinese New Year the Buddha invited all the animals in his kingdom to come before him. Unfortunately, for reasons best known to the animals, only 12 turned up. The first to arrive was the Rat, followed by the Ox, Tiger, Rabbit, Dragon, Snake, Horse, Goat, Monkey, Rooster, Dog and finally Pig. In gratitude, the Buddha decided to name a year after each of the animals and that those born during that year would inherit some of the personality of that animal. Therefore those born in the year of the Ox would be hardworking, resolute and stubborn, just like the Ox, while those born in the year of the Dog would be loyal and faithful, just like the Dog. While it is not possible that everyone born in a particular year can have all the characteristics of the sign, it is incredible what similarities do occur, and this is partly where the fascination of Chinese horoscopes lies.

In addition to the 12 signs of the Chinese zodiac there are five elements and these have a strengthening or moderating influence upon the signs. Details about the effects of the elements are given in each of the chapters on the signs.

To find out which sign you were born under, refer to the tables on the following pages. As the Chinese year is based on the lunar year and does not start until late January or early February, it is particularly important for anyone born in those two months to check carefully the dates of the Chinese year in which they were born.

Also included, in the appendix, are two charts showing the compatibility between the signs for personal and business relationships and details about the signs ruling the different hours of the day. From this it is possible to locate your ascendant and, as in Western astrology, this has a significant influence on your personality.

In writing this book I have taken the unusual step of combining the intriguing nature of Chinese horoscopes with the Western desire to know what the future holds, and have based my interpretations upon various factors relating to each of the signs. Over the years in which *Your Chinese Horoscope* has been published I have been pleased that so many have found the sections on the forthcoming year of interest and hope that the horoscope has been constructive and useful. Remember, though, that at all times you are master of your own destiny.

I sincerely hope that *Your Chinese Horoscope 2015* will prove interesting and helpful for the year ahead.

The Chinese Years

Ox	6 February	1913	to	25 January	1914
Tiger	26 January	1914	to	13 February	1915
Rabbit	14 February	1915	to	2 February	1916
Dragon	3 February	1916	to	22 January	1917
Snake	23 January	1917	to	10 February	1918
Horse	11 February	1918	to	31 January	1919
Goat	1 February	1919	to	19 February	1920
Monkey	20 February	1920	to	7 February	1921
Rooster	8 February	1921	to	27 January	1922
Dog	28 January	1922	to	15 February	1923
Pig	16 February	1923	to	4 February	1924
Rat	5 February	1924	to	23 January	1925
Ox	24 January	1925	to	12 February	1926
Tiger	13 February	1926	to	1 February	1927
Rabbit	2 February	1927	to	22 January	1928
Dragon	23 January	1928	to	9 February	1929
Snake	10 February	1929	to	29 January	1930
Horse	30 January	1930	to	16 February	1931
Goat	17 February	1931	to	5 February	1932
Monkey	6 February	1932	to	25 January	1933
Rooster	26 January	1933	to	13 February	1934
Dog	14 February	1934	to	3 February	1935
Pig	4 February	1935	to	23 January	1936
Rat	24 January	1936	to	10 February	1937
Ox	11 February	1937	to	30 January	1938
Tiger	31 January	1938	to	18 February	1939
Rabbit	19 February	1939	to	7 February	1940
Dragon	8 February	1940	to	26 January	1941

Snake	27 January	1941	to	14 February	1942
Horse	15 February	1942	to	4 February	1943
Goat	5 February	1943	to	24 January	1944
Monkey	25 January	1944	to	12 February	1945
Rooster	13 February	1945	to	1 February	1946
Dog	2 February	1946	to	21 January	1947
Pig	22 January	1947	to	9 February	1948
Rat	10 February	1948	to	28 January	1949
Ox	29 January	1949	to	16 February	1950
Tiger	17 February	1950	to	5 February	1951
Rabbit	6 February	1951	to	26 January	1952
Dragon	27 January	1952	to	13 February	1953
Snake	14 February	1953	to	2 February	1954
Horse	3 February	1954	to	23 January	1955
Goat	24 January	1955	to	11 February	1956
Monkey	12 February	1956	to	30 January	1957
Rooster	31 January	1957	to	17 February	1958
Dog	18 February	1958	to	7 February	1959
Pig	8 February	1959	to	27 January	1960
Rat	28 January	1960	to	14 February	1961
Ox	15 February	1961	to	4 February	1962
Tiger	5 February	1962	to	24 January	1963
Rabbit	25 January	1963	to	12 February	1964
Dragon	13 February	1964	to	1 February	1965
Snake	2 February	1965	to	20 January	1966
Horse	21 January	1966	to	8 February	1967
Goat	9 February	1967	to	29 January	1968
Monkey	30 January	1968	to	16 February	1969
Rooster	17 February	1969	to	5 February	1970
Dog	6 February	1970	to	26 January	1971
Pig	27 January	1971	to	14 February	1972
Rat	15 February	1972	to	2 February	1973
Ox	3 February	1973	to	22 January	1974
Tiger	23 January	1974	to	10 February	1975
Rabbit	11 February	1975	to	30 January	1976

Dragon	31 January	1976	to	17 February	1977
Snake	18 February	1977	to	6 February	1978
Horse	7 February	1978	to	27 January	1979
Goat	28 January	1979	to	15 February	1980
Monkey	16 February	1980	to	4 February	1981
Rooster	5 February	1981	to	24 January	1982
Dog	25 January	1982	to	12 February	1983
Pig	13 February	1983	to	1 February	1984
Rat	2 February	1984	to	19 February	1985
Ox	20 February	1985	to	8 February	1986
Tiger	9 February	1986	to	28 January	1987
Rabbit	29 January	1987	to	16 February	1988
Dragon	17 February	1988	to	5 February	1989
Snake	6 February	1989	to	26 January	1990
Horse	27 January	1990	to	14 February	1991
Goat	15 February	1991	to	3 February	1992
Monkey	4 February	1992	to	22 January	1993
Rooster	23 January	1993	to	9 February	1994
Dog	10 February	1994	to	30 January	1995
Pig	31 January	1995	to	18 February	1996
Rat	19 February	1996	to	6 February	1997
Ox	7 February	1997	to	27 January	1998
Tiger	28 January	1998	to	15 February	1999
Rabbit	16 February	1999	to	4 February	2000
Dragon	5 February	2000	to	23 January	2001
Snake	24 January	2001	to	11 February	2002
Horse	12 February	2002	to	31 January	2003
Goat	1 February	2003	to	21 January	2004
Monkey	22 January	2004	to	8 February	2005
Rooster	9 February	2005	to	28 January	2006
Dog	29 January	2006	to	17 February	2007
Pig	18 February	2007	to	6 February	2008
Rat	7 February	2008	to	25 January	2009
Ox	26 January	2009	to	13 February	2010
Tiger	14 February	2010	to	2 February	2011

Rabbit	3 February	2011	to	22 January	2012
Dragon	23 January	2012	to	9 February	2013
Snake	10 February	2013	to	30 January	2014
Horse	31 January	2014	to	18 February	2015
Goat	19 February	2015	to	7 February	2016

Note

The names of the signs in the Chinese zodiac occasionally differ, although the characteristics of the signs remain the same. In some books the Ox is referred to as the Buffalo or Bull, the Rabbit as the Hare or Cat, the Goat as the Sheep and the Pig as the Boar.

For the sake of convenience, the male gender is used throughout this book. Unless otherwise stated, the characteristics of the signs apply to both sexes.

Welcome to the
Year of the Goat

Whether clambering over mountain rocks or grazing in lush green fields, there is an air of contentment about the goat. Unless troubled by some threat, he is generally at ease with himself and his genial nature will have a bearing on events in his own year.

On the world stage, the emphasis will be on reconciliation. Some troubled and warring nations will now take steps to seek peace and adopt measures that will allow them to be more accepted by the world community. Important settlements will be reached and this will be a year for dialogue, diplomacy and greater understanding. It was, for instance, in the last Goat year, 2003, that India and Pakistan restored full diplomatic ties and brought to an end years of conflict in Kashmir, and other Goat years have seen the historic Camp David peace talks, the signing of the SALT II nuclear weapons agreement and the abolition of apartheid in South Africa. The stated reason for the 2003 invasion of Iraq was to rid the nation of weapons of mass destruction and so make the world a safer place. This drive for security – and understanding – will be very evident this year.

In addition to the many high-level meetings that will characterize the year, industrialists and political leaders will be keen to stimulate trade, and significant agreements are likely to be made between countries and other trading communities. Many governments will invest heavily in infrastructure programmes to attract investment and create jobs as well as improve conditions. The accent will be on growth and moving forward, and the economies of many countries will benefit as a result.

Much attention will also be focused on environmental matters, particularly on protecting the world's resources, and there will be a corresponding increase in the use of renewable energy, with many authorities promoting a cleaner and greener message. Indeed, the theme of Expo 2015, which will be held in Milan, will be 'Feeding the Planet, Energy for Life' and the focus will be on the availability of food and water and the state of nutrition and health in years to come.

There is also likely to be significant growth in the organic food industry, with many people paying greater attention to their diet and making positive changes to their lifestyle. Humanitarian issues, too, will feature prominently, with international bodies launching major initiatives as well as increasing awareness of the suffering of some of the peoples of the world. Again, some remarkable achievements can ensue, and the year will see some regions transformed as a result. Interestingly, it was in the previous Goat year that the World Health Organisation was alerted to the threat of the SARS virus and what followed was the most effective response to an epidemic in history.

This will also be an election year in Britain. Over the long campaign, considerable volatility will be seen as the issues are hotly debated. It will be a searching campaign, too, with much attention focused on considering alternative ways forward. The result may not be as clear-cut as some may wish.

Goat individuals are born under the sign of art, and the arts can look forward to an exciting and innovative year. In many countries, major exhibitions and cultural events will capture the imagination. New artists, with their own distinctive styles, will come to prominence, and in the theatre and cinema major productions that enthral many.

The fashion industry will also see the emergence of new trends, with some distinctive styles and even some bizarre embellishments being introduced. The Goat year is all for style, colour and experimentation.

Goat years can be groundbreaking; it was in a Goat year that the Beatles released their concept album *Sgt Pepper's Lonely Hearts Club Band*, which not only featured songs destined to become classics but was famed for its iconic cover. Goat years are times of self-expression and creativity, and a feel-good factor is likely to be evident in much that is produced this year.

The Goat year will also bring excitement. On the sports field, new records will be created and some particularly competitive tournaments will take place. For the sports enthusiast, the year will contain many delights, with the Rugby World Cup, for example, generating great interest not only in the competing nations but also beyond.

And the beyond too will be significant this year, as the NASA space probe *Dawn* is scheduled to explore the dwarf planet Ceres and *New Horizons*, another spacecraft, to fly by and study Pluto. During the year outer space will reveal yet of its more secrets.

Another aspect of the Goat year is that it favours relationships and the family. It is a time when many people will spend more time with others and appreciate what they have in their lives. Many people in love will also come together, cement relationships, marry and start a family.

Overall, Goat years offer hope, although, as is always the way, there will also be flashpoints, tragedy and disasters. During this year, certain territories could be affected by heatwaves and there will also be moments of volatility – goats can, after all, be fickle! – but the underlying trend will be one of consensus, growth and moving forward. Over the year not only will historic agreements be forged and solutions found to some of the world's concerns, but the individual will enjoy a more balanced lifestyle and realize inner potential.

For us all, the Goat year offers possibility and I hope that by using your strengths, you will prosper as well as find contentment.

I wish you good luck and good fortune.

Your
Chinese
Horoscope
2015

5 February 1924 to 23 January 1925 — *Wood Rat*

24 January 1936 to 10 February 1937 — *Fire Rat*

10 February 1948 to 28 January 1949 — *Earth Rat*

28 January 1960 to 14 February 1961 — *Metal Rat*

15 February 1972 to 2 February 1973 — *Water Rat*

2 February 1984 to 19 February 1985 — *Wood Rat*

19 February 1996 to 6 February 1997 — *Fire Rat*

7 February 2008 to 25 January 2009 — *Earth Rat*

The Rat

The Personality of the Rat

To see,
and to see what others do not see.
That is true vision.

The Rat is born under the sign of charm. He is intelligent, popular and loves attending parties and large social gatherings. He is able to establish friendships with remarkable ease and people generally feel relaxed in his company. He is a very social creature and is genuinely interested in the welfare and activities of others. He has a good understanding of human nature and his advice and opinions are often sought.

The Rat is a hard and diligent worker. He is also very imaginative and is never short of ideas. However, he does sometimes lack the confidence to promote his ideas and this can often prevent him from securing the recognition he deserves.

The Rat is very observant and many Rats have made excellent writers and journalists. The Rat also excels at personnel and PR work and any job that brings him into contact with people and the media. His skills are particularly appreciated in times of crisis, for the Rat has an incredibly strong sense of self-preservation. When it comes to finding a way out of an awkward situation, he is certain to be the one who comes up with a solution.

The Rat loves to be where there is a lot of action, but should he ever find himself in a very bureaucratic or restrictive environment he can become a stickler for discipline and routine. He is also something of an opportunist and is constantly on the lookout for ways in which he can improve his wealth and lifestyle. He rarely lets an opportunity go by and can become involved in so many plans and schemes that he sometimes squanders his energies and achieves very little as a result. He is also rather gullible and can be taken in by those less scrupulous than himself.

Another characteristic of the Rat is his attitude towards money. He is very thrifty and to some he may appear a little mean. The reason for this is purely that he likes to keep his money within his family. He can be most generous to his partner, his children and close friends and relatives. He can also be generous to himself, for he often finds it impossible to deprive himself of any luxury or object he fancies. He is very acquisitive and can be a notorious hoarder. He also hates waste and is rarely prepared to throw anything away. He can be rather greedy and will rarely refuse an invitation to a free meal or a complimentary ticket to a lavish function.

The Rat is a good conversationalist, although he can occasionally be a little indiscreet. He can be highly critical of others – for an honest and unbiased opinion, the Rat is a superb critic – and will sometimes use confidential information to his own advantage. However, as he has such a bright and irresistible nature, most people are prepared to forgive him his slight indiscretions.

Throughout his long and eventful life the Rat will make many friends and will find that he is especially well suited to those born under his own sign and those of the Ox, Dragon and Monkey. He can also get on well with those born under the signs of the Tiger, Snake, Rooster, Dog and Pig, but the rather sensitive Rabbit and Goat will find him a little too critical and blunt for their liking. The Horse and Rat will also find it difficult to get on with each other – the Rat craves security and will find the Horse's changeable moods and rather independent nature a little unsettling.

The Rat is very family orientated and will do anything to please his nearest and dearest. He is exceptionally loyal to his parents and can himself be a very caring and loving parent. He will take an interest in all his children's activities and see that they want for nothing. He usually has a large family.

The female Rat has a kindly, outgoing nature and involves herself in a multitude of different activities. She has a wide circle of friends, enjoys entertaining and is an attentive hostess. She is also conscientious about the upkeep of her home and has good taste in home furnishings. She is most supportive to the other members of her family and, due to her resourceful, friendly and persevering nature, can do well in practically any career she chooses.

Although the Rat is essentially outgoing, he is also a very private individual. He tends to keep his feelings to himself and while he is not averse to learning what other people are doing, he resents anyone prying too closely into his own affairs. He also does not like solitude and if he is alone for any length of time he can easily get depressed.

The Rat is undoubtedly very talented, but he does sometimes fail to capitalize on his many abilities. He has a tendency to become involved in too many schemes and chase after too many opportunities at once. If he can slow down and concentrate on one thing at a time, he can become very successful. If not, success and wealth can elude him. But, with his tremendous ability to charm, he will rarely, if ever, be without friends.

The Five Different Types of Rat

In addition to the 12 signs of the Chinese zodiac there are five elements and these have a strengthening or moderating influence on the signs. The effects of the five elements on the Rat are described below, together with the years in which they were exercising their influence. Therefore Rats born in 1960 are Metal Rats, Rats born in 1972 are Water Rats, and so on.

Metal Rat: 1960

This Rat has excellent taste and certainly knows how to appreciate the finer things in life. His home is comfortable and nicely decorated and he likes to entertain and mix in fashionable circles. He has considerable financial acumen and invests his money well. On the surface he appears cheerful and confident, but deep down he can be troubled by worries that are quite often of his own making. He is exceptionally loyal to his family and friends.

Water Rat: 1972

The Water Rat is intelligent and very astute. He is a deep thinker and can express his thoughts clearly and persuasively. He is always eager to learn and is talented in many different areas. He is usually very popular, but his fear of loneliness can sometimes lead him into mixing with the wrong sort of company. He is a particularly skilful writer, but can get sidetracked very easily and should try to concentrate on just one thing at a time.

Wood Rat: 1924, 1984

The Wood Rat has a friendly, outgoing personality and is popular with his colleagues and friends. He has a quick, agile brain and likes to turn his hand to anything he thinks may be useful. His one fear is insecurity, but given his intelligence and capabilities, this fear is usually unfounded. He has a good sense of humour, enjoys travel and, due to his highly imaginative nature, can be a gifted writer or artist.

Fire Rat: 1936, 1996

The Fire Rat is rarely still and seems to have a never-ending supply of energy and enthusiasm. He loves being involved in some form of action, be it travel, following up new ideas or campaigning for a cause in which he fervently believes. He is an original thinker and hates being bound by petty restrictions or the dictates of others. He can be forthright in his views but can sometimes get carried away in the excitement of the moment and commit himself to various undertakings without thinking through all the implications. Yet he has a resilient nature and with the right support can go far in life.

Earth Rat: 1948, 2008

This Rat is astute and very level-headed. He rarely takes unnecessary chances and while he is constantly trying to improve his financial status, he is prepared to proceed slowly and leave nothing to chance. He is probably not as adventurous as the other types of Rat and prefers to remain in familiar territory rather than rush headlong into something he knows little about. He is talented, conscientious and caring towards his loved ones, but at the same time can be self-conscious and worry a little too much about the image he is trying to project.

Prospects for the Rat in 2015

The Year of the Horse (31 January 2014–18 February 2015) will have not been the easiest for the Rat. Some situations could have frustrated him and he could also have faced niggling problems. In addition, his relations with others will have needed care. Although he is usually skilful in this area, some disagreements may have arisen and, uncharacteristically, he may have misread some situations.

In the remaining months of the Horse year he will need to remain on his mettle. This is no time for rush, risk or jumping to conclusions, and should he have misgivings over any matter, he should check the facts and wait for matters to become clear.

However, while the aspects advise caution, the closing months of the Horse year can be important ones for the Rat. In his work, he should make full use of his skills and take advantage of any chances to widen his role. By being active now, he can improve his prospects for the future, especially for the much-improved Goat year to come.

With the closing months of the year often being an expensive time, the Rat would also do well to be disciplined in his spending and wary of risk or extravagance.

The year's end can see an increase in social activity, including the chance to meet up with some people the Rat doesn't often get to see. He will also value spending more time with his loved ones, although he does need to remain mindful in all his relations with others. Inattention or lapses could cause awkward moments. Throughout the Horse year the Rat needs to be careful and aware. Fortunately, most Rats are, and many will fare reasonably well in the closing quarter of the Horse year, but it is generally a time for caution and vigilance.

The Goat year starts on 19 February, and as it begins, if not shortly before, many a Rat will sense a change taking place. This is likely to be a greatly improved year, with new opportunities emerging and progress much easier. Indeed, any Rats who have struggled or faced disappointments in recent times should turn their attention to the future rather than dwell on what has gone before. For quite a few, this will be a year of opportunity, with the chance to make substantial headway.

Also, should the Rat have any concerns or niggling problems as the Goat year starts, he should see if these can be addressed. Discussion could be helpful, as could advice from those with expert knowledge. Action taken early on in the year can lead to the easing of some outstanding concerns.

The Rat's work situation is especially encouraging, with the Rat having more chance to profit from his strengths. Whether he remains where he is or decides to move on, he can not only achieve some good results this year but also impress others. As a result, when new openings occur or promotion opportunities arise, he will be excellently placed to benefit. Many Rats could also benefit from openings created by restructuring or new initiatives in their place of work. March, April, August and October could see some important developments, but in Goat years opportunities can arise quickly and need acting upon without delay.

For Rats looking for work, the Goat year may provide the very opportunity they have been seeking for some time. The Rat's resourcefulness and keen personality will impress prospective employers and, once in a position, many Rats will work hard to establish themselves in their new role. For those who secure a new position or see a change of duties early on in the year, there could be the chance to take on further responsibilities late in 2015 or early 2016.

For Rats whose work involves communication or has an expressive element, this can be a particularly successful year, and these Rats should make the most of their ideas and the opportunities that come their way. Goat years favour innovation and professional development.

Rats who enjoy creative pursuits should also look to further their skills in some way. This can be an exciting and stimulating time for them. It is also an excellent year for taking on new challenges and if there is a particular activity that appeals to the Rat, he should aim to find out more. Both existing and new interests can be rewarding this year.

Finances can also see an improvement, with some Rats finding ways to supplement their income through a personal interest or an enterprising idea. However, while the income of many Rats is set to increase, the Rat does need to stay in control of his budget. If he is able, any provision he can make for more major plans, or savings for his future, could help both his present and longer-term situation.

The personable Rat always values his relations with others and here again the aspects are much improved this year. Any Rats who have experienced some strains of late will find this an excellent time to try and ease these. By reaching out, talking more and, importantly, giving more time to others, they may be able to strengthen some relationships which have encountered difficulties in recent times. Here the Rat's input and willingness can be an important factor.

This emphasis on improved relationships extends to family life. Sharing ideas, home projects and other activities can all lead to many enjoyable times – and achievements. Goat years favour togetherness.

Affairs of the heart are also splendidly aspected, and for any Rat who is currently alone or has had some personal upset, the Goat year heralds a brighter time. Chance can play a significant part, with a fortuitous meeting transforming the lives of quite a few unattached Rats over the year. May, June, August and September could be particularly active months both for socializing and for meeting others.

Although the aspects are very much on the Rat's side this year, one area he must not neglect is his well-being. With an often busy lifestyle, he does need to keep himself in good form. Some personal care and attention, including watching his diet and general level of exercise, can make an important difference this year. Rats, do take note.

Overall, the Year of the Goat will suit the Rat's personality. Being resourceful and keen to make the most of his opportunities, he will welcome the chances that arise during it. Whether through improved work prospects, the chance of a new job, the satisfaction that personal interests can bring or the benefits of stronger relations with others, he can enjoy an often special year.

The Metal Rat

The last few years will have brought their challenges for the Metal Rat and not everything will have gone as smoothly as he would have liked. However, with the start of the Goat year, his prospects will be much more encouraging. Any Metal Rats nursing frustrations or keen to reach certain objectives will, in particular, benefit from redoubling their efforts at this time. With resolve, much can now be accomplished, and the Metal Rat will be able to put some more recent disappointments firmly behind him.

Work prospects are especially encouraging and many Metal Rats will be able to use the specialist knowledge they have built up to advantage. Whether this involves taking on new responsibilities, overseeing initiatives, securing promotion or building on their skills in a different capacity, the Goat year encourages moving forward. Any Metal Rats who have been disappointed with their recent progress or find themselves frustrated in their current role will, in particular, find that this is a year to seize the initiative and seek out a better position. As many will discover, once they start to make enquiries, developments can quickly follow on. Goat years are *not* ones for standing still.

Also, initiative will carry great weight this year and all Metal Rats, especially those involved in presentation and more creative areas, should capitalize on their strengths. Their skills, ideas and input will often be well received.

For Metal Rats seeking work or hoping for the chance to switch to something new, the Goat year can also open up some exciting possibilities. Although the job-seeking process can be frustrating, by widening the scope of what they are prepared to consider these Metal Rats may well be able to secure a new and often very different position, and will welcome the challenge in front of them. Late February to early May, August and October could see important developments, although throughout the year the Metal Rat needs to keep alert for openings and ways in which he can further his skills.

With the Goat year favouring culture, Metal Rats who have interests which are in any way artistic should aim to spend some time developing their talents, perhaps by enrolling on a course to add to their knowledge. Similarly, Metal Rats who have creative aspirations would find it useful to promote their work. Personal interests, whether creative or in other spheres, can be of considerable value to the Metal Rat this year.

Progress made at work and in other areas can also help financially, and many Metal Rats will enjoy an increase in income over the year. Some may also benefit from funds from another source. However, the Metal Rat will need to keep a close watch on his outgoings, otherwise extra funds could quickly be spent, and not always in the most effective way. Whenever possible, he should aim to set money aside for particular plans and requirements. By managing his resources well, he will get to do more. With financial discipline and awareness, he can make this a fortunate year.

With his amiable nature, the Metal Rat values his relations with others, and his home and social life will both see much activity. Socially, he will appreciate any chances to meet up with his friends, and some with expert knowledge could be especially helpful when he has a decision to make. In addition, his personal interests and changes in his workplace can lead to him making some important new connections. This is a year which encourages reaching out and any Metal Rats who have had personal difficulties in recent times or are feeling lonely will find that by participating in local activities and taking up any chances to go out, they can come into contact with others and add new meaning (and joy) to their lifestyle. New friendships and, for some, romantic opportunities can help make this a special time. May, June and August to early October could see the most social activity.

The Metal Rat's home life will also see important developments, with the Metal Rat in frequent demand as loved ones seek his advice. Quite often he will have to divide his time up carefully to help both younger relations and those more senior, but throughout the year he will value his role at the heart of family life. While this is likely to be a busy time, there will also be highlights to enjoy. These may not only include the Metal Rat's own successes, but also the achievements of a younger relation. Travel is also likely to be appreciated by all concerned. While often busy, the Metal Rat's home life can be special and rewarding.

Overall, the Year of the Goat is an encouraging one for the Metal Rat, although he does need to seize his opportunities. Whether he is making more of his ideas and talents, furthering his personal interests or looking to build on his work situation, he will find this is a year which favours a purposeful approach. However, he has great experience behind him and an engaging personal manner, and by making the most of these advantages he can look forward to enjoying some well-deserved success.

Tip for the Year
Be resolute. Make plans and act on them. With determination, you can achieve a great deal. This is a year of opportunity for you. Use it well.

The Water Rat

The Water element can strengthen the creative and communicative qualities of a sign and this is particularly the case for the Water Rat. Always adept at expressing himself and coming up with ideas, he is set to do well this year. Indeed, after the challenges he may have faced in recent times, this year can bring a welcome change in fortune.

As the year starts, though, the Water Rat should set himself some objectives to work towards. This is no time for sitting on the sidelines or waiting for opportunities to emerge – the year favours action.

One area which can particularly benefit from the improved aspects is the Water Rat's work situation. The many Water Rats who are already established in a particular industry will have the chance to take their career further, while the aspects are also encouraging for those seeking a position or a change.

Water Rats who are already settled where they are will find that developments can open up new positions and there could be opportunities for promotion or to move to another sector. Some may be offered training which can lead on to other possibilities or have an idea which they are able to develop as the year progresses.

Water Rats who are looking for work should actively follow up suitable openings but also explore other possibilities. Sometimes courses may be available which can widen and update their skills, or they may decide to consider a different type of work. Whatever they choose to do, by being active and showing initiative, both to employment advisers and prospective employers, these Water Rats will not only be given valuable assistance but may also be successful in their quest. It is the Water Rat's talents, personality and drive which will deliver results this year. March to early May, August and October could see important work developments, but whenever opportunities arise, they do need to be acted upon promptly, before the impetus is lost.

With the aspects favouring initiative, this is also an excellent year for the Water Rat to further his personal interests. Creative pursuits could develop particularly well, with some ideas or projects meeting with a pleasing response. Any Water Rats who do not have a current interest or would welcome a new challenge should keep alert for possibilities. With this being a year that favours personal development, any new interests that are followed through can bring considerable personal benefit.

Quite a few Water Rats will also give some consideration to their well-being over the year. By seeking advice about diet and exercise, they may be able to introduce changes that make a noticeable difference.

Finances can also see an improvement this year. Many Water Rats are likely to both increase their income and benefit from a gift or additional payment. However, the Water Rat will have many demands on his resources and should budget carefully and set money aside for specific requirements. In particular, major purchases for the home need to be costed carefully. In some cases it could be prudent to wait for special opportunities. Here the Water Rat's alertness and patience may well help him to make purchases on favourable terms.

With his outgoing nature, he will also welcome the social opportunities of the year. Not only will he value his chances to chat with his friends and get important feedback on his thoughts and concerns, but his work and interests could lead to him meeting some new people who could quickly become important. May, June and mid-July to early October could see the most social opportunities.

For the unattached, the Goat year can also bring unexpected and glorious romance, with a chance meeting transforming the Water Rat's life. On a personal level, he will certainly find himself in demand, with some special times to enjoy.

This will also be a busy year domestically and it is important that there is good dialogue between everyone in the household. Here the Water Rat's input can lead to a lot going ahead, although decisions should not be rushed and sufficient time allowed for practical activities and considering more major purchases. The Goat year can also bring some unexpected opportunities, including the chance to travel or take a holiday at short notice. Some of the Water Rat's ideas may also lead to some memorable family occasions.

Water Rats who are parents will be keen to support their children, particularly if they are facing important decisions concerning their education or work choices. Here the Water Rat's ability to listen and advise can be of particular value.

In so many respects the Goat year offers considerable scope for the Water Rat. It is a time to decide on what he wants to achieve and then work purposefully towards it. He will not only be helped by his background and personality but also by the opportunities that will arise over the year. On quite a few occasions, serendipity will prove a special friend. This is very much a year for personal growth and the positive and willing Water Rat can enjoy some fine successes.

Tip for the Year
Be active and involved. Put forward ideas, build on strengths and keep alert for opportunities. This can be an exciting time. Make the most of it, for there is much to be gained.

The Wood Rat

'Diligence leads to riches', as the Chinese proverb reminds us, and the effort the Wood Rat puts into his various activities this year will reward him well. In many ways this can be an encouraging time for him, although in the light of previous developments there will be quite a few Wood Rats who start the year disappointed with recent progress or nursing some regret. These Wood Rats should try to draw a line under what has gone before and focus their attention on the present. In particular, if the Wood Rat has specific objectives to meet or ideas he would like to explore, this is a time to take action and see what materializes. With a confident, determined approach, much can come to pass, but the Wood Rat does need to be the instigator.

This is especially the case in his work situation. For Wood Rats who are following a particular career, this is an excellent time to progress to a new level. Sometimes this will occur as more senior staff move on and create promotion opportunities, but if not and it looks difficult to move forward in the Wood Rat's current place of work, he should investigate openings elsewhere. He knows he has great potential and he should not allow himself to languish this year.

For Wood Rats who are dissatisfied with their present situation or seeking work, the Goat year offers change and opportunity. Although the job-seeking process will be demanding, by making enquiries and actively following up vacancies (sometimes in a different capacity from what they have done before), many of these Wood Rats will be successful in gaining a position on which they can build in the future. March, April, August, October and January 2016 could see important developments, but throughout the year chances can arise suddenly and need to be acted upon before they are lost.

Progress made at work will also help financially and in addition the Wood Rat's astute nature will assist him with some transactions and purchases, especially concerning his accommodation. However, with many outgoings likely, he will need to control his budget carefully. Also, if entering into an agreement at any time, he should check the terms and, if appropriate, obtain professional advice. Financially, he can fare well this year, but he does need to be thorough.

As far as his personal interests are concerned, this can also be an encouraging year. Wood Rats who are creatively inclined should make full use of their talents and consider promoting their ideas and work. Also, no matter what interests the Wood Rat may have, it is important that he sets time aside to pursue them. The Goat year favours personal growth, and developing his personal interests can bring the Wood Rat pleasure and keep his often busy lifestyle in balance.

This Goat year can also be personally memorable. Some Wood Rats may decide to marry or settle down with their partner or see an addition to their family. Affairs of the heart are splendidly aspected and Wood Rats who are unattached will have an excellent chance to meet someone who is destined to become significant.

Throughout the year the Wood Rat will also value the support of his family and close friends. With ideas to consider, decisions to take and work changes likely, he may be particularly grateful for their first-hand knowledge and assistance. Throughout the year he should not hesitate to ask for advice should his situation warrant it.

In addition, he will enjoy his social life, including the way certain interests bring him into contact with others. New friends and contacts can be important both now and in the future. May, June and August to early October could see the most social opportunities and the Wood Rat should aim to make the most of them. This is a year to be active and involved. Much can be gained as a consequence.

Domestically, too, this will be a busy year. Accommodation matters could be prominent, with some Wood Rats deciding to move to more convenient accommodation or carry out improvements on their home. A lot of time and effort is likely to be spent on practical activities and while these may sometimes be exasperating, by the year's end the Wood

Rat will often be surprised and delighted by how much has been achieved.

Another feature of the Goat year is the sudden opportunities it can bring and throughout the year the Wood Rat needs to keep alert, particularly as unforeseen developments can make certain tasks and decisions easier. In some instances, just mentioning an idea can set important wheels in motion or lead to a helpful suggestion being made. Serendipity, luck and an unexpected helping hand can all play a welcome part in this domestically fulfilling year.

With his determined nature and many personal strengths, the Wood Rat has great potential and this year will offer him the chance to make more of himself. To reap the benefits he will need to look to move his situation forward, but throughout the year he will value his relations with others, and personal developments can help make this a splendid and memorable time.

Tip for the Year
Follow through on your dreams. With your abilities and the excellent opportunities that will come your way, you can achieve a lot this year. This is a time for action and for realizing your potential. You have a lot to gain.

The Fire Rat

The significance of this Goat year for the Fire Rat should not be underestimated. With many Fire Rats embarking on important stages in their education, seeking to establish themselves in their work and/or facing key personal choices, the decisions they take during it can shape the next few years. In many of his undertakings, the Fire Rat will be assisted by the year's favourable aspects, although to make the most of his potential he will need to apply himself and take charge.

For the many Fire Rats involved in education, there will be considerable amounts to study, new subject areas to master and some exacting deadlines. Although these Fire Rats will sometimes be daunted by what is expected of them, by remaining organized and working consistently, they can make valuable progress and discover new talents. In some cases, what they study now could alert them to subjects they will choose to specialize in later. In others, there will be the chance to switch to a more appropriate course. For many Fire Rats, this will be a year of self-discovery in which they gain strengths and knowledge they can build on in the future.

With a lot resting on what they choose to do now, it is important these Fire Rats make the most of the resources available to them, including the facilities in their place of education. They may also benefit from seeking advice from their tutors on the choices they have to make or asking for assistance if facing difficulties.

For Fire Rats in work, again the year can bring far-reaching decisions. Those already established in a position will often be offered the chance to take on greater duties. By being willing and showing commitment, they may well find one opportunity paving the way for another. Taking advantage of training schemes can also help both their present and future prospects.

For Fire Rats who are unfulfilled in their present work and keen to move on, as well as those seeking a position, the Goat year can open up interesting opportunities. To benefit, these Fire Rats may need to consider types of work that are different from their original choice. However, by keeping alert, actively following up vacancies and seizing the chances they are offered, they can not only gain valuable work experience but also establish an important base which they can build on, sometimes quite quickly. March, April, August and October and January 2016 could see particularly encouraging developments.

The Fire Rat can also see an improvement in his financial position over the year and may benefit from a gift or extra sum of money. However, in view of his busy lifestyle and the many plans and purchases he will have in mind, he will need to be disciplined in spending and budget ahead for certain requirements. Also, rather than rushing into purchases, if he takes the time to make comparisons and wait for favourable buying opportunities, he can save himself unnecessary outlay. This is a year for careful financial management.

It can, however, be an encouraging time for personal interests. Fire Rats with creative talents could derive particular pleasure from taking their ideas further. Many will also benefit from the encouragement of others and be on inspired form. By being willing to embrace what becomes available to them, all Fire Rats can make this a satisfying and potentially successful year.

For many Fire Rats, affairs of the heart can also bring some glorious times. Love, romance and special friendships can all play a big part this year. Changes in the Fire Rat's situation can also lead to new friendships. May, June and August to early October could see the most social activity. However, in this busy and full year, a note of warning does need to be sounded: with a busy social life and some demanding days and late nights, the Fire Rat does need to give himself the chance to catch up. Overtiring himself, overindulging himself or paying scant attention to his diet could leave him not at his best. This can be an exciting year, but the Fire Rat does need to strike a sensible balance.

Also, although he is often immersed in his own activities, he would do well to share his thoughts with family members as well as contribute to family life. Not only will good dialogue help rapport, but if the Fire Rat is able to express his ideas, he will find those close to him better able to understand and assist. In addition, some expertise the Fire Rat may have, whether technical or in some other capacity, could prove useful to a more senior relative and be of more value than he may realize at the time. In this respect, as with so much this year, a great deal can follow on from the Fire Rat's willingness to be open and involved.

Overall, the Year of the Goat is rich in possibility and there will be chances for the Fire Rat to show more of his potential as well as make important headway in his education or work. This will require discipline and application, but by believing in himself the Fire Rat can make valuable progress as well as help determine the course of the next few years. On a personal level, this can be an exciting year, with the Fire Rat making the most of his strengths and his many social opportunities.

Tip for the Year
Believe in yourself. Skills, qualifications and experience gained over the year can open up opportunities for you. Make the most of today, for it can lead to an exciting tomorrow.

The Earth Rat

The Earth Rat has a talent for using his time well and as the Goat year starts he will almost certainly have projects he is keen to pursue as well as a myriad of activities to keep him busy. However, while a lot can go well for him, it is important that he keeps an open mind. Situations may change and plans should not be set in stone this year.

It is also important that when he has an idea, the Earth Rat consults those around him and listens to their views. Sometimes just the process of discussion can give him fresh thoughts to consider and set plans in motion. Good dialogue can assist him in many of his undertakings this year, including home and domestic projects, travel, personal interests or any matters preying on his mind. Sometimes professionals can give important advice as well. By seeking the opinions of others (and sometimes a helping hand), the Earth Rat will find that a lot can be achieved this year.

One area which can bring particular satisfaction will be his personal interests. Creative activities are especially well aspected, and Earth Rats who enjoy art, writing, music or craftwork could take delight in developing their talents. The Goat year offers great possibilities for the willing. Earth Rats who have been considering learning another skill, trying a different pursuit or following up a new area of interest will also benefit from putting their ideas into practice. As family connections are important to the Earth Rat, some may enjoy spending time researching aspects of family history. Whatever his interests, the Earth Rat will find this an ideal year for developing them in some way.

In addition, he should also give some consideration to his own wellbeing over the year. If he does not take regular exercise, he should seek medical advice on activities that may help. Here again, he could benefit from the suggestions from others, and in some cases start a pleasurable new activity. The Goat year can open up many possibilities.

Travel may also feature prominently over the year and many Earth Rats will have the chance to visit areas they have long wanted to see. Some will also enjoy finding out more about their own area, perhaps by visiting places of interest. The Earth Rat's enquiring nature can lead to many enjoyable occasions.

Another pleasing aspect of the year will be the strokes of luck the Earth Rat will enjoy. These will not only include the way certain plans are fortuitously advanced but the special offers the Earth Rat is able to take advantage of, including travel-wise.

Financially, too, the aspects are encouraging, with many Earth Rats benefiting from the receipt of extra funds. However, the Earth Rat will need to remain disciplined and budget for specific requirements. The more control he exercises, the more he will be able to benefit.

With his genial nature, the Earth Rat will welcome meeting up with his friends during the year and some of them will be able to offer specific advice based on personal knowledge. New activities can also bring him into contact with other people and any Earth Rat who is lonely will find that taking part in community activities or joining a local group can be good ways to meet others.

The Earth Rat can also look forward to some exciting developments in his domestic life. Many Earth Rats will see the birth of grandchildren or great-grandchildren. The Earth Rat will take a caring interest in the different activities of family members and there will be times this year when he will feel justifiably proud of their achievements. Also, just as he is keen to support close relatives, so he in turn will benefit from what they are able to do for him, whether it is providing assistance with practical tasks or offering technical advice. Shared activities can also be enjoyable. Whether the Earth Rat and others are tackling projects together or going to places of interest, they can enjoy many memorable occasions. In so many ways, this can be a fulfilling and stimulating time for the Earth Rat.

Overall, with his ideas and talents and the good support he is likely to enjoy, the Earth Rat can achieve a great deal. He does need to be flexible in some undertakings, but he will be pleased by the range of things he is able to do as well as delight in some of his new activities. This is an encouraging year full of possibility.

Tip for the Year
Don't be restrictive in your outlook. Follow up ideas, try out new activities and keep alert for emerging opportunities. This is a year to explore, to be inventive – and to enjoy yourself.

Famous Rats

Ben Affleck, Ursula Andress, Louis Armstrong, Lauren Bacall, Dame Shirley Bassey, Kathy Bates, Irving Berlin, Kenneth Branagh, Marlon Brando, Charlotte Brontë, Jackson Browne, George H. W. Bush, Glen Campbell, Jimmy Carter, Jeremy Clarkson, Aaron Copland, Cameron Diaz, David Duchovny, Duffy, T. S. Eliot, Eminem, Colin Firth, Pope Francis I, Clark Gable, Liam Gallagher, Al Gore, Hugh Grant, Lewis Hamilton, Thomas Hardy, Prince Harry, Charlton Heston, Buddy Holly, Mick Hucknall, Henrik Ibsen, Jeremy Irons, Samuel L. Jackson, LeBron James, Jean-Michel Jarre, Scarlett Johansson, Gene Kelly, Avril Lavigne, Jude Law, Gary Lineker, Lord Andrew Lloyd Webber, Ian McEwan, Katie Melua, Claude Monet, Olly Murs, Richard Nixon, Ozzy Osbourne, Brad Paisley, Sean Penn, Katy Perry, Philippe I, King of the Belgians, Sir Terry Pratchett, Ian Rankin, Lou Rawls, Burt Reynolds, Rossini, William Shakespeare, James Taylor, Leo Tolstoy, Henri Toulouse-Lautrec, Spencer Tracy, the Prince of Wales, George Washington, the Duke of York, Emile Zola.

6 February 1913 to 25 January 1914 — *Water Ox*

24 January 1925 to 12 February 1926 — *Wood Ox*

11 February 1937 to 30 January 1938 — *Fire Ox*

29 January 1949 to 16 February 1950 — *Earth Ox*

15 February 1961 to 4 February 1962 — *Metal Ox*

3 February 1973 to 22 January 1974 — *Water Ox*

20 February 1985 to 8 February 1986 — *Wood Ox*

7 February 1997 to 27 January 1998 — *Fire Ox*

26 January 2009 to 13 February 2010 — *Earth Ox*

The Ox

The Personality of the Ox

The more considered the way,
the more considerable the journey.

The Ox is born under the signs of equilibrium and tenacity. He is a hard and conscientious worker and sets about everything he does in a resolute, methodical and determined manner. He has considerable leadership qualities and is often admired for his tough and uncompromising nature. He knows what he wants to achieve in life and, as far as possible, will not be deflected from his ultimate objective.

The Ox takes his responsibilities and duties very seriously. He is decisive and quick to take advantage of any opportunity that comes his way. He is also sincere and places a great deal of trust in his friends and colleagues. He is, nevertheless, something of a loner. He is a quiet and private individual and often keeps his thoughts to himself. He also cherishes his independence and prefers to set about things in his own way rather than be bound by the dictates of others or influenced by outside pressures.

The Ox tends to have a calm and tranquil nature, but if something angers him or he feels that someone has let him down, he can have a fearsome temper. He can also be stubborn and obstinate and this can lead him into conflict with others. Usually he will succeed in getting his own way, but should things go against him he is a poor loser and will take any defeat or setback extremely badly.

The Ox is often a deep thinker and rather studious. He is not particularly renowned for his sense of humour and does not take kindly to new gimmicks or anything too innovative. He is too solid and traditional for that and prefers to stick to the more conventional norm.

His home is very important to him and in some respects he treats it as a private sanctuary. His family tends to be closely knit and the Ox will make sure that each member does their fair share around the house. He tends to be a hoarder, but he is always well organized and neat. He also places great importance on punctuality and there is nothing that infuriates him more than to be kept waiting, particularly if it is due to someone's inefficiency. The Ox can be a hard taskmaster!

Once settled in a job or house the Ox will quite happily remain there for many years. He does not like change and he is also not particularly keen on travel. He does, however, enjoy gardening and other outdoor pursuits and he will often spend much of his spare time out of doors. He is usually an excellent gardener and whenever possible will make sure he has a large area of ground to maintain. He usually prefers to live in the country rather than the town.

Due to his dedicated and dependable nature the Ox will usually do well in his chosen career, providing he is given enough freedom to act on his own initiative. He invariably does well in politics, agriculture and careers that need specialized training. He is also very gifted artistically and many Oxen have enjoyed considerable success as musicians or composers.

The Ox is not as outgoing as some and it often takes him a long time to establish friendships and feel relaxed in another person's company. His courtships are likely to be long, but once he is settled he will remain devoted and loyal to his partner. He is particularly well suited to those born under the signs of the Rat, Rabbit, Snake and Rooster. He can also establish a good relationship with the Monkey, Dog, Pig and another Ox, but he will find that he has little in common with the whimsical and sensitive Goat. He will also find it difficult to get on with the Horse, Dragon and Tiger – the Ox prefers a quiet and peaceful existence and those born under these three signs tend to be a little too lively and impulsive for his liking.

The female Ox has a kind and caring nature and her home and family are very much her pride and joy. She always tries to do her best for her partner and can be a most conscientious and loving parent. She is an excellent organizer and a very determined person who will often succeed in getting what she wants in life. She usually has a deep interest in the arts and is often a talented artist or musician.

The Ox is a very down-to-earth character. He is sincere, loyal and unpretentious. He can, however, be rather reserved and to some he may appear distant and aloof. He has a quiet nature, but underneath he is very strong-willed and ambitious. He has the courage of his convictions and is often prepared to stand up for what he believes to be right, regardless of the consequences. He inspires confidence and trust and throughout his life he will rarely be short of people who are ready to support him.

The Five Different Types of Ox

In addition to the 12 signs of the Chinese zodiac there are five elements and these have a strengthening or moderating influence on the signs. The effects of the five elements on the Ox are described below, together with the years in which they were exercising their influence. Therefore Oxen born in 1961 are Metal Oxen, Oxen born in 1973 are Water Oxen, and so on.

Metal Ox: 1961

This Ox is confident and very strong-willed. He can be blunt and forth-right in his views and is not afraid of speaking his mind. He sets about his objectives with a dogged determination, but he can become so involved in his various activities that he can be oblivious to the thoughts and feelings of those around him, and this can sometimes be to his detriment. He is honest and dependable and will never promise more than he can deliver. He has a good appreciation of the arts and usually has a small circle of very good and loyal friends.

Water Ox: 1973

This Ox has a sharp and penetrating mind. He is a good organizer and sets about his work in a methodical manner. He is not as narrow-minded as some of the other types of Ox and is more willing to involve others in his plans and aspirations. He usually has very high moral standards and is often attracted to careers in public service. He is a good judge of character and has such a friendly and persuasive manner that he usually experiences little difficulty in securing his objectives. He is popular and has an excellent way with children.

Wood Ox: 1925, 1985

The Wood Ox conducts himself with an air of dignity and authority and will often take a leading role in any enterprise in which he becomes involved. He is very self-confident and is direct in his dealings with others. He does, however, have a quick temper and has no hesitation in speaking his mind. He has tremendous drive and willpower and an extremely good memory. He is particularly loyal and devoted to the members of his family and has a most caring nature.

Fire Ox: 1937, 1997

The Fire Ox has a powerful and assertive personality and is a hard and conscientious worker. He holds strong views and has very little patience when things do not go his way. He can also get carried away in the excitement of the moment and does not always take into account the views of those around him. He nevertheless has many leadership qualities and will often reach positions of power, eminence and wealth. He usually has a small group of loyal and close friends and is very devoted to his family.

Earth Ox: 1949, 2009

This Ox sets about everything he does in a sensible and level-headed manner. He is ambitious but also realistic in his aims and is often prepared to work long hours to secure his objectives. He is shrewd in financial and business matters and is a very good judge of character. He has a quiet nature and is greatly admired for his sincerity and integrity. He is also very loyal to his family and friends and his views are often sought.

Prospects for the Ox in 2015

The Ox will have seen a lot happen in the Horse year (31 January 2014–18 February 2015) and in the remaining months he will need to keep his wits about him.

Quite a few Oxen will face an increased workload at this time and a lot will be asked of them. However, there will be scope for making progress and, for those seeking a position, taking on something new. September and late November could see encouraging developments, even if some positions offered are on a temporary basis only.

The year's end will also see an increase in spending and to prevent mistakes or unnecessary outlay the Ox will need to manage his resources well and allow sufficient time when considering more substantial purchases.

The closing months of the year will also bring great activity to his social life. In addition to meeting up with his friends, he could be invited to some lively occasions and find a friend passing on some surprising news.

Similarly, in his home life there will be a lot to do, often including making travel plans for later on in the year. Being a good organizer, the Ox will attend to many of the arrangements himself, but it is also important that he talks his plans over with those around him, especially with so much happening at this time of year. Despite all the activity, he will enjoy some special family gatherings at the close of the year.

The Year of the Goat starts on 19 February and will be a mixed one for the Ox. Oxen are careful, methodical and practical, but Goat years are times of change, with a lot happening very quickly. The Ox may not feel entirely comfortable with either the developments or the general tenor of the year, but it can bring important benefits and on a personal level there will be some particularly good times for the Ox to enjoy.

One of the more favourable aspects of the year concerns his home life. The Ox will often content himself with various projects, with his practical nature coming to the fore. As one project is completed, another will often suggest itself, and the Ox will be able to fill his time in satisfying and productive ways. In addition, he will find himself at the heart of family life, with many looking to him for advice or a helping hand and valuing his solid and dependable nature. For an honest opinion the Ox has few equals and over the year he will assist many people and could advise on a potentially significant matter. The Goat year will also have its memorable domestic occasions and promises to be a full and pleasing time.

The Ox's social life can also reward him well. His personal interests will often have a good social element and throughout the year he will value the support of his friends. Whenever he has concerns he could find it helpful to share these and, if applicable, seek the advice of those with first-hand experience. In this variable year it is important that the Ox does not feel alone. 'A worry shared *is* a worry halved.'

In view of the pressures he may face, it is also important that the Ox pays some attention to his own well-being and allows himself time to enjoy the rewards his efforts bring. Oxen who do not currently lead a balanced lifestyle will find that taking up activities in their area could open up some beneficial possibilities, possibly again with a social element. April, May, August and December could see the most social activity.

For the unattached, romance too can brighten the year. In true Ox fashion, some romances may take some time to get established, but by the year's end quite a few Oxen will be enjoying the passions of true love. Romantically, this can be an exciting year.

In work matters, however, it can be a demanding time. For Oxen who are established in their role, the year will bring its vexations, with many changes taking place and new procedures impacting on the work these Oxen have to do. Oxen favour tradition, while Goat years see change – and inevitable teething problems. For the majority of Oxen, the best policy this year is to concentrate on what is required and do the best they can in not always easy situations. However, while this may be frustrating, the experience many Oxen have built up could be especially appreciated when problems need addressing. Amid the pressures, progress *is* possible, and when it occurs, it will be well deserved.

For Oxen who are looking to improve their position by moving elsewhere or seeking work, again the Goat year can be tricky. Openings could be limited, competition keen and opportunities may vanish if not seized quickly. However, the Ox is tenacious and his commitment may well enable him to secure a position, possibly in a field that is new to him. Here again the Goat year will require flexibility, but provided the Ox is prepared to adapt and learn, he can gain experience that he can build on in the future. April, June and September to early November will see particularly encouraging developments.

Where finance is concerned, however, the Ox will need to be thorough. Throughout the year he should keep careful control of his budget and check the terms and obligations if entering into any major agreement. In particularly complex matters, professional advice would be wise. Also, if tempted to speculate, the Ox should be aware of potential liabilities. Financial matters need close attention this year and risks should be avoided.

In general, the Goat year will be a challenging one for the Ox. Sudden changes can disrupt his plans, but by doing his best in often volatile situations, he can discover new strengths and make modest progress. Importantly, he will enjoy the support of his family and close friends, and his domestic life is likely to be a source of pride and happiness. Personal interests can help his lifestyle balance, and for the unattached, romance can add excitement to the year. Overall, a tricky time, but with some important benefits mixed in.

The Metal Ox

One of the fine qualities of the Metal Ox is his conscientious nature. When he sets out to do something, he sets out to do it well. He is also tenacious and prepared to work long and hard for what he wants. However, in the Goat year, despite his best endeavours, his progress could be muted and there could be some niggling problems to address. Nevertheless, the year will have its brighter moments too.

In view of prevailing aspects, it is, though, important that the Metal Ox liaises well with others rather than acts independently. That way, he will not only be better able to gauge what it is best to do but also be more a part of what is going on. Some Metal Oxen are loners, but this is very much a time for involvement.

At work the Metal Ox could see considerable change, with some of the more traditional ways of doing things (which he prefers) being supplanted. Although he may be uncomfortable with certain develop-ments, it is a case of focusing on what is required and making the best of his situation. He also needs to keep informed about ideas under consideration and be an active member of any team rather than on the periphery. With care, he can make his presence and expertise felt, but he does need to proceed mindfully, liaise well and pick the right moments.

Although progress will not be easy, the year will, however, still bring some opportunities. In some cases, the changes that take place will provide the ideal chance for the Metal Ox to develop his skills in another capacity. For Metal Oxen who are in a rut, the Goat year can open up some interesting and timely possibilities.

The majority of Metal Oxen will remain with their present employer over the year, but in an often changed role. For those intent on change or seeking work, the Goat year will be challenging. Openings may be limited, but here again the Metal Ox's tenacious qualities can be brought to bear, and by keeping alert and seeking expert advice (communication is so important this year), he may succeed in his quest. Opportunities do need to be seized without delay, but over the year many Metal Oxen will have the chance to take on a new challenge. April, June and September to early November could see interesting possibilities.

In financial matters, the Metal Ox will again need to be careful and aware. When considering major transactions, he should allow himself the time to compare costs and options. This is no year for rush or risk. He should also keep watch over his budget and make early provision for plans and obligations. The better his control, the better he will fare.

A feature of the Goat year is that it favours personal development and, being practical, the Metal Ox could derive considerable pleasure from extending his interests. Also, should a new subject or activity intrigue him, he should aim to find out more. If he has let his personal interests fall away in recent years, this would be a good time to remedy this. Goat years encourage exploring talents and in this sometimes tricky one the Metal Ox's interests could be of considerable benefit to him.

Further pleasure can come from travel. Some opportunities could arise at short notice, and while the Metal Ox may prefer to plan ahead, taking advantage of last-minute offers could lead to some enjoyable times, especially in the spring and summer.

Although the Metal Ox can be a private individual, it is also important that he stays in regular contact with his friends and is prepared to discuss any matters on his mind. The support – and assistance – of others can make a real difference to some situations this year, but to benefit the Metal Ox does need to be forthcoming. April, May, August and December and January 2016 could see the most social activity.

For Metal Oxen who are unattached, the Goat year offers strong romantic possibilities, with a chance meeting likely to prove significant. Goat years can spring their surprises *and* special moments.

Home life can also bring contentment to many Metal Oxen. Although various family members will often be busy with their own activities, the Metal Ox's talents at bringing everyone together will be especially appreciated. He will do a lot to support others and it is essential that he also talks over his own activities and concerns. He will not only find this can be helpful in itself, but also that it can strengthen rapport and understanding. Good communication is a key requisite of the Goat year.

With some of his more practical plans for the home, the Metal Ox will need to be flexible. As snags and delays arise (as they will), projects may have to be revised. Admittedly, this may not suit the Metal Ox's orderly nature, but Goat years can be changeable and the Metal Ox will have to adapt accordingly.

Overall, in 2015 the Metal Ox will need to keep his wits about him. However, while he may view some of the developments of the year with misgiving, there will be scope for him to further what he does in both his work and his personal interests. He will also value the support of those close to him, although to benefit fully he does need to be open. A sometimes awkward year, but a full and interesting one.

Tip for the Year

Watch your independent tendencies. Make a point of talking to others and seeking their opinions and support. By being a team player, you will fare much better this year. In addition, stay alert for fresh developments and be prepared to adjust accordingly. Goat years require awareness and a flexible approach, and what happens in this one can prove significant.

The Water Ox

This will be a time of change and fast-moving developments for the Water Ox and his resourcefulness and talent for thinking out of the box will prove of great value.

In his home life this can be a busy and often exciting time. The Water Ox will often be keen to forge ahead with plans, although, in keeping with the volatile nature of the year, these can be subject to change, including major rethinks. However, if he is adaptable, the Water Ox will often be able to delight in his home improvements. Spending quality time with his loved ones will also lead to some memorable occasions, and if the Water Ox has particular ideas, he should put these forward. His input can add greatly to the quality of home life.

Water Oxen who are parents will offer important encouragement as their children face exams, have decisions to make or grapple with awkward matters. Here the Water Ox's ability to empathize and guide can be of especial value. More senior relations too will have reason to be grateful for his time and assistance.

Domestically, this will be a busy year, but despite the demands, the Water Ox will feel great contentment as he sees the results of his efforts.

Busy though he may be, it is important that he does not neglect his social life. Contact with others is very important this year and whenever possible the Water Ox should take up the invitations he receives and go to events that appeal to him. In some instances, especially if he is alone, it could be well worth considering joining a local interest group. April, May, August and December could see the most social activity.

For some Water Oxen who are currently unattached, the year can also see the start of a special and possibly significant romance.

The Water Ox should also give time to his personal interests and consider developing his ideas. His resourcefulness can open up interesting possibilities. Creative activities could be especially satisfying this year.

In work matters, however, he will need to proceed carefully. With changes underway and an often heavy workload, he will find his skills and patience frequently tested. Throughout the year he will need to liaise well with colleagues and be actively involved in his place of work. Commitment, communication and willingness to learn are all so important this year. While situations may be demanding, the Water Ox will nevertheless have an excellent chance to prove himself and extend his knowledge. His knack for solving problems and ability to deal with pressure can particularly impress others, and quite a few Water Oxen will ultimately have the chance to take on greater responsibilities.

Some Water Oxen, however, will not feel fulfilled where they are and be keen to make a change. For these Water Oxen, as well as those seeking work, the Goat year can open up some potentially exciting possibilities. The employment situation may be difficult, but Goat years favour change, and by looking to adapt their skills, many Water Oxen could be offered an interesting new position. This could entail considerable learning and change of routine, but the Water Ox will relish the challenge. April, June and late August to early November could see particularly encouraging developments, but throughout the year the Water Ox should follow up ideas, seek advice and keep alert for openings.

In view of his plans and commitments, however, he will need to be especially careful in money matters. This includes keeping a close watch on spending and taking his time when considering major purchases or transactions. If he has any uncertainties over the terms or cost implications, he *must* address these before proceeding. This is no time for risk, carelessness *or* assumptions. Money matters require discipline and care.

Overall, the Goat year will be a demanding one for the Water Ox. The pressures may be considerable, but the Water Ox has great strength of character and by demonstrating his skills and using his time well, he can accomplish a great deal. In his work, his commitment and ability to adjust can lead to new responsibilities and his achievements may pave the way to other possibilities in the near future. His relations with others will also be of value to him and a great help throughout the year. Conditions may not always be easy, but they will highlight the gifts and fortitude of many a Water Ox and make his rewards this year all the more deserved.

Tip for the Year

Proceed carefully and mindfully. Pay heed to the views of those around you and be prepared to adjust as situations change. This may be a challenging year, but what you undertake now can be of both present *and* future value. Also, spend time with those who are special to you. Their love and support can be significant.

The Wood Ox

This year marks the start of a new decade in the Wood Ox's life. Hopeful, determined and in true Wood Ox style *resolute*, he will be keen to make the most of it. Although it may not always be an easy year, what he accomplishes during it can have considerable bearing on the better times that await.

One feature of the Goat year is that situations can be volatile, and the Wood Ox, who likes to be sure of his ground, will find some events giving rise to uncertainty. However, while he may have his misgivings about certain developments, on several occasions they may ultimately prove of value. As Henry Ford noted, 'Problems are opportunities in disguise,' and so it will be for many Wood Oxen this year.

At work, many Wood Oxen will already be established in a particular role and keen to take their career to a new level. However, progress may not be easy this year and these Wood Oxen would do well to broaden the range of positions they are prepared to consider. Important headway *is* possible this year, but it may involve a substantial change of duties.

This also applies to Wood Oxen who are seeking work or looking to make a change. Rather than restrict their search to one particular type of work, they should widen its scope, as well as seek the advice of employment officials. By showing their resolve and willingness to learn, many will be given the chance to prove themselves in a new way. April, June and September to early November could see key developments.

To help their situation, all Wood Oxen will need to work closely with others throughout the year and seize any chances to raise their profile. More independent-minded Wood Oxen, do take note. Contact and commitment are vital to success this year.

Although many Wood Oxen will see a modest rise in income over the year, money matters need to be handled with great care. With important purchasing decisions likely, as well as personal and travel costs, there will be many demands on the Wood Ox's resources. Throughout the year he needs to budget carefully and check the terms of any new agreement he enters into. Rush or lack of care could lead to regret. Wood Oxen, do be careful and thorough.

With this being their thirtieth year, many Wood Oxen will have travel on the agenda. Again, this needs to be carefully budgeted for, but for quite a few Wood Oxen, it could be a highlight of their year.

The Wood Ox can also derive considerable pleasure from his personal interests. No matter whether he prefers practical pursuits, creative activities or the outdoors, the Goat year can open up interesting possibilities, and by being game, the Wood Ox will be pleased with how many of his plans develop. Wood Oxen who are keen to do something different (and many will feel the time is ripe for a new challenge) will find that if they follow up possibilities, their actions can bring unforeseen benefits, including, in some cases, extending their social circle and getting out and about more. Goat years may have their awkward aspects, but they do offer scope and diversity.

This will also be an important year domestically. Many Wood Oxen will have been thinking through plans for their accommodation and changes that might make their lifestyle easier. Although some of these will be for the longer term, it is important that the Wood Ox talks his ideas over with those close to him, including more senior relations. By considering possibilities, costing options and combining views, he may be able to set his plans in motion. Some may develop in a different way from what was originally proposed, but by the year's end many Wood Oxen will be pleased with what they have undertaken.

Amid all the activity, the Goat year will also have its special moments. Not only will his loved ones be keen to mark the Wood Ox's thirtieth birthday in style, but some Wood Oxen could see an addition to their family. All will enjoy sharing activities, making plans and encountering the surprises the year will bring. Personally, this can be a full and interesting time.

The Wood Ox can also benefit from the year's social opportunities and may well find himself in increasing demand as the year progresses. Late March to early June, August and December could see the most social activity.

For the unattached, affairs of the heart can add considerable excitement to the year, with quite a few Wood Oxen meeting their future partner in a way that seemed destined to be.

As the Wood Ox enters his thirtieth year, he will have hopes and aspirations he will be keen to realize. However, he will acknowledge that some of these will require great effort as well as an element of luck. In the Goat year, progress *is* possible and some personal hopes may well be realized, but the Wood Ox will need to be flexible in attitude and adapt to situations as they arise. By rising to the year's challenges, however, he will be preparing himself for the opportunities that await in the future. He may not have a particularly easy start to his thirties, but his efforts *will*, in time, prevail. In all he does, he should draw on the support of those around him. Many people believe in him and, despite the challenges this year, there will be many special times to share.

Tip for the Year

Look to extend your skills and interests. What happens this year will often happen for a reason and significant possibilities can open up for you. Also, value your loved ones. They are special and can play an important part in making your thirtieth year special too.

The Fire Ox

This will be a busy and demanding year for the Fire Ox. Not only will he have a lot to do and decide upon, but he could also encounter problems with some of his activities. Goat years can be challenging, but it is by rising to the challenges that the Fire Ox will identify strengths he can build on. Indeed, what he discovers about himself this year will prepare him for the substantial advances he can make over the next few years.

During the Goat year it is, though, important that the Fire Ox remains open-minded. That way he can not only gain more from the opportunities that come his way but also broaden his scope for later. As a forward-thinker, he may already have formed some ideas about what he would like to do next, but in the Goat year flexibility is required.

For the many Fire Oxen in education this will be an important year, especially as they near the end of courses or start new academic work. A lot will be expected of them and they will need to be disciplined and focused. Also, working consistently throughout the year rather than leaving a lot to the last moment will not only make their studying more satisfying but their results that much better. There may be pressures this year but the Fire Ox could also find new opportunities emerging. Different courses may be offered to him, new specialisms may appeal or he may discover an educational establishment that is more suitable for what he wants to do. Much can become available in the Goat year, but to benefit the Fire Ox should do what he feels is right for him, even if this means revising his original intentions.

In view of the importance of his current decisions, the Fire Ox should also make the most of the advice and information available to him. Some education and employment experts may be able to give new insight into what he may be considering or suggest alternative ways forward, and he would do well to be open-minded.

In addition to his studying, the Fire Ox will be encouraged by the way certain of his personal interests develop, perhaps through new skills and knowledge or new equipment. Goat years particularly encourage creative endeavour and this can be an exciting time, especially for Fire Oxen who enjoy the performing arts, music and other creative pursuits.

The Fire Ox's social life will also be abuzz with activity, with parties and other social occasions to look forward to and lively times to enjoy with his close circle of friends. For Fire Oxen who find themselves in a new environment and/or feeling lonely, there will be good opportunities to meet like-minded people and forge what can become long-standing friendships. For some Fire Oxen the Goat year can have the added excitement of romance. On a personal level, this can be a busy and pleasing year. Late March to early June, August, December and January 2016 are likely to see the most social activity.

For Fire Oxen in work or seeking work the Goat year can, however, be tricky. Those already in a position may find some of their work routine and feel they are not making the most of their potential. Changes may suddenly be introduced, too, and these Fire Oxen may feel unprepared and uncomfortable with the developments. Goat years can bring their challenging moments, but during this one many Fire Oxen will be able to use their current position as a springboard to something better, either where they are or elsewhere.

Fire Oxen seeking work will find that putting in that extra effort when making an application can greatly improve their prospects. It could be helpful for them to find out more about the company and work involved so they can emphasize their strengths and any relevant experience. Online research can yield up-to-date information which can impress at interview. Effort will be needed, but the Fire Ox is resolute by nature and may succeed in securing that all-important foothold on the employment ladder. April, June and late August to early November could see encouraging developments.

Throughout the year, however, the Fire Ox will need to keep a close watch on spending and, as far as possible, remain within his budget. He may have an active social life, and many other plans too, but the year requires financial control. He should also be wary about making purchases too hurriedly and be circumspect about anything risky. Financial matters are poorly aspected this year. Fire Oxen, take note.

Overall, this will be an active and demanding year for the Fire Ox, but it will also be an important one. What he does now can determine the course of the next few years. During the year he needs to remain open to possibility and not be too wedded to one idea or plan. He also should take advantage of the support available to him. This is a year for effort, but its rewards can be far-reaching.

Tip for the Year
Be focused and use your time well. Although some situations may be difficult, they can give you the opportunity to learn and prove yourself. Do make the most of the year, for it can provide the skills, ideas and sometimes qualifications needed for future progress.

The Earth Ox

The Goat year can be a time of considerable change and during it the Earth Ox will get to experience a great deal. A fair amount will go well for him, but he does need to be prepared for some snags. However, while the aspects may be mixed, the Earth Ox can still look forward to some special times.

The key to so much this year will be mindfulness. As the Earth Ox sets about his activities, he does need to take into account the views of others. Also, he needs to *communicate*. The redoubtable Earth Ox likes to set his own course, but this is no time for single-mindedness or acting too independently. Consultation and flexibility will lead to far more being achieved – and fewer awkward moments too.

In his home life, if the Earth Ox has plans he would like to carry out or learns of equipment that might make certain tasks easier, it is important that he talks these through and explores the options. Similarly, when tackling practical projects, he should draw on the willingness of others to assist. This is very much a year which favours combined effort.

Also, in view of the cultural activity that characterizes the Goat year, if the Earth Ox sees events that appeal to him or learns of special occasions that he can enjoy with those around him, it is important that he shares his ideas before the chance is lost. Throughout the year he does need to be forthcoming – which some of the more stolid Earth Oxen tend not to be!

The Earth Ox's dependable nature will, however, come to the fore when offering important support to family members, including perhaps on a sensitive matter. His advice will mean more than he may realize. If a grandparent, he will also enjoy encouraging his grandchildren and will value the often close bond he shares with them. The Goat year can see some happy family times.

It also has a spontaneous element to it and the Earth Ox could be caught by surprise by the way opportunities suddenly open up. It may be that he receives an invitation to stay with relatives or friends at short notice or is attracted by a last-minute travel offer. To benefit, he will need to seize the opportunity and be flexible in his planning. Goat years have an immediacy about them which may not always sit comfortably with the Earth Ox's psyche but can nevertheless bring benefits.

The Earth Ox's social life can also bring considerable pleasure, although again he will need to make the most of the opportunities that arise. Personal interests can also lead to some interesting social occasions, and Earth Oxen who are feeling lonely will find that joining a local group of enthusiasts can be of great value. Late March to early June, August and December could see the most social activity, and for the unattached, the Goat year has romantic possibilities too. In essence this year shines a spotlight on the Earth Ox's relations with others and he does need to be open and aware and watch any independent tendencies.

One area which calls for especial care is finance. Earth Oxen who have recently retired could have adjustments to make and complex correspondence to deal with concerning policies and entitlements. In any difficult matter the Earth Ox does need to obtain advice and seek clarification if necessary. All Earth Oxen need to be disciplined in controlling their budget and take their time when considering major transactions. 'It is better to be safe than sorry.'

More positively, the Earth Ox's personal interests can bring him great satisfaction, although these too can undergo considerable change. It could be that he decides to embark on a new challenge or pursue an idea he has been contemplating for some time. For some Earth Oxen, new equipment or knowledge can add impetus to a particular activity.

In addition, some Earth Oxen will pay greater attention to their well-being, perhaps by starting a new fitness discipline or joining an activity group. With proper guidance, they can make a noticeable difference to how they feel, and their activities can often have a fun and possibly social element too. Here again, the Goat year can open up many interesting possibilities.

Overall, however, in 2015 the Earth Ox will need to be thorough, cautious and aware. This is no time for risk, especially in financial matters and important correspondence. Also, the Earth Ox does need to liaise with others rather than act independently. That way his year will not only be more pleasurable but he will also have a better chance of benefiting from the support and opportunities that will be available. If he bears this in mind, he can make this an interesting and generally satisfying year.

Tip for the Year
Be mindful and communicative. Others can do a lot for you *if you let them*. So open up and share, participate and be receptive to the new. That way your year can be that much more enriching.

Famous Oxen

Lily Allen, Hans Christian Andersen, Gemma Arterton, Johann Sebastian Bach, David Blaine, Napoleon Bonaparte, Albert Camus, Jim Carrey, Charlie Chaplin, George Clooney, Bill Cosby, Diana, Princess of Wales, Marlene Dietrich, Walt Disney, Patrick Duffy, Jessica Ennis-Hill, Jane Fonda, Edward Fox, Michael J. Fox, Peter Gabriel, Elizabeth George, Richard Gere, Ricky Gervais, William Hague, Handel, King Harald V of Norway, Adolf Hitler, Dustin Hoffman, Hal Holbrook, Anthony Hopkins, Billy Joel, King Juan Carlos of Spain, Tony Keith, John Key, B. B. King, Keira Knightley, Mark Knopfler, Burt Lancaster, Bruno Mars, Queen Mathilde of Belgium, Chloë Moretz, Kate Moss, Eddie Murphy, Jack Nicholson, Leslie Nielsen, Bill Nighy, Barack Obama, Gwyneth Paltrow, Oscar Peterson, Lionel Richie, Wayne Rooney, Tim Roth,

Rubens, Meg Ryan, Amanda Seyfried, Jean Sibelius, Bruce Springsteen, Meryl Streep, Lady Thatcher, Alan Titchmarsh, Scott F. Turow, Vincent van Gogh, Zoë Wanamaker, Sigourney Weaver, the Duke of Wellington, Arsène Wenger, W. B. Yeats.

26 January 1914 to 13 February 1915 — *Wood Tiger*

13 February 1926 to 1 February 1927 — *Fire Tiger*

31 January 1938 to 18 February 1939 — *Earth Tiger*

17 February 1950 to 5 February 1951 — *Metal Tiger*

5 February 1962 to 24 January 1963 — *Water Tiger*

23 January 1974 to 10 February 1975 — *Wood Tiger*

9 February 1986 to 28 January 1987 — *Fire Tiger*

28 January 1998 to 15 February 1999 — *Earth Tiger*

14 February 2010 to 2 February 2011 — *Metal Tiger*

The Tiger

The Personality of the Tiger

It's
the zest,
the enthusiasm,
the giving the little bit more,
that makes the difference.
And opens up so much.

The Tiger is born under the sign of courage. He is a charismatic figure and usually holds very firm views. He is strong-willed and determined and sets about most of his activities with tremendous energy and enthusiasm. He is very alert and quick-witted and his mind is forever active. He is a highly original thinker and is nearly always brimming with new ideas or full of enthusiasm for some new project or scheme.

The Tiger adores challenges and loves to get involved in anything that he thinks has an exciting future or that catches his imagination. He is prepared to take risks and does not like to be bound either by convention or the dictates of others. He likes to be free to act as he chooses and at least once during his life he will throw caution to the wind and go off and do the things he wants to do.

The Tiger does, however, have a somewhat restless nature. Even though he is often prepared to throw himself wholeheartedly into a project, his initial enthusiasm can soon wane if he sees something more appealing. He can also be rather impulsive and there will be occasions in his life when he acts in a manner he later regrets. If he were to think things through or be prepared to persevere in his various activities, he would almost certainly enjoy a greater degree of success.

Fortunately the Tiger is lucky in most of his enterprises, but should things not work out as he hoped, he is liable to suffer from severe bouts of depression and it will often take him a long time to recover. His life often consists of a series of ups and downs.

He is, however, very adaptable. He has an adventurous spirit and rarely stays in the same place for long. In the early stages of his life he is likely to try his hand at several different jobs and he will also change his residence fairly frequently.

The Tiger is very honest and open in his dealings with others. He hates any sort of hypocrisy or falsehood. He is also well known for being blunt and forthright and has no hesitation in speaking his mind. He can be rebellious at times, particularly against any form of petty authority, and while this can lead him into conflict with others, he is never one to shrink from an argument or avoid standing up for what he believes is right.

The Tiger is a natural leader and can rise to the top of his chosen profession. He does not, however, care for anything too bureaucratic or detailed, and he does not like to obey orders. He can be stubborn and obstinate and throughout his life he likes to retain a certain amount of independence in his actions and be responsible to no one but himself. He likes to consider that all his achievements are due to his own efforts and he will not ask for support from others if he can avoid it.

Ironically, despite his self-confidence and leadership qualities, he can be indecisive and will often delay making a major decision until the very last moment. He can also be sensitive to criticism.

Although the Tiger is capable of earning large sums of money, he is rather a spendthrift and does not always put his money to best use. He can also be most generous and will often shower lavish gifts on friends and relations.

The Tiger cares very much for his reputation and the image that he tries to project. He carries himself with an air of dignity and authority and enjoys being the centre of attention. He is very adept at attracting publicity, both for himself and the causes he supports.

The Tiger often marries young and he will find himself best suited to those born under the signs of the Pig, Dog, Horse and Goat. He can also get on well with the Rat, Rabbit and Rooster, but will find the Ox and Snake a bit too quiet and serious for his liking and will be highly irritated by the Monkey's rather mischievous and inquisitive ways. He will also find it difficult to get on with another Tiger or a Dragon – both partners will want to dominate the relationship and could find it difficult to compromise on even the smallest of matters.

The Tigress is lively, witty and a marvellous hostess at parties. She takes great care over her appearance and is usually most attractive. She can be a very doting mother and while she believes in letting her children have their freedom, she makes an excellent teacher and will ensure that her children are well brought up and want for nothing. Like her male counterpart, she has numerous interests and likes to have sufficient independence and freedom to go off and do the things she wants to do. She has a most caring and generous nature.

The Tiger has many commendable qualities. He is honest, courageous and often a source of inspiration to others. Providing he can curb the wilder excesses of his restless nature, he is almost certain to lead a fulfilling and satisfying life.

The Five Different Types of Tiger

In addition to the 12 signs of the Chinese zodiac there are five elements and these have a strengthening or moderating influence on the signs. The effects of the five elements on the Tiger are described below, together with the years in which they were exercising their influence. Therefore Tigers born in 1950 and 2010 are Metal Tigers, Tigers born in 1962 are Water Tigers, and so on.

Metal Tiger: 1950, 2010

The Metal Tiger has an assertive and outgoing personality. He is very ambitious, and while his aims may change from time to time, he will work relentlessly until he has obtained what he wants. He can, however, be impatient for results and become highly strung if things do not work out as he would like. He is distinctive in his appearance and is admired and respected by many.

Water Tiger: 1962

This Tiger has a wide variety of interests and is always eager to experiment with new ideas or satisfy his adventurous nature by going off to explore distant lands. He is versatile, shrewd and has a kindly nature. He tends to remain calm in a crisis, although he can be annoyingly indecisive at times. He communicates well with others and through his many capabilities and persuasive nature usually achieves what he wants in life. He is also highly imaginative and is often a gifted orator or writer.

Wood Tiger: 1914, 1974

The Wood Tiger has a friendly and pleasant personality. He is less independent than some of the other types of Tiger and more prepared to work with others to secure a desired objective. However, he does have a tendency to jump from one thing to another and can easily become distracted. He is usually very popular, has a large circle of friends and invariably leads a busy and enjoyable social life. He also has a good sense of humour.

Fire Tiger: 1926, 1986

The Fire Tiger sets about everything he does with great verve and enthusiasm. He loves action and is always ready to throw himself wholeheartedly into anything that catches his imagination. He has many leadership qualities and is capable of communicating his ideas and enthusiasm to others. He is very much an optimist and can be most generous. He has a likeable nature and can be a witty and persuasive speaker.

Earth Tiger: 1938, 1998

This Tiger is responsible and level-headed. He studies everything objectively and tries to be scrupulously fair in all his dealings. Unlike other Tigers, he is prepared to specialize in certain areas rather than get distracted by other matters, but he can become so involved in what he is doing that he does not always take into account the opinions of those around him. He has good business sense and is usually very successful in later life. He has a large circle of friends and pays great attention to both his appearance and his reputation.

Prospects for the Tiger in 2015

The Tiger likes to be active and occupied, and the busy nature of the Horse year (31 January 2014–18 February 2015) will suit him well. This is a generally encouraging time and a lot can happen in the closing months.

As the Tiger sets about his activities, he will find opportunities arising quickly. In his work, developments can lead him to taking on additional responsibilities, with scope for an increased role should he wish. Some Tigers may be tempted by a position elsewhere, while those seeking work could find an opportunity or training scheme that could have an important bearing on their future. September and late November could see considerable activity work-wise.

The Tiger is well known for his generous streak and would do well to make early provision for increased spending during the later months of the year. Some Tigers could also enjoy some money luck at this time, perhaps by way of a bonus or extra payment.

Socially and domestically, the Tiger will be in demand, and if possible, he should aim to spread out his commitments rather than have a lot concentrated in a short space of time. September, December and the New Year will be busy, and for Tigers enjoying romance, this can add sparkle to the year's end.

The Year of the Goat starts on 19 February and the Tiger will have definite hopes for it. Enterprising, resourceful and with ideas aplenty, he will regard this as a year for decisive action. He will fare reasonably well, but Goat years are fickle and during them the best-laid plans may not always proceed in the manner intended. In 2015 the Tiger will need to keep his wits about him.

One positive aspect of the Goat year is that it is a time for ideas, creativity and fresh approaches, and here the Tiger is in his element. In his work in particular, when changes are introduced, new approaches are needed or problems occur, he will often have suggestions to make or find his experience helping in some way. As a result he will have the chance to make headway this year, including through promotion or the offer of a better position elsewhere. However, while the aspects are encouraging, the Tiger will need to be disciplined and focused. Sometimes his initial enthusiasm can wane and he can get distracted by other matters. Should he relax his efforts this year or spread his attention too widely (always a risk in Goat years), problems could loom. Tigers, take note.

In addition the Tiger should pay careful attention to his relations with colleagues. This includes consulting them regularly about current developments and being aware of their points of view. The greater the Tiger's contribution this year, the more support he will enjoy and the more that will become possible for him.

For Tigers who are seeking work or a change, the Goat year has good possibilities in store. In addition to following up vacancies in the type of work he favours, the Tiger could find it helpful to consider other ways in which he could use his skills. His thinking could open up new opportunities and result in the offer of a potentially important position. March, June, July and October could be important months for work matters.

Another encouraging aspect concerns the Tiger's personal interests. With his enquiring nature and capacity for coming up with ideas, he can derive a lot of pleasure from them this year. If something intrigues him, he should take action and see what develops. The Goat year offers the Tiger considerable scope.

In view of his commitments and plans and likelihood of good travel possibilities, however, he will need to manage his resources carefully. With a certain amount of discipline, he can fare well, but he should watch his general spending and avoid yielding to too many unplanned purchases, otherwise some activities planned for later in the year may need to be curtailed. Tigers, take note and keep control of your purse-strings. Also, keep your belongings safe. A loss could be upsetting.

The Tiger's home life will see much activity and there will need to be good liaison and some quality time set aside for sharing, otherwise general busyness and lack of communication could lead to misunderstandings and tension. The Tiger does need to be mindful of this and should try not to conduct everything at such a heady pace.

As he will frequently find himself inspired this year, he will, however, often be keen to go ahead with plans for the home. Some of these could make a noticeable difference, especially in efficiency and energy saving, but he should avoid starting too many projects all at once. Sometimes his enthusiasm can get the better of him. Also, plans are liable to change this year and he will need to be adaptable.

Busy though the Tiger's home life will be, it will contain many pleasures and the closing months of the year may well be marked by some special family news, a particular occasion or the opportunity of additional travel.

With his genial nature, the Tiger is always keen to enjoy his social life and this will not disappoint him this year. Changes and new pursuits will introduce him to new people and he will have an interesting mix of events to go to during the year. March, April, July and August could see the most social activity. However, while usually mindful of others, the Tiger does need to take into account his friends' views and be aware of arrangements that have been agreed upon. With so much going on, being preoccupied and not keeping his diary up to date could cause problems.

For the unattached Tiger, however, there is the prospect of significant romance. Quite a few Tigers will meet their future partner in the Goat year.

Overall, the year is filled with possibility for the Tiger, and his inventiveness, drive and enthusiasm will allow him to do a great deal. In view of the volatility of the year, he does need to take into account prevailing conditions and the views of others rather than proceed regardless. However, with awareness and flexibility, he will find his efforts rewarding him well. A full and satisfying year.

The Metal Tiger

This will be a year of interesting developments for the Metal Tiger and while some plans will be affected by change, he will emerge from it with many accomplishments to his credit.

One particular strength of the Metal Tiger is his ability to put himself across to others. Often eloquent, he is always persuasive, interesting and the source of some very fine ideas. In the Goat year these qualities will serve him well and whenever he is in a position in which he can be of influence or put forward ideas, his input can be telling. He can impress quite a few people and reap considerable benefits.

This particularly applies to his work situation. Many Metal Tigers will be affected by change, especially as colleagues (some long-standing and also good friends) move on or new ways of working are introduced. At such times the Metal Tiger's experience can be brought to bear, and by making a contribution and liaising well with others, he may find himself playing an increased role. For Metal Tigers whose work involves self-expression or creativity, this can be an especially active and success-ful time.

Many Metal Tigers will be fully involved in their work this year and immerse themselves in their often changed duties, but there will also be some who decide to retire or reduce their working hours. These Metal Tigers should pay close attention to the paperwork they receive and the terms offered. These do need to be checked thoroughly and if anything is unclear the Metal Tiger needs to ask for clarification and, if necessary, seek professional advice. Where officialdom is concerned, this is no year to be lax.

This also applies to finance. For Metal Tigers who retire, important financial adjustments will be needed, and for those who have expensive plans, careful budgeting will be required. This is no year to proceed on too much of an ad hoc basis. In addition, financial forms and insurance documents need to be dealt with carefully and the Metal Tiger should keep important items secure. Extra vigilance is advised this year.

If possible, however, the Metal Tiger should make provision for a holiday, as a rest in a carefully chosen destination can do him good.

Goat years can also be marked by notable events such as exhibitions, concerts and sporting spectacles, and if any of these (including some held locally) appeal to the Metal Tiger, he should try to go. Goat years can be culturally rich and some events will whet the Metal Tiger's interest.

The Metal Tiger will also be encouraged by the way he is able to further certain of his own interests. He is likely to have the chance to take them in new directions or try out something different. Goat years can open up exciting possibilities, but the Metal Tiger needs to be prepared to take advantage of these. Metal Tigers who are newly retired or would welcome a new activity, do keep alert for opportunities.

Personal interests can also lead to the Metal Tiger meeting others and, in some cases, being introduced to a new circle of people. For the unattached, the Goat year is not without romantic interest. At most times of the year the Metal Tiger will have things to do, with March, April, July and August seeing the most social opportunities.

The Metal Tiger's home life will also keep him busy. In addition to his own activities, he will do much to assist those close to him. Younger relations could be particularly grateful for his help. He will also be keen to proceed with certain domestic plans, including, for a few, a move. However, as the Metal Tiger will quickly find, the Goat year can inject a certain unpredictability into proceedings. New possibilities may arise, problems and delays occur and original requirements change. The Metal Tiger will need to accept that certain activities will take longer than anticipated. However, by the year's end, some ambitious home projects and purchases will have been successfully completed and the benefits appreciated by all.

Overall, this will be an active and interesting year for the Metal Tiger, although he will need to be flexible with some of his plans. However, the Metal Tiger is adroit and can often turn situations to his advantage. This can be a varied but satisfying year for him and his many qualities will serve him well.

Tip for the Year

Make more of your ideas and creative talents. Set yourself a project, develop an interest or take up something new. Also, be alert for opportunity, for positive action can make this an interesting and enriching time.

The Water Tiger

Goat years encourage personal growth and by embracing this one, the Water Tiger can do well. This will be an important year for him, but it is essential that he is not too narrow in his thinking. He possesses a quick and innovative mind, however, and this can lead to a lot opening up for him during the year. And in addition he will be helped by his resourceful streak.

Goat years are also changeable, with even the best-laid plans subject to alteration. The Water Tiger will experience this several times throughout the year. However, while there may be moments of uncertainty, new opportunities can arise. Throughout the year the Water Tiger needs to keep alert and be swift to respond.

In his work this can be a particularly eventful time. With the experience he has behind him, he will have the opportunity to extend his role and take on more specialist tasks. Although this will be welcome, his new duties may sometimes be different from what he was expecting. As a result, he will need to rise to the challenge and make the most of situations *as they are*. Some parts of the year will test him, but also give him the chance to prove himself. For Water Tigers whose work involves artistic expression or creative input, this can be a particularly rewarding and productive time.

For Water Tigers who are seeking work or keen to move elsewhere, the Goat year can hold unexpected developments. By widening the scope of their search, many will secure an interesting position in a new line of work. There will often be a considerable change of routine involved and much to learn, but Goat years encourage the Water Tiger to explore and expand on his capabilities. March, late May, June to early August and October could see significant developments.

The progress the Water Tiger makes at work can bring an increase in income and some Water Tigers may also find ways to add to this through an interest or enterprising idea. However, to make the most of his resources, the Water Tiger will need to manage his financial situation carefully. Also, if entering into any new agreement, he should check the terms and conditions. Goat years are not ones for risk or haste. In addition, the Water Tiger should keep valuable belongings safe. A loss could upset and inconvenience him. Water Tigers, be warned.

In his personal interests, the Water Tiger should again look to develop his skills. The Goat year encourages creative endeavour and Water Tigers who enjoy artistic pursuits should promote their talents. The year can be rich in cultural activity and some Water Tigers will enjoy visiting exhibitions and attending concerts as well as furthering their interests through courses or study programmes. Although the Water Tiger may have many demands on his time, it is important that he does not neglect his own interests.

The Goat year can also give rise to some interesting travel opportunities. Some Water Tigers could be tempted by interest-related events and should see what can be organized. As with so much this year, travel opportunities can arise in unexpected fashion and many Water Tigers will enjoy special occasions and breaks which have sometimes been hastily arranged.

With his genial nature, the Water Tiger enjoys company and over the year can look forward to some interesting social occasions. He may find himself helped by the advice of a close friend, and in some cases discussing ideas with his friends can lead to a certain synergy developing and interesting possibilities following on. The active mind of the Water Tiger may well be ignited by a flash of inspiration when talking to another person this year. Late February to April, July, August and early September could see the most social activity.

For Water Tigers who are alone and have experienced some personal difficulty, the Goat year will bring the chance to turn the corner. New activities, new friendships and, for quite a few, new romance can all brighten the year. In spite of their pressures, Goat years can be personally special.

The Water Tiger's home life will see much activity and tasks, decisions and plans will all need to be talked over and, as situations change, modified accordingly. Throughout the year the Water Tiger should ensure that home life is not *always* conducted in a whirl and should spend some quality time with his loved ones. This is very much a year that favours togetherness. It will contain several special family occasions, with a lot happening in the last quarter.

Overall, the Water Tiger will see a tremendous amount happen this year, and when he looks back, he will be surprised by all the changes that have taken place. Throughout the year there will be successes and enjoyable times, especially as ideas and interests develop, although there will also be times of uncertainty and pressure. However, the Water Tiger is blessed with an inventive and enthusiastic nature, and by making the most of what happens, adjusting as required and seizing his opportunities, he can gain a lot from the Goat year. And throughout, he will value the support of those around him.

Tip for the Year
Be open to opportunity. By taking advantage of what occurs and putting your ideas forward, you can see interesting developments following on. Be game, be adventurous and use your talents well. This year has much to offer you.

The Wood Tiger

Interesting times await the Wood Tiger! As the Goat year starts, he will have definite plans in mind and, in characteristic fashion, will set about them with purpose and resolve. However, as he will soon discover, Goat years have a way of their own. Plans will be subject to change and some interesting (and often unexpected) chances will arise along the way. This can be a generally good year for the Wood Tiger, but he does need to adapt and to make the most of emerging opportunities.

This will be especially the case in his work situation. During the year many Wood Tigers will be affected by new ways of working and, despite some initial reservations, will need to embrace them. In some cases they could entail additional training or new duties, but if the Wood Tiger shows willingness, there will often be the chance for him to play a greater role. However, some opportunities will arise with little warning this year and to benefit the Wood Tiger will need to be quick. In particular, Wood Tigers whose work involves an element of creative expression should make the most of their talents. Inventive and resourceful, they will find that some of what they put forward can develop in an encouraging way.

For Wood Tigers who are seeking a change from their current position, as well as those seeking work, the Goat year is again one of interesting possibility. By widening the scope of his search, discussing his options with employment officials and perhaps taking advantage of training incentives, the Wood Tiger can uncover new possibilities. Goat years can have some curious twists and turns, and quite a few Wood Tigers will end this one working in an area quite different from what they have done before. Whenever the Wood Tiger sees an opportunity, he should act upon it without delay, but March, June, July and October could see potentially important developments.

Progress at work will allow many Wood Tigers to increase their income and some will also benefit from the receipt of extra funds. However, the Wood Tiger will need to keep control of his outgoings, otherwise anything extra could be quickly spent, and not always in the most effective way. To go ahead with his plans, including home and equipment purchases and travel, he will need to budget carefully. He will also need to be vigilant when entering into any new agreement, deal with correspondence promptly and ensure his insurance policies cover his needs. Items of personal value should also be looked after carefully. This is very much a year to be vigilant and thorough.

Although the Wood Tiger will often be kept busy with his various commitments, it is also important he allows time for recreational pursuits. If sedentary for much of the day, he will particularly benefit from those that allow him additional exercise. His interests can also provide a welcome contrast to his more usual activities and the Goat year encourages trying the new. Creative activities are excellently aspected and should the Wood Tiger want to make more of a certain idea or talent, now is the time. Those who enjoy writing could find this an especially satisfying (and sometimes therapeutic) activity.

The Wood Tiger should also not allow the demands of the year to prevent him from going to any social occasions that appeal to him. These can both bring him pleasure and provide valuable lifestyle balance. Contacts with close friends too can be helpful, not only in allowing the Wood Tiger to discuss ideas he may be considering but also in enabling him to benefit from the perceptive advice of another person. Late February to the end of April and July to early September could see the most social activity.

For the unattached Wood Tiger, changes in work or new interests taken up over the year can lead to meeting new people, and one of these, perhaps met by chance, can become important as the year develops.

Domestically, the Wood Tiger will see much activity. As commitments and routines alter, adjustments will be needed. The Wood Tiger and his loved ones are also likely to be facing some key decisions and it is important that these are talked through and the implications considered. The Goat year requires good liaison, dialogue and co-operation. In addition, when embarking on practical projects, the Wood Tiger will need to show some flexibility. Initial ideas and requirements are apt to change and plans will need to be revised accordingly. However, amid the sometimes hectic activity, there will be special times to mark, with shared activities, including trips out or a possible holiday, doing everyone good.

The Year of the Goat offers considerable scope for the Wood Tiger and with care and willingness he can benefit from what occurs during it. In his work he will often have good chances to further his skills and can widen his options for the future. Personal interests too will allow him to use his ideas and creativity. Throughout the year he will value the support of those around him and shared activities are favourably aspected. Overall, an encouraging year, although the Wood Tiger does need to keep alert and make the most of his opportunities.

Tip for the Year
Look to make more of your ideas and special talents. Also, keep your lifestyle in balance and preserve time for those who are special to you as well as to enjoy personal pursuits.

The Fire Tiger

The Fire Tiger sets about life with considerable energy and during the Goat year yet again he will be involved in a great many activities. There will be triumphs and encouraging developments, but mixed in with these will be disappointments and challenges. However, what Fire Tiger experiences can have long-term value. This may not be an easy or straightforward year, but will be an action-packed and significant one!

Throughout the year the Fire Tiger will need to remain aware of developments and communicate well with those around him. Immersing himself so much in his own activities that he loses sight of the broader picture could mean he misses out on emerging opportunities.

This will be especially the case in his work. For Fire Tigers who are well established where they are or pursuing a particular career, changes are afoot. If the Fire Tiger is in a large organization, there could be the opportunity for him to transfer to another department or substantially change his duties. Some of what is asked of him may not be what he had envisaged but may nevertheless provide him with valuable new experience. The ambitious Fire Tiger will have high hopes for the future and any strengths he can highlight now can be instrumental in his later success. Goat years favour resourcefulness and a keen 'can do' approach, and here many a Fire Tiger can shine.

The majority of Fire Tigers will stay where they are over the year, although with an often considerable change of duties. However, for those who feel their position can be bettered elsewhere or are seeking work, again the Goat year has encouraging prospects. To help in their quest, these Fire Tigers should actively make enquiries, and if they see an opening or are drawn towards a new type of work, they should find out more. In many cases their initiative can reward them with a position they can build on in the future. A few Fire Tigers may also be successful in securing a position following a rejection, which, while disappointing at the time, could turn out to be a blessing in disguise. Such are the workings of this interesting but curious Goat year. March, June to early August and October could see particularly interesting developments.

Progress at work can lead to an increase in income and some Fire Tigers may also find ways to supplement their earnings through a personal interest or enterprising idea. However, while any financial upturn will help the Fire Tiger carry out certain plans he may have (including accommodation-wise), he will need to manage his resources carefully. To be over-extravagant or not make sufficient allowance for his commitments could result in economies later. Budgets need to be adhered to in the Goat year. The Fire Tiger should also be thorough when dealing with important correspondence and take especial care when entering into an agreement. It would also be worth him making sure that his insurance policies are sufficient for his needs and up to date. A lapse could result in problems. He should also take extra care with valuables. A loss could upset and inconvenience him. Fire Tigers, take note.

Although the Fire Tiger *will* need to be disciplined with spending, if possible he should try to make allowance for a holiday this year. Even if he decides not to travel too far, a change of scene can do him a lot of good. With the year's emphasis on culture, some exhibitions or places of interest could appeal to him. The Goat year will be a frequently inspiring time.

With this in mind, the Fire Tiger should also set aside time for recreational pursuits. Creative activities are well aspected and Fire Tigers who enjoy writing, art or some other form of self-expression should explore their talents, while Fire Tigers who have let their interests lapse or who would welcome a personal challenge should keep alert for new activities to pursue.

The Fire Tiger's interests and recreational activities will often have an enjoyable social element to them and he will benefit from meeting other enthusiasts and having the chance to form new friendships and potentially valuable contacts. For the unattached, a meeting in chance circumstances could prove significant. Late February to the end of April and July to mid-September could see the most social activity.

This also promises to be an eventful year domestically, with important decisions to make, activities to carry out (including parenthood for some and/or supporting more senior family members) and plans to see through. However, projects do need to be kept fluid. Over the year some plans may alter quite considerably and discussion will be needed. There may be several ways forward and some of what occurs may take a curious course but in the end work in the Fire Tiger's favour. However, although he will be kept busy, the Goat year can be an exciting time. August could be a particularly special month in many a Fire Tiger household.

Overall, this will be a full year for the Fire Tiger and when he looks back at the end of it, he will be astonished by the changes that have occurred and the experience he has gained. It is a year to venture, to be active and make the most of what occurs. Goat years may bring their uncertainties and pressures but they also have their opportunities, which the resourceful Fire Tiger can turn to his advantage. An eventful and satisfying year.

Tip for the Year
Enjoy your talents. With your ideas, ambitions and hopes, you can make this year the prelude to future success. Also, be open to possibility. Unexpected opportunities can arise this year. Don't close your mind to them. They can bring far-reaching benefits.

The Earth Tiger

For Earth Tigers born in 1998 this will be an active and interesting year with some important, though unanticipated, opportunities. With a game attitude and their usual keenness, these young Earth Tigers will enjoy much of the year and can do their prospects considerable good.

Throughout the year they would, though, do well to remember the Chinese proverb 'Diligence leads to riches.' If they put in the effort and use their time well, they can gain the skills needed to progress. In their education in particular, many will now have more chance to concentrate on their preferred subject areas. As a result, their studying can not only become more satisfying but also open up new possibilities. In some cases the facilities now available to them will allow them to do more or some work they have undertaken will alert them to options to consider in the near future.

The Goat year favours creative activity and Earth Tigers who are interested in the arts should make the most of their ideas. For the keen musician, artist, writer or drama student, the year can open up exciting possibilities.

The Earth Tiger's personal interests can also bring him much pleasure, and here again new ideas, teaching and equipment can lead to him doing more.

Goat years are excellent for exploring capabilities, and Earth Tigers who are in work or seeking work will also find that if they seize their chances to learn, they can gain valuable experience that they can build on in the future.

The young Earth Tiger will also appreciate the camaraderie of his friends during the year. Not only can interests often be shared, and much fun had in the process, but the Earth Tiger will value the support and understanding of those around him. Often his friends will have similar concerns to his own, and by being open and talking these through, he will often be helped and reassured. A close friend can be especially important in this regard. As a result of new activities, many Earth Tigers will find their social circle widening and, for a few, the Goat year can have romantic possibilities. At most times of the year the young Earth Tiger will have activities to do and parties and other occasions to look forward to, with late February to April and July to mid-September likely to be particularly lively months.

In view of the items the Earth Tiger will be keen to buy this year, together with his various interests and activities, he will need to manage his spending carefully, however, and be wary of too many impulse buys. When considering anything expensive, he should seek advice from others. Extra time and consideration will lead to more appropriate decisions.

In his home life too, the Earth Tiger should be forthcoming and willing to discuss his hopes, activities and concerns. This will not only be helpful for general family rapport but also allow close relations to better understand and support him. Also, rather than remain in his room for long periods (a tendency of many teenagers), he would find it helpful to come out now and then and give some assistance around the home. This may be appreciated more than he may realize.

The Goat year can bring unexpected opportunities and the Earth Tiger may also have the chance to visit some places at relatively short notice or to go to special events. When possible, he should aim to do so. The Goat year will do a lot to satisfy his enquiring nature.

For the Earth Tiger born in 1938, the Goat year will also have interesting developments in store. Again, some will be travel related, with the Earth Tiger enjoying any chances to visit family members (including some who may live some distance away) as well as places of interest. Cultural activities and local entertainments could also bring pleasure to many Earth Tigers.

The more senior Earth Tiger can also derive a great deal of satisfaction from his personal interests, especially the way he can put his often extensive knowledge to good use. He may delight in contact with other enthusiasts, too, and in the new ideas that follow on. This can be an inspiring time.

Throughout the year the Earth Tiger will also be very much involved in family activities and will appreciate the support and kindness of those around him. He will be equally glad to reciprocate, with advice (tactfully given) to a younger relation being of especial value.

When dealing with money matters and important correspondence, the Earth Tiger will, however, need to be thorough and check anything that is unclear. To make assumptions or give important matters scant attention could be to his disadvantage. Earth Tigers, take note and seek help when necessary.

Whether born in 1938 or 1998, the Earth Tiger can make the Goat year a pleasing and satisfying one. For both it is a year to enjoy developing ideas and for sharing these and other activities. For the Earth Tiger born in 1998, it is also a year to build up skills. The effort he puts in now is an investment in his future.

Tip for the Year
Be open-minded and willing to try out new activities. If you broaden your skills, you can find important benefits following on. Also, seek support. With help, more can open up for you. This is a year of interesting possibility and potential reward. Enjoy it – and use it well.

Famous Tigers

Paula Abdul, Amy Adams, Kofi Annan, Sir David Attenborough, Christian Bale, Victoria Beckham, Beethoven, Jamie Bell, Tony Bennett, Tom Berenger, Chuck Berry, Usain Bolt, Jon Bon Jovi, Sir Richard Branson, Matthew Broderick, Emily Brontë, Garth Brooks, Mel Brooks, Isambard Kingdom Brunel, Agatha Christie, Charlotte Church, Suzanne Collins, Robbie Coltrane, Bradley Cooper, Sheryl Crow, Tom Cruise, Penelope Cruz, Charles de Gaulle, Lana De Rey, Leonardo DiCaprio, Emily Dickinson, David Dimbleby, Drake, Dwight Eisenhower, Queen Elizabeth II, Enya, Roberta Flack, Frederick Forsyth, Jodie Foster, Megan Fox, Lady Gaga, Crystal Gayle, Ellie Goulding, Buddy Greco, Germaine Greer, Ed Harris, Hugh Hefner, William Hurt, Ray Kroc, Shia LaBeouf, Stan Laurel, Jay Leno, Groucho Marx, Karl Marx, Marilyn Monroe, Demi Moore, Alanis Morissette, Rafael Nadal, Robert Pattinson, Jeremy Paxman, Marco Polo, Beatrix Potter, Renoir, Nora Roberts, Kenny Rogers, the Princess Royal, Dylan Thomas, Liv Ullman, Jon Voight, Julie Walters, H. G. Wells, Oscar Wilde, Robbie Williams, Tennessee Williams, Sir Terry Wogan, Stevie Wonder, William Wordsworth.

14 February 1915 to 2 February 1916 — *Wood Rabbit*

2 February 1927 to 22 January 1928 — *Fire Rabbit*

19 February 1939 to 7 February 1940 — *Earth Rabbit*

6 February 1951 to 26 January 1952 — *Metal Rabbit*

25 January 1963 to 12 February 1964 — *Water Rabbit*

11 February 1975 to 30 January 1976 — *Wood Rabbit*

29 January 1987 to 16 February 1988 — *Fire Rabbit*

16 February 1999 to 4 February 2000 — *Earth Rabbit*

3 February 2011 to 22 January 2012 — *Metal Rabbit*

The Rabbit

The Personality of the Rabbit

Whenever
Wherever
With whoever.
Always I try to understand.
Without this, one flounders.
But with understanding,
at least you have a chance.
A good chance.

The Rabbit is born under the signs of virtue and prudence. He is intelligent, well mannered and prefers a quiet and peaceful existence. He dislikes any sort of unpleasantness and will try to steer clear of arguments and disputes. He is very much a pacifist and tends to have a calming influence on those around him. He has wide interests and usually a good appreciation of the arts and the finer things in life. He also knows how to enjoy himself and will often gravitate to the best restaurants and nightspots in town.

The Rabbit is a witty and intelligent speaker and loves being involved in a good discussion. His views and advice are often sought by others and he can be relied upon to be discreet and diplomatic. He will rarely raise his voice in anger and will even turn a blind eye to matters that displease him just to preserve the peace. He likes to remain on good terms with everyone, but he can be rather sensitive and takes any form of criticism very badly. He will also be the first to get out of the way if he sees any form of trouble brewing.

The Rabbit is a quiet and efficient worker and has an extremely good memory. He is very astute in business and financial matters, but his degree of success often depends on the conditions that prevail. He hates being in a situation which is fraught with tension or where he has to make sudden decisions. Wherever possible he will plan his various activities with the utmost care and a good deal of caution. He does not like to take risks and does not take kindly to change. Basically, he seeks a secure, calm and stable environment, and when conditions are right he is more than happy to leave things as they are.

The Rabbit is conscientious and because of his methodical and ever-watchful nature he can often do well in his chosen profession. He makes a good diplomat, lawyer, shopkeeper, administrator or priest, and he excels in any job where he can use his superb skills as a communicator. He tends to be loyal to his employers and is respected for his integrity and honesty, but if he ever finds himself in a position of great power he can become rather intransigent and authoritarian.

The Rabbit attaches great importance to his home and will often spend a lot of time and money maintaining and furnishing it and fitting it with all the latest comforts – the Rabbit is very much a creature of comfort! He is also something of a collector and there are many Rabbits who derive much pleasure from collecting antiques, stamps, coins, *objets d'art* or anything else which catches their eye or particularly interests them.

The female Rabbit has a friendly, caring and considerate nature, and will do all in her power to give her home a happy and loving atmosphere. She is also very sociable and enjoys holding parties and entertaining. She has a great ability to make the maximum use of her time and although she involves herself in numerous activities, she always manages to find time to sit back and enjoy a good read or a chat. She has a great sense of humour, is very artistic and is often a talented gardener.

The Rabbit takes considerable care over his appearance and is usually smart and well turned out. He also attaches great importance to his relations with others and matters of the heart are particularly important to him. He will rarely be short of admirers and will often have several serious romances before he settles down. He is not the most faithful of signs, but he will find that he is especially well suited to those born under the signs of the Goat, Snake, Pig and Ox. Due to his sociable and easy-going manner he can also get on well with the Tiger, Dragon, Horse, Monkey, Dog and another Rabbit, but he will feel ill at ease with the Rat and Rooster, as both these signs tend to speak their mind and be critical in their comments and the Rabbit just loathes any form of criticism or unpleasantness.

The Rabbit is usually lucky in life and often has the happy knack of being in the right place at the right time. He is talented and quick-witted, but he does sometimes put pleasure before work and wherever possible will opt for the easy life. He can at times be a little reserved and suspicious of the motives of others, but generally will lead a long and contented life and one which – as far as possible – will be free of strife and discord.

The Five Different Types of Rabbit

In addition to the 12 signs of the Chinese zodiac there are five elements and these have a strengthening or moderating influence on the signs. The effects of the five elements on the Rabbit are described below, together with the years in which they were exercising their influence. Therefore Rabbits born in 1951 and 2011 are Metal Rabbits, Rabbits born in 1963 are Water Rabbits, and so on.

Metal Rabbit: 1951, 2011

This Rabbit is capable, ambitious and has very definite views on what he wants to achieve in life. He can occasionally appear reserved and aloof, but this is mainly because he likes to keep his thoughts to himself. He has a quick and alert mind and is particularly shrewd in business matters. He can also be very cunning in his actions. He has a good appreciation of the arts and likes to mix in the best circles. He usually has a small but very loyal group of friends.

Water Rabbit: 1963

The Water Rabbit is popular, intuitive and keenly aware of the feelings of those around him. He can, however, be rather sensitive and take things too much to heart. He is very precise and thorough in everything he does and has an exceedingly good memory. He tends to be quiet and at times rather withdrawn, but he expresses his ideas well and is highly regarded by his family, friends and colleagues.

Wood Rabbit: 1915, 1975

The Wood Rabbit is likeable, easy-going and very adaptable. He prefers to work in a group rather than on his own and likes to have the support and encouragement of others. He can, however, be rather reticent in expressing his views and it would be in his own interests to become a little more open and let others know how he feels on certain matters. He usually has many friends, enjoys an active social life and is noted for his generosity.

Fire Rabbit: 1927, 1987

The Fire Rabbit has a friendly, outgoing personality. He likes socializing and being on good terms with everyone. He is discreet and diplomatic and has a very good understanding of human nature. He is also strong-willed and provided he has the necessary backing he can go far in life. He does, not, however, suffer adversity well and can become moody and depressed when things are not working out as he would like. He has a particularly good manner with children, is very intuitive and there are some Fire Rabbits who are even noted for their psychic ability.

Earth Rabbit: 1939, 1999

The Earth Rabbit is a quiet individual, but nevertheless very astute. He is realistic in his aims and prepared to work long and hard in order to achieve his objectives. He has good business sense and is invariably lucky in financial matters. He also has a most persuasive manner and usually experiences little difficulty in getting others to fall in with his plans. He is held in high esteem by his friends and colleagues and his views are often sought and highly valued.

Prospects for the Rabbit in 2015

In the Horse year (31 January 2014–18 February 2015) a lot will have happened very quickly and in what remains of it the Rabbit will be kept busy. Sometimes he may wish he was under less pressure or had more time available to attend to certain matters, but amid all the activity there will be several occasions he will particularly appreciate.

In his domestic and social life there will be a lot to do and where possible the Rabbit should try to plan ahead and so ease some of the pressure later.

The hectic pace will extend to work matters, with the Rabbit often finding his workload increasing as well as additional issues (some of which may concern colleagues) requiring attention. He will need to remain focused, but some of the demanding situations he will be faced with can highlight his skills and be to his future benefit.

For Rabbits seeking work, important opportunities may arise in the later part of the Horse year and positions taken on at this time could have good potential for future development. August, November and January 2016 could be significant.

By nature, the Rabbit is careful, thorough and likes to be in control, and some parts of the rather volatile Horse year will have been challenging for him. However, many a Rabbit will have proved himself and now be well placed to build on his accomplishments in the more encouraging Year of the Goat.

The Goat year is one of the most favourably aspected years for the Rabbit. Starting on 19 February, it is a time for moving forward and enjoying some pleasing and sometimes overdue success.

One of the major strengths of the Rabbit is his ability to get on well with other people. He not only listens but also empathizes, and this is appreciated by almost all who come into contact with him. This year his personal skills will serve him well, bringing him additional support and aiding his progress. Indeed, as the Goat year starts, the Rabbit could find it helpful to talk to his loved ones about his hopes for the year. Some of his plans could quickly take shape. February and March can be particularly constructive months and some early decisions will help get the Goat year off to a positive start.

The Rabbit's work prospects are especially encouraging and there will be the chance for him to make more effective use of his strengths. The many Rabbits who have experienced recent change or who take on new duties early in 2015 will have the chance to become established in their new role and achieve their objectives. For many this will be a far more fulfilling time than recent months. Also, as a result of staff movements and other changes, there will be excellent promotion prospects. However, when openings arise or the Rabbit is made an offer, he needs to respond quickly. In Goat years speed and initiative are of the essence.

For Rabbits who feel their prospects are limited where they are, who would welcome the chance to do something different or who are seeking work, the Goat year can again have significant developments in store. To help in their quest, these Rabbits should talk to those who are able to assist and follow up their suggestions. By taking the initiative and showing resolve, they can be rewarded with an important opportunity. Furthermore, once in a position, these Rabbits will have the chance to establish themselves in their new role. Goat years are encouraging and this one will see many Rabbits feeling more inspired than they have for some while. Late February to the end of April and September could see important developments.

The progress the Rabbit enjoys at work can also help financially. However, to make the most of this, the Rabbit will need to consider major purchases carefully and take the time to check the details and implications of any agreement he enters into. Proceeding in haste could lead to unfortunate oversights. The Rabbit is usually diligent in money matters, but in this generally good year he must not be lulled into complacency or rush decisions unnecessarily. Rabbits, take note.

In view of the encouraging aspects of the year, the Rabbit will be keen to pursue his personal interests, and whether he is developing an existing skill or trying out something different, he will take pleasure in what he does and the sometimes ambitious projects he carries out. Here again this is a year of interesting and ultimately pleasing possibilities. It is also a time when the arts enjoy increased prominence, and many Rabbits will make the most of this by going to concerts, exhibitions or special events.

With his genial nature, the Rabbit enjoys company and can look forward to many convivial occasions this year. He will also welcome the opportunity to run his ideas by his good friends and could be considerably helped by suggestions they make. Work changes can also lead to him making important connections. This is an excellent time for networking. Any Rabbits who start the year in low spirits could find it helpful to take an interest in what is happening in their community. By becoming more active and involved, many of these Rabbits will see a brightening in their situation. March, May, July, September and December could see the most social activity.

Affairs of the heart can also make the year special. Some unattached Rabbits will meet their future partner, while for those newly in love this can be a heady time.

In his home life, the Rabbit will be the instigator of many of the improvements that will take place over the year. Where interior design is concerned, his sense of style will be evident and several areas of his home will benefit from a makeover. He will also do a lot to encourage his loved ones and will delight in some family news, especially in the last quarter of the year. Travel can also bring much pleasure. Overall the Rabbit's home life will be both active and rewarding.

The aspects are very much on the Rabbit's side this year but, as with any year, problems will sometimes raise their head. When they do, it could be because the Rabbit has made assumptions or not fully taken into account his own situation and the implications involved. To make the most of the year, he does need to be thorough, check facts and think through the best approach. Extra care and attention can make a real difference. Generally, though, the Goat year offers excellent prospects for the Rabbit. His personal life is favourably aspected and for the unattached, significant romance can beckon, while at work there will be many chances for him to use his strengths and make good headway. This is a good year for him and one to enjoy.

The Metal Rabbit

The Metal Rabbit has a happy knack of using his time well and he will be pleased with how many of his activities proceed during the Goat year. Unlike some years, when he may feel events are outside his control, during this one he will feel more in charge. He will also be able to use his skills to telling effect. The Metal Rabbit is an adept communicator and in the Goat year not only will discussion lead to additional support but also help get some activities underway. The Metal Rabbit is good at enthusing others and he can reap the benefits this year.

At work there will be important decisions to make, possibly including the option for the Metal Rabbit to retire or alter his working schedule in some way. If affected, he should consider the implications carefully and seek clarification should any terms or arrangements be unclear. With care and good advice, he will be satisfied with the decisions he takes and the opportunities (including sometimes more free time) that follow on. For Metal Rabbits who are dissatisfied with their situation or feeling staid, the Goat year can bring the change they have been seeking.

For the Metal Rabbits who continue in work, the Goat year can also bring important developments. As personnel change, many of these Metal Rabbits will find themselves focusing on more specific tasks, including possibly mentoring junior colleagues. For those whose work involves an element of creativity, this can be an inspiring time and they can enjoy some notable success.

There will also be some Metal Rabbits who are seeking work or keen to change their position, perhaps in order to reduce their hours or commute. Although their quest may be difficult, they could be helped by talking to contacts and former colleagues and 'keeping their ears open' for opportunities. Something they hear about could be just right for them. Late February to the end of April, September and early October could see important developments.

The Metal Rabbit will also have some important financial decisions to take over the year and those who retire will have adjustments to make. To make the most of his position, and also when considering significant purchases, the Metal Rabbit needs to take his time, compare options and seek appropriate advice. Where finance is concerned, this is a year to be thorough and avoid risk.

If possible, the Metal Rabbit should try to make provision for a holiday, and with many special events being held this year, if something appeals to him, he should try to attend. Over the year many Metal Rabbits will derive great pleasure from what they are able to do, visit and see.

Another encouraging aspect concerns the Metal Rabbit's interests. He will often be keen to set himself a new challenge and again his creativity will be to the fore. Metal Rabbits who are newly retired will find that their interests will often take on more meaning. Some could have a pleasing social element too. Whether making contact with other enthusiasts independently or joining a local group, the Metal Rabbit will enjoy the chance to talk over ideas, receive feedback and share knowledge. Metal Rabbits who have recently changed their circumstances or are alone will find time spent on interests and recreational pursuits can add a lot to their year.

There will also be the chance for many Metal Rabbits to add to their circle of friends and acquaintances, and those involved in some aspect of their community could find their involvement increasing over the year and their services much appreciated. March, May, July, September and December could see the most social opportunities.

In so much that happens this year, the Metal Rabbit will value the support given by those close to him. When he is facing decisions, he will often find that by talking his options over, he will be able to clarify his thoughts. He will also do much to advise both younger and more senior relations. In addition, quite a lot of his time will be spent on home improvements. While certain plans may initially be problematic, important comforts will ultimately follow on. Holidays and special occasions will also be appreciated. Domestically, this promises to be an active year, with a lot concentrated at the beginning and very end.

The Metal Rabbit is a good judge of situations and likes to make plans and set himself objectives. In the Goat year, a lot will go in his favour and by gaining support and working towards what he wants, he will achieve a great deal. He is in the driving seat this year and can benefit from some excellent opportunities.

Tip for the Year

Share your ideas and hopes with others and then act. Much is possible. Enjoy your strengths, enjoy the satisfaction your activities can bring and enjoy the year.

The Water Rabbit

The Water Rabbit is quietly ambitious and sets about his activities without fuss. As the Goat year starts he will sense that his prospects are much improved and that with effort, and a certain amount of luck, he can accomplish a great deal. And his instincts will not let him down: this can be an active and auspicious year for him.

One of the most encouraging features of the year is the way that ideas can gain momentum. Many of the Water Rabbit's suggestions will be taken further and he can enjoy several notable outcomes.

In his work considerable progress is possible. Water Rabbits who have been in the same organization for some while will find their in-house knowledge and expertise may lead to a greater role. This will often be through promotion or the chance to transfer to another sector, and may be something the Water Rabbit has been working towards for some time. Such are the aspects that once in a new position he may soon be offered additional responsibilities. Goat years have scope *and* potential.

The aspects are also encouraging for Water Rabbits who decide to move on from where they are or are seeking work. Chance can play a big part and by exploring possibilities and following up ideas, they may be offered an interesting opportunity. Sometimes this may involve retraining and altering routines, but these Water Rabbits will welcome the opportunity. Late February to the end of April, September and early October could see particularly encouraging developments, but when an opportunity arises or the Water Rabbit has a flash of inspiration, he needs to act upon it *at the time*. Others may also set up useful introductions or put in a good word on his behalf. A lot can work in his favour this year, though he may not be aware of all of it.

The Water Rabbit's achievements at work can lead to an increase in income and he may also benefit from the receipt of extra funds. Financially, this can be an improved year, although when dealing with important correspondence he needs to be attentive and thorough. Haste – or, equally, delay and missed deadlines – could be to his detriment. Similarly, when considering sizeable purchases, he should take the time to make comparisons and consider cost and suitability. The greater his care, the better his eventual decision.

When possible, he should budget for a holiday. Travel could be a high-light this year. Goat years favour culture and many Water Rabbits will gain particular pleasure from exhibitions, attractions and places of inter-est. The Water Rabbit should also keep alert for events held in his area, including touring shows. Goat years can offer a veritable cultural feast.

Although often busy with commitments, it is also important that the Water Rabbit sets time aside for his personal interests. These can not only bring balance to his lifestyle but also be an important outlet for his talents. Creative activities are particularly well aspected and Water Rabbits who enjoy pursuits which call for visual awareness, such as photography, can derive considerable satisfaction from what they do.

Any Water Rabbit who does not take regular exercise should also aim to build some into his schedule, after seeking advice on what might be suitable.

The Water Rabbit's interests can also bring him into contact with others, and some people he meets over the year will quickly warm to him. This is an excellent year for networking and Water Rabbits who are feeling lonely or have experienced personal difficulty can see an important shift in fortune. New acquaintances, interests, social groups and, for some, romance can all add brightness to their year. March, May, July, September and December could be particularly lively months, but at most times of the year the Water Rabbit will have things to look forward to.

The considerable activity and variety of the Goat year can also be seen in the Water Rabbit's home life. Again he will be keen to go ahead with certain plans, but while he may have specific outcomes in mind, practical projects do need to be fully discussed, and adjusted as required. Also, finer details should not be rushed and costs should be carefully considered and budgeted for. Some exciting plans can take shape this year, but the Water Rabbit needs to be thorough and take his time.

The Goat year will also contain some notable domestic highlights. Not only will some of the Water Rabbit's own successes delight his loved ones, but there will also be other family achievements to mark. Shared interests, trips and other occasions will also be appreciated, and the year will offer a good mix of things to do. The last quarter will be especially busy.

When the genial, aware and determined Water Rabbit sets his mind on an objective, he works hard to achieve it. In 2015 his diligence will reward him well. By acting on his ideas and keeping alert for opportunities, he can make good progress. In both his work and personal interests he will have excellent opportunities to use his strengths, and his relations with others will aid his progress. With his skills, personable manner and drive, he can make this a constructive year.

Tip for the Year
This is a year for progress. However, do be thorough. A little extra attention can make a big difference, both in adding to your success and preventing mistakes. Also, value those around you. Their love, encouragement and advice can be significant.

The Wood Rabbit

An exciting year ahead! This year marks the start of a new decade in the Wood Rabbit's life and will not only contain surprises but also some significant opportunities. Plans the Wood Rabbit has been working towards can now be realized – or at least taken much further. This can be a lucky year and a good one.

To get the best from it the Wood Rabbit will, though, need to show some flexibility. Events can happen quickly and he will need to seize the moment. To delay or hesitate could lead to chances being missed. Time is of the essence.

This will especially be the case in his work situation. Opportunities to further his career may arise suddenly, perhaps through the need to cover for absent colleagues or deal with an unexpectedly high workload. By making the most of these situations, the Wood Rabbit will not only have the chance to widen his skills but also to strengthen his prospects. In many cases, sudden developments can turn out to be excellent opportunities.

The majority of Wood Rabbits will stay where they are this year, though in an often wider role. However, some will be tempted to look elsewhere, perhaps feeling the time is right to take their career in a new direction. Here again the Goat year can have unanticipated developments in store. Exciting doors can open for the Wood Rabbit, but he needs to be quick and willing to embrace the new.

This also applies to Wood Rabbits who are seeking work. By widening the scope of what they are prepared to consider, they can be successful in obtaining an interesting new position. Late February to the end of April and September to mid-October could see significant opportunities.

Progress at work can lead to many Wood Rabbits enjoying a noticeable increase in income. However, in view of his many activities and commitments, the Wood Rabbit may find that anything extra is quickly absorbed, and he could find it helpful to keep accounts so he can track spending and budget wisely. With good control, he will be able to do – and enjoy – that much more. Also, when dealing with important paperwork, he needs to be thorough and check the small print. Although usually careful, he could find mistakes or lapses resulting in inconvenience and extra cost. Wood Rabbits, do be vigilant.

With this being an active time, travel could feature prominently, with many Wood Rabbits not only enjoying a special holiday to mark their fortieth year but also taking advantage of invitations or other chances to go away. With cultural activities favourably aspected, many will be inspired by places, exhibitions or events they get to see.

In addition the Wood Rabbit should set aside time for his personal interests. These too are capable of developing in new ways this year.

The Goat year can give rise to much social activity, too, and the good rapport the Wood Rabbit enjoys with so many will be an important factor in his success. March, May, July, September and December could be particularly active months, and Wood Rabbits who start the year alone or who have seen a recent change in personal circumstances will discover that new friendships (including one with strong romantic possibility) can bring new joy to their lives.

The prospects are also good domestically. Loved ones will often be keen to mark the Wood Rabbit's fortieth birthday in style and may have some surprises lined up as well. Parts of the year will certainly have a celebratory feel. However, with so much happening, there will need to be good co-operation between everyone in the Wood Rabbit's household, and some flexibility too, as routines change and new possibilities arise. Where more practical activities are concerned, timescales may be fluid and initial ideas subject to change. During the year, family members will need to pull together. However, while some months will be pressured, there will still be some special times to enjoy.

The Year of the Goat not only marks the Wood Rabbit's fortieth year but during it he will feel ready to take on new challenges. And if he seizes his opportunities, he can make important headway. He will also value the support and love shown by others as well as some of the surprises this full and interesting year can bring. It is not only his fortieth year but in many respects a significant one too.

Tip for the Year
You know deep down that you are capable of great things. So, take action. Believe in yourself and go forth and realize your dreams. Also, value your loved ones and enjoy their love and support.

The Fire Rabbit

Many Fire Rabbits will have high hopes for the Year of the Goat. With ambitions they are keen to realize, they will regard this as a year for action. And they can fare well. Not only will their determined stance help, but throughout the year they will be assisted by others and also by circumstance. However, Goat years can proceed in unexpected ways and the Fire Rabbit will need to adapt as required. Considerable progress awaits, but it may not come in exactly the form envisaged. Goat years have their surprises.

The Fire Rabbit sets great store by his relations with others, and throughout the year the support and advice he receives can be instrumental in much that unfolds. To fully benefit, though, the Fire Rabbit does need to be willing to talk over ideas and seek advice from experts. With backing and helpful input, he will achieve far more.

This need for good dialogue applies to most areas of his life, but with this a year of some key personal plans, it is especially important in his personal life. By sharing hopes and combining efforts with those who are close to him, the Fire Rabbit will find some plans quickly getting underway. These could be accommodation matters (with some Fire Rabbits deciding to move), major acquisitions for the home or other goals, but whatever he wishes to carry out, the Fire Rabbit will find that concerted action can lead to some exciting times.

Many a Fire Rabbit will also benefit from fortunate developments over the year. It could be that what he wants to purchase suddenly becomes available or another good offer presents itself. Over the year the Fire Rabbit needs to make the most of what arises, even if it involves making adjustments to plans and timescales.

In addition to practical matters, the Goat year will give rise to some splendid personal times. Interests the Fire Rabbit can share can bring particular pleasure and there is likely to be a spontaneous edge to events. It could be that chances to go away for a short break or holiday suddenly arise, especially in late summer, or a spur of the moment treat is suggested. Whatever happens, the Goat year will offer a good mix of things to do and some Fire Rabbits will also be involved in some significant personal decisions. In many ways this can be an important and special time.

The Fire Rabbit will also enjoy the social activities the Goat year can bring. Not only will he value the support and (often pertinent) advice of long-standing friends but also the variety of occasions that take place. As a result of some of these, he will have the chance to meet many new people and this in itself can be important. As has often been found, the more people you know, the more likely you are to hear of opportunities or know of someone in a position to help you. Some of the people the Fire Rabbit meets now can be especially helpful to him. March, May, July, September and December could see the most social activity.

For Fire Rabbits who are unattached, romantic prospects are promising and will appear as if by ordained by fate.

The Goat year also encourages personal interests and is an excellent time to explore and promote ideas. Accordingly, if the Fire Rabbit sees a course or finds other ways to develop what he does, it would be worth following it up.

The aspects are also encouraging work-wise. Many of the Fire Rabbits following a particular career will feel ready to move to a new level and be alert for promotion opportunities or chances to widen their experience. In some instances, circumstances early on in the year will help. Quite a few Fire Rabbits will be able to make progress where they are, but for others events may take a curious course. It could be that a contact alerts the Fire Rabbit to an opening elsewhere or puts in a recommendation on his behalf (friends and contacts can play a big part in the Fire Rabbit's life this year) or his experience leads to another employer offering him a position. There can be excellent chances for him to further his career this year.

For Fire Rabbits who are unfulfilled where they are and those seeking work, the year can also bring important chances. Again friends and contacts can be helpful, as can those the Fire Rabbit approaches for advice. Through them, he may learn of possibilities worth pursuing. Some of what arises may be substantially different from what he has done before, but may present an interesting new challenge *and* prospects for the future. Late February to the end of April and the month of September could see particularly encouraging developments but at any time during the year if the Fire Rabbit detects an opportunity he should act quickly. Initiative can bring good results this year.

Progress at work may lead to an increase in income over the year, but with some exciting personal plans in store, the Fire Rabbit will need to keep strict control over his spending and budget in advance for specific requirements. He also needs to be thorough when dealing with paperwork and seek advice if anything is unclear. Mistakes, delays or ignorance of the implications of finer details could all work to his disadvantage. Finances do need attention and good management.

The Fire Rabbit has an engaging personality. He may sometimes seem quiet, but he is nevertheless determined and has a skilful way of achieving his aims. This can be a successful and often lucky year for him and by promoting his ideas and seizing his opportunities, he can achieve a lot. In his personal life there will be exciting times to enjoy and he will often be helped by the support of others. He will have much in his favour this year and can make this a successful time.

Tip for the Year

This is a year of great possibility for you. Move towards your goals with determination, but be prepared to adapt as situations require. Also, use any chances to raise your profile. The more active you are, the more opportunities can emerge. On a personal level, enjoy the love and support of those who are special to you. They can add much joy to your year as well as be important factors in your success.

The Earth Rabbit

The Goat year suits the Earth Rabbit's personality well. Encouraging freedom of thought and offering the chance to explore ideas and capabilities, it has a lot of potential for him.

For the Earth Rabbit born in 1999, the year can see some particularly important developments. In their education, many of these young Earth Rabbits will have the chance to decide on areas they would like to concentrate on and their decisions will often have a bearing on the future direction of their career. It is important that these Earth Rabbits let their own views be known to others but also listen carefully to the advice they are given. With proper consideration, they will be able to welcome the new opportunities opening up for them and many will feel more inspired by their studies and can make encouraging headway as the year progresses.

The Goat year can also give rise to additional opportunities. The Earth Rabbit could find himself starting a new subject, learning an additional skill or making better use of his resources. Goat years encourage experimenting and exploring. In addition, with the arts strongly favoured, those who enjoy music, drama or another creative pursuit should make the most of their talents. For the keen and interested, this can be an inspiring time.

The Earth Rabbit can benefit from the year in other respects as well, including, for many, growing in outward confidence. He will welcome his social opportunities and value the camaraderie of friends. Whether he is sharing interests, enjoying team activities or meeting like-minded people, he will find that a lot of fun can be had this year.

It is also important that he talks to those at home about his activities, hopes and the decisions he has to make, and seeks their advice when necessary. If he is forthcoming, they will be better able to help.

The Goat year can give rise to some interesting travel opportunities and whether the young Earth Rabbit is going on holiday, visiting places of interest or attending events, he will find this is a time that is rich in activity. With a game approach and an open mind, he will enjoy a lot of what he does. And this is the essence of the Goat year – it is one for making the most of what arises and for experimenting, exploring and building on strengths. The young Earth Rabbit has an exciting future ahead of him and can lay the foundation for that future this year.

For the Earth Rabbit born in 1939, again ideas and activities can bring pleasure. The Earth Rabbit sets about his pursuits with care, and yet again this year he will enjoy the way many of his plans evolve.

In his home life he will take particular satisfaction in setting about tasks he has long thought about. This could include sorting out storage areas, replacing outdated equipment and having a general efficiency drive. Some of what the Earth Rabbit does will take longer than anticipated but could yield some surprises, perhaps even long-lost items.

The Earth Rabbit will also be grateful for the support of family members and their assistance can make a major difference, particularly with more awkward tasks. Should the Earth Rabbit have concerns at any time, it is important that he voices these and seeks advice, including, if need be, the opinion of experts. However, just as he will benefit from the help he receives, so he in turn will do much to support those close to him, especially younger family members.

He will also enjoy the opportunities he has to travel as well as to involve himself in his community. With his keen and alert nature, he will often have things to do, visit or see, with some local events or social groups bringing particular delight.

The Earth Rabbit is generally adept at dealing with financial matters, but in the Goat year extra attention is required. Forms and other financial paperwork, although irksome, do need to be checked, dealt with promptly and kept carefully. If the Earth Rabbit is uncertain or concerned about anything, he should check the facts carefully. Similarly, time spent considering more major purchases and getting advice on what best meets his criteria will lead to better decisions. This is a time for increased financial care.

Overall, whether born in 1939 or 1999, the Earth Rabbit can gain a lot from the year. It is a time to go ahead with ideas, explore possibilities and enjoy the company and support of others. It can be a satisfying year and, especially for the Earth Rabbit born in 1999, it is one that can offer the chance to gain the skills he will need in the future. A pleasing and constructive year.

Tip for the Year
Don't set about your activities in isolation – involve others. With their input and advice, you can gain so much more from this favourable year.

Famous Rabbits

Margaret Atwood, Drew Barrymore, David Beckham, Harry Belafonte, Ingrid Bergman, St Bernadette, Jeff Bezos, Kathryn Bigelow, Michael Bublé, Nicolas Cage, Lewis Carroll, Fidel Castro, John Cleese, Confucius, Marie Curie, Johnny Depp, Novak Djokovic, Albert Einstein, George Eliot, W. C. Fields, James Fox, Cary Grant, Ashley Greene, Edvard Grieg, Oliver Hardy, Seamus Heaney, Tommy Hilfiger, Bob Hope,

Whitney Houston, Helen Hunt, John Hurt, Anjelica Huston, Enrique Iglesias, E. L. James, Henry James, Sir David Jason, Angelina Jolie, Michael Jordan, Michael Keaton, John Keats, Enda Kenny, Lisa Kudrow, Gina Lollobrigida, George Michael, Sir Roger Moore, David Moyes, Andy Murray, Mike Myers, Brigitte Nielsen, Graham Norton, Michelle Obama, Jamie Oliver, George Orwell, Edith Piaf, Brad Pitt, Sidney Poitier, Romano Prodi, Ken Russell, Emeli Sandé, Elisabeth Schwarzkopf, Neil Sedaka, Jane Seymour, Maria Sharapova, Neil Simon, Frank Sinatra, Sting, Quentin Tarantino, J. R. R. Tolkien, KT Tunstall, Tina Turner, Luther Vandross, Sebastian Vettel, Queen Victoria, Muddy Waters, Orson Welles, Hayley Westenra, Walt Whitman, Will-i-Am, Robin Williams, Kate Winslet, Tiger Woods.

3 February 1916 to 22 January 1917 — *Fire Dragon*

23 January 1928 to 9 February 1929 — *Earth Dragon*

8 February 1940 to 26 January 1941 — *Metal Dragon*

27 January 1952 to 13 February 1953 — *Water Dragon*

13 February 1964 to 1 February 1965 — *Wood Dragon*

31 January 1976 to 17 February 1977 — *Fire Dragon*

17 February 1988 to 5 February 1989 — *Earth Dragon*

5 February 2000 to 23 January 2001 — *Metal Dragon*

23 January 2012 to 9 February 2013 — *Water Dragon*

The Dragon

The Personality of the Dragon

I like giving things a go.
Sometimes I succeed,
sometimes I fail.
Sometimes the unexpected happens.
But it is the giving things a go
and the stepping forward
that make life so interesting.

The Dragon is born under the sign of luck. He is a proud and lively character and has a tremendous amount of self-confidence. He is also highly intelligent and very quick to take advantage of any opportunity. He is ambitious and determined and will do well in practically anything he attempts. He is also something of a perfectionist and will always try to maintain the high standards he sets himself.

The Dragon does not suffer fools gladly and will be quick to criticize anyone or anything that displeases him. He can be blunt and forthright in his views and is certainly not renowned for being either tactful or diplomatic. He does, however, often take people at their word and can occasionally be rather gullible. If he ever feels that his trust has been abused or his dignity wounded, he can sometimes become very bitter and it will take him a long time to forgive and forget.

The Dragon is usually very outgoing and is particularly adept at attracting attention and publicity. He enjoys being in the limelight and is often at his best when he is confronted by a difficult problem or tense situation. In some respects he is a showman and he rarely lacks an audience. His views are highly valued and he invariably has something interesting – and sometimes controversial – to say.

He also has considerable energy and is often prepared to work long and unsocial hours in order to achieve what he wants. He can, however, be rather impulsive and does not always consider the consequences of his actions. He also has a tendency to live for the moment and there is nothing that riles him more than to be kept waiting. The Dragon hates delay and can get extremely impatient and irritable over even the smallest of hold-ups.

The Dragon has an enormous faith in his abilities, but he does run the risk of becoming over-confident and unless he is careful he can sometimes make grave errors of judgement. While this may prove disastrous at the time, he does have the tenacity and ability to bounce back and pick up the pieces again.

The Dragon has such an assertive personality, so much willpower and such a desire to succeed that he will often reach the top of his chosen profession. He has considerable leadership qualities and will do well in positions where he can put his own ideas and policies into practice. He is usually successful in politics, show business, as the manager of his own department or business, and in any job that brings him into contact with the media.

The Dragon relies a tremendous amount on his own judgement and can be scornful of other people's advice. He likes to feel self-sufficient and there are many Dragons who cherish their independence to such a degree that they prefer to remain single throughout their lives. However, the Dragon will often have numerous admirers and many will be attracted by his flamboyant personality and striking looks. If he does marry, he will usually marry young, and will find himself particularly well suited to those born under the signs of the Snake, Rat, Monkey and Rooster. He will also find that the Rabbit, Pig, Horse and Goat make ideal companions and will readily join in with many of his escapades. Two Dragons will also get on well together, as they will understand each other, but the Dragon may not find things so easy with the Ox and Dog, as both will be critical of his impulsive and somewhat extrovert manner. He will also find it difficult to form an alliance with the Tiger, for the Tiger, like the Dragon, tends to speak his mind, is very strong-willed and likes to take the lead.

The female Dragon knows what she wants in life and sets about everything she does in a determined and positive manner. No job is too small for her and she is often prepared to work extremely hard to secure her objectives. She is immensely practical and somewhat liberated. She hates being bound by routine and petty restrictions and likes to have sufficient freedom to go off and do what she wants to do. She will keep her house tidy, but is not one for spending hours on housework – there are far too many other things that she prefers to do. Like her male counterpart, she has a tendency to speak her mind.

The Dragon usually has many interests and enjoys sport and other outdoor activities. He also likes to travel and often prefers to visit places that are off the beaten track rather than head for popular tourist destinations. He has a very adventurous streak in him and providing his financial circumstances permit – and the Dragon is usually sensible with his money – he will travel considerable distances during his lifetime.

The Dragon is a very flamboyant character and while he can be demanding of others and in his early years rather precocious, he will have many friends and will nearly always be the centre of attention. He has charisma and so much confidence that he can often become a source of inspiration to others. In China he is the leader of the carnival and he is also blessed with an inordinate share of luck.

The Five Different Types of Dragon

In addition to the 12 signs of the Chinese zodiac there are five elements and these have a strengthening or moderating influence on the signs. The effects of the five elements on the Dragon are described below, together with the years in which they were exercising their influence. Therefore Dragons born in 1940 and 2000 are Metal Dragons, Dragons born in 1952 and 2012 are Water Dragons, and so on.

Metal Dragon: 1940, 2000

This Dragon is very strong-willed and has a particularly forceful personality. He is energetic, ambitious and tries to be scrupulous in his dealings with others. He can also be blunt and to the point and usually has no hesitation in speaking his mind. If people disagree with him or are not prepared to co-operate, he is more than happy to go his own way. He usually has very high moral values and is held in great esteem by his friends and colleagues.

Water Dragon: 1952, 2012

This Dragon is friendly, easy-going and intelligent. He is quick-witted and rarely lets an opportunity slip by. However, he is not as impatient as some of the other types of Dragon and is prepared to wait for results rather than expect everything to happen at once. He has an understanding nature and is willing to share his ideas and co-operate with others. His main failing is a tendency to jump from one thing to another rather than concentrate on the job in hand. He has a good sense of humour and is an effective speaker.

Wood Dragon: 1964

The Wood Dragon is practical, imaginative and inquisitive. He loves delving into all manner of subjects and can quite often come up with some highly original ideas. He is a thinker and a doer and has the drive and commitment to put many of his ideas into practice. He is more diplomatic than some of the other types of Dragon and has a good sense of humour. He is very astute in business matters and can also be most generous.

Fire Dragon: 1916, 1976

This Dragon is ambitious, articulate and has a tremendous desire to succeed. He is a hard and conscientious worker and is often admired for his integrity and forthright nature. He is very strong-willed and has considerable leadership qualities. He can, however, rely a bit too much on his own judgement and fail to take into account the views and feelings of others. He can also be rather aloof and it would certainly be in his own interests to let others join in more with his various activities. He usually enjoys music, literature and the arts.

Earth Dragon: 1928, 1988

The Earth Dragon tends to be quieter and more reflective than some of the other types of Dragon. He has a wide variety of interests and is keenly aware of what is going on around him. He also has clear objectives and usually has no problems in obtaining support and backing for any of his ventures. He is very astute in financial matters and often able to accumulate considerable wealth. He is a good organizer, although he can at times be rather bureaucratic and fussy. He mixes well with others and has a large circle of friends.

Prospects for the Dragon in 2015

The Dragon likes to live life to the full. He has great energy and resolve and will have welcomed many of the opportunities the Horse year (31 January 2014–18 February 2015) will have opened up. A lot is still set to happen in the remaining months, although to make the most of this time, the Dragon needs to be careful not to overreach himself and spread his attention too widely.

At work, many Dragons will have the chance to draw on their expertise and win plaudits for what they do in sometimes challenging situations. Some may also have the opportunity to vary their role. The closing months of the Horse year, especially October, could contain interesting chances.

The Dragon's judgement can also help him financially at this time, particularly in view of the purchases he will be keen to make. By keeping alert and investigating different outlets, he could be fortunate in what he buys, whether for himself, for others or for the home.

Domestically and socially, he will be in demand. December and early January will be particularly busy. However, amid all the activity, the Dragon will need to liaise well with others and watch his independent tendencies. Also, should a rumour or another matter concern him, he does need to check the facts rather than make assumptions. While this is a generally favourable time for him, he needs to remain mindful of others.

*   *   *

The Year of the Goat starts on 19 February and will be a variable one for the Dragon. He likes to get on and do things, but could find progress middling at best. However, Goat years also have their benefits and the Dragon's personal life and general lifestyle balance will often be much improved. This is, though, a year to proceed carefully.

At work, rather than being intent on making major advances, many Dragons will decide to concentrate on their current role. As a result, they will not only have more chance to put their knowledge and skills to good effect but also to enjoy some professionally satisfying results. As the year proceeds, many could benefit from additional training or fresh objectives and see a widening of their role. Although the Goat year may lack the opportunities of some, it can still be a constructive one, with the Dragon able to concentrate on his strengths.

For Dragons who decide to move on from their present position and those seeking work, the year will be challenging. Obtaining a new position will not be easy, but the Dragon is redoubtable and if he actively follows up opportunities, his drive, enthusiasm and sheer tenacity will lead to chances being given. This may take time, but whenever challenged, the Dragon invariably shows great strength of character and is often able to win through.

An important feature of the Goat year is that it favours innovation and Dragons who work in a creative environment will often welcome the chance to be part of the idea-generating process. Goat years do have scope for the Dragon to make headway in work matters, but he needs to work within the parameters set and liaise closely with colleagues rather than be a lone voice. Dragons, take careful note.

April, July, September and November could see significant work developments, but generally the second half of the year will be easier than the first.

A major benefit of the year will be the way the Dragon is able to pursue his interests. Rather than always be looking ahead, though, this is an excellent time to take stock and enjoy what he can do *now*. Some Dragons may look at projects they have long considered or subjects that have intrigued them for a while and decide to find out more. Others may enrol on courses or study programmes or give some thought to their lifestyle and well-being. They can derive considerable benefit from their actions over the year.

The aspects also encourage travel and the Dragon should try to give himself a break at some point. Whether he decides to travel a considerable distance or somewhere within easy reach, he will appreciate what he gets to see and do. Spring and late summer could see some pleasing opportunities.

In view of travel possibilities as well as his other commitments, the Dragon will need to manage his financial situation well. Important purchases and transactions should be carefully considered and costed rather than rushed, and if tempted by anything speculative, the Dragon should think through the implications. Without sufficient attention, he could misjudge a certain issue and incur a loss. Financially, this is a year for careful control.

With his engaging manner and wide interests, however, the Dragon can look forward to an active and pleasing social life. Whether chatting with existing friends or making new ones, he will enjoy the many social opportunities that come his way. April, June, August and December could see considerable social activity.

For the unattached, romantic prospects are promising, with a chance meeting potentially becoming significant.

The Dragon will also enjoy sharing his ideas with family members and will not only be encouraged but could also find a pooling of thoughts leads to more taking place. Goat years favour collective effort. Also, rather than conducting his home life in a whirl, he should ensure that time is set aside for activities everyone can appreciate, such as watching a film, enjoying a good meal or going on a special trip or weekend away. Here again, Goat years are ideal for getting life into better balance.

Overall, although the Dragon's actual progress may be modest this year compared to some, this can still be a constructive time for him. The Dragon may like to live life in the fast lane, but sometimes even he has to slow down, and this is an ideal year to do so. To make the most of it, the Dragon should immerse himself in his current activities, give time to his own interests and development, and strive for a good lifestyle balance. Then next year, when more substantial opportunities will come his way, he will be ready.

The Metal Dragon

The element of Metal gives a sign greater resolve and this certainly holds true for the Metal Dragon. Determined, purposeful and with clear-cut views, he is a redoubtable figure who makes things happen. However, in this Goat year he cannot expect everything to go his way. Although he will continue to set about his activities with great energy, to get the best from the year he will need to watch his independent tendencies and adapt as required. This is a year to toe the line.

For the Metal Dragon born in 1940, this can be a busy and interesting year, but he does need to seek support for his activities. To be too self-willed or not pay sufficient regard to what others recommend could cause difficulties. Metal Dragons, take note and remember that this is a year favouring consensus and a combined approach.

As always, the more senior Metal Dragon will have given thought to what he would like to see happen over the year. To help his plans come to fruition, he should discuss them with his family, close friends and, should anything require specialist input, professionals. By being forthcoming and receptive to what others advise, he could see some plans quickly set in motion. A further feature of the year is an element of serendipity. Sometimes ideas that have been discussed could be realized due to a stroke of luck.

Over the year many Metal Dragons will take great pleasure in home improvements, including smartening certain areas and installing new equipment. Some may also mount an efficiency drive and declutter storage areas. Home projects can be satisfying and often beneficial this year.

The Goat year can also bring some fine travel opportunities. Some Metal Dragons will take advantage of last-minute offers or decide to go away on whim, and the spontaneity can add an exciting element to their travels.

The Metal Dragon can also derive considerable pleasure from his personal interests and should set time aside to explore ideas and, if artistically inclined, enjoy his creations. Goat years encourage self-expression and many Metal Dragons will be enthused by their activities. Again, if these Metal Dragons can share their thinking with others, this can give the ideas added momentum.

It could also be to the Metal Dragon's advantage to take note of what is happening locally. There could be social groups to join and, with the year's emphasis on culture, exhibitions to see or places of interest to visit. By being aware and involved, the Metal Dragon can take advantage of the variety of activities that are on offer this year.

In addition, he will often delight in shared family occasions and the support he is able to give close relations. Socially, too, he will welcome his chances to meet up with friends and attend events. Late March, April, June, August and December are likely to be particularly full and interesting months.

However, although the Metal Dragon is usually thorough when dealing with correspondence and finance, in the Goat year he does need to give these extra attention and seek advice on anything that is unclear or of concern. To misinterpret what is required or not take all the implications into account could be to his disadvantage. Metal Dragons, take note and be attentive.

Also, throughout the year the Metal Dragon needs to be mindful of others and watch his independent tendencies. The more he consults others and shares his ideas and activities, the richer his year can be.

For Metal Dragons born in 2000, it is also a case of being receptive and aware this year. Particularly in his education, by embracing what is available, the young Metal Dragon can advance his skills and knowledge as well as participate in more activities. This is a year that very much rewards commitment. Unfortunately, though, a trait of some Metal Dragons is to be self-willed, and some will close their mind to current opportunities and in time come to rue their attitude. For the overly independent and narrow-minded, Goat years can disappoint and frustrate. Metal Dragons, do take note.

Throughout the year, the Metal Dragon will be helped by being more forthcoming and talking about his hopes, activities and concerns. That way, he will find that others are not only better able to help, but also that, particularly in the home, rapport is enhanced.

The Goat year encourages creativity and Metal Dragons who are interested in developing their skills will find this an ideal time to take advantage of the opportunities, including tuition, available to them. Here again, a willing attitude will lead to far more being gained – and enjoyed.

With travel well aspected, many Metal Dragons will also enjoy the chance to visit new areas over the year, including some exciting attractions. The Goat year will certainly provide a good mix of things to do.

During the year, both the younger and more senior Metal Dragon will be involved in a great many activities and can fare reasonably well. However, the key is to curb their go-it-alone tendencies. This is a time for them to share their thoughts and be a part of what is happening. With this in mind, the alert and eager Metal Dragon can make this a rewarding year.

Tip for the Year
There is strength in numbers. Be forthcoming and seek support for your plans. That way, more will become possible. Time spent on your interests and skills can also be particularly rewarding.

The Water Dragon

There are some years which seem effortless and when much is achieved and some which are difficult, bringing problem after problem. For the Water Dragon this can be a reasonable year, although it is one to keep expectations modest. Rather than strive for too much, the Water Dragon should take stock and enjoy getting his lifestyle into better balance. In this respect, the year can have considerable personal value.

Many Water Dragons will find it helpful to take some moments at the start of the Goat year to consider what they would now like to do. Their ideas could include ways to make more of particular strengths, activities they may have wondered about taking up but not had the chance to pursue as well as things they may be keen to correct, including perhaps a bad habit or niggling problem. By considering how these can be best addressed, the Water Dragon will find his efforts bringing results. Also, if he talks his thoughts over with those around him he will find this helps concentrate minds and leads to actions being taken and solutions found. Goat years favour consensus and if the Water Dragon involves others in his plans, far more will come to fruition.

In addition to tackling plans and implementing ideas in the home, he should also encourage shared activities with his loved ones. These could include going to events happening in his local area, pursuing mutual interests or just setting time aside to enjoy together. With travel well aspected, quite a few Water Dragons will be keen to go away for a break, and whether this is just for a few days or a longer holiday, they can enjoy some treasured occasions. June, July and December may see some particularly pleasing personal and family times, and throughout the year there will be an element of spontaneity to events, as new ideas occur and travel possibilities arise.

Many Water Dragons will also see the birth of a grandchild or great-grandchild, and the Water Dragon himself offering time and assistance to younger family members.

He will also be keen to follow through more personal ideas this year. These could include taking more exercise and/or improving his diet. By seeking medical guidance on what is most suitable and following the recommendations, he will be pleased with what he is able to do. He may even be enthused by a new fitness regime!

He will also welcome the social opportunities that his interests and activities can bring and the chance to talk over ideas (and sometimes a few niggles) with close friends. For some unattached Water Dragons, the Goat year can have romantic possibilities. It is a time favouring personal matters and capable of surprise. Socially, April, June, August and December could be particularly pleasing months.

In work, progress is possible, but may be modest. For all Water Dragons, but particularly those who have experienced change of late, this is a time when they would do best to focus on their current role and use their specialist skills to advantage. This way, many will be able to make this a satisfying year and will have the chance to have useful input in their place of work. Those around them will often value their extensive knowledge and some Water Dragons will do much to assist junior colleagues. For those who work in creative environments, this can be a particularly inspiring time, and many will enjoy the chance to implement their ideas as the year progresses.

The majority of Water Dragons will remain where they are over the year, but a few will decide the time is right for change, perhaps feeling they have accomplished all they can in their present position. For these Water Dragons, and those currently seeking work, the Goat year can bring surprises. By not being too restrictive in the nature of the work they are considering, many could secure a position which uses their skills in new ways as well as suits their circumstances better. Sometimes friends or close contacts can also be helpful in their quest. Work-wise, April, July, September and November could be important months.

With family expenses, travel and the ideas he is keen to pursue, the Water Dragon will need to keep a close watch on spending, however, and plan ahead for more substantial outgoings. Also, if tempted by anything speculative, he should be wary. Rush, risk and oversight could all lead to problems. Water Dragons, take note and manage your finances well.

The Water Dragon possesses considerable enthusiasm and likes to set himself meaningful targets. However, rather than regarding this as a year for major advance, he should see it as a time to pay attention to his lifestyle and aspirations. This is an excellent year to try out his ideas (some of which he may have had for a long time), enjoy his interests and spend time with those who are special to him. By bringing some balance to his lifestyle and giving himself the chance to make more of his talents, he can make this a personally valuable and satisfying time.

Tip for the Year
Enjoy your personal interests and give yourself the opportunity to rediscover talents that may have been dormant for some time. Also, preserve time to enjoy with those who are close to you. On a personal level, this can be a richly rewarding year.

The Wood Dragon

The Wood Dragon will have seen a lot happen in recent years, some good, some disappointing. This year he will have a chance to take stock and make changes. The significance of some of his decisions should not be underestimated.

One of the strengths of the Wood Dragon is his ability to forge good connections with others and throughout the year it is important that he talks to those around him about possibilities he is considering. Also, if he knows someone with expert knowledge or relevant experience in an area that is of concern to him, he should seek their opinion. With good advice and the synergy talk can sometimes create, he will find some of his decisions can be made considerably easier. More independent-minded Wood Dragons, do bear this in mind. Input and support can help you so much this year.

At work, the Goat year can have considerable significance, and Wood Dragons following a particular career will have a good chance to put their specialist knowledge to greater use and work towards what could be challenging objectives. In the process they can not only highlight strengths but also do their reputation a lot of good. Many will gain new insights into their capabilities and prepare themselves for the more substantial opportunities that lie ahead, especially in the following Monkey year. In addition, anything they can do to raise their profile can be to their advantage.

For Wood Dragons who decide to move on from where they are, as well as those seeking work, again the Goat year can shape future directions. Although the job-seeking process will be difficult, by not being too restrictive in the type of position they are considering, many of these Wood Dragons could secure entry into a new type of work. This could involve a change of routine and a lot of learning, but many Wood Dragons will establish themselves in their new role and look forward to building on their position in subsequent years. Late March, April, July, September and November could see particularly interesting developments, but the chief value of this Goat year is the opportunity it will bring for the Wood Dragon to prove himself in an often different capacity.

It is also an excellent year to devote time to personal interests, explore ideas and talents and enjoy some 'me time'. Some Wood Dragons may be tempted by new interests and forms of recreation, possibly with a keep-fit element. By giving themselves the chance to follow these up, they can reap the benefits. This is an excellent year to strive for a better lifestyle balance and the Wood Dragon will find some attention to his own well-being of particular advantage.

With his keen and curious nature, he will also enjoy going to various events over the year, and his many friends and wide interests will provide him with an interesting mix of things to do.

He will delight in the social opportunities that arise over the year, and the helpfulness of certain friends can be of real value. April, June, August and December are likely to be particularly full and interesting months socially, and for some unattached Wood Dragons, sudden romance could beckon.

In view of all the Wood Dragon's plans, he will, however, need to be disciplined in money matters and keep a close watch on outgoings. This is a year for good financial management. Also, if entering into any important agreement or considering anything even remotely speculative, he should check the facts and, if applicable, obtain professional advice. Risks or oversights could be to his disadvantage.

The Wood Dragon's home life will see much activity and, with the Wood Dragon and others involved in work or other changes, routines will need adjusting. Extra effort and support at busy times will help. With practical undertakings, combined effort will also lead to better and faster results, and by the end of the year some aspects of home life will be noticeably improved. The Wood Dragon will also value some of the shared activities of the year, possibly mutual interests, trips out or the celebration of personal successes. Spring and late summer could see interesting developments in many a Wood Dragon household.

Overall, the Goat year can be a constructive one for the Wood Dragon and can prepare him for the success that lies ahead, especially next year. It is also an excellent time for personal development and for achieving a better lifestyle balance. The Wood Dragon will also be helped by the support and goodwill of those around him. By being open to opportunity and receptive to support, he can end the year generally content with what he has achieved.

Tip for the Year

Be focused and make the most of your time. What you do now can prepare you for some of the excellent opportunities soon to emerge. Also, give thought to your own development and share your thinking with others. This can be a potentially valuable year with far-reaching significance.

The Fire Dragon

Ambitious, hopeful and determined, the Fire Dragon invests great energy in his activities and invariably makes an impact. His judgement is usually good and he chooses his moments well. Over the years his skills will have allowed him to do a lot as well as opened up many opportunities for him. However, in the Goat year, his prospects are variable. There will be successes and some personal highlights, but progress may not be easy. Indeed, rather than regard this as a year of rapid advancement, he would do better to view it as one to take stock and prepare the ground for future aspirations. Used in this way, it can be a highly valuable time.

In his work, rather than looking too far ahead, the Fire Dragon would do well to make the most of his present position and use any chances to network and add to his area of expertise. By concentrating on his current objectives, he can not only become more established but also strengthen his reputation. As the year progresses, complex matters and additional pressures can bring the chance for him to prove himself in new ways.

The majority of Fire Dragons will decide to remain with their present employer over the year and have the chance to extend their role as new possibilities and staff movements occur, but for those keen to move on or seeking work, the Goat year can have important consequences. The job-seeking process can be difficult, but the Fire Dragon knows he has the ability to do well. What he needs is a chance. By widening the scope of his search, he could discover types of work which allow him to use his skills in new ways and have good potential for later development. By seeking out such opportunities and showing initiative in his application and at interview (including finding out more about the company and duties on offer), he will give himself the best chance of securing a position. April, July, September and November could see encouraging developments.

In general this year the Fire Dragon will need to be thorough and attentive. This particularly applies to money matters. He will need to keep a tight rein on outgoings and make early provision for commitments and plans. If he enters into a new agreement, it is important that he checks the terms and obligations and addresses any uncertainties. In addition, he should be wary of speculation and unnecessary risk. This is a year for vigilance, and misjudgements or poor budgeting will cause problems.

A more positive aspect of the year concerns the Fire Dragon's personal interests and general lifestyle. Although he will have many commitments, if he preserves time for his own interests, he will not only find these beneficial but also that new ideas (or new interests) will inspire him to do more. Goat years encourage self-expression and personal development. Some Fire Dragons may take up a new exercise discipline and enjoy working towards targets they set themselves.

The Fire Dragon's interests can also have a pleasing social element and, if applicable, he could benefit from joining a local group and meeting other enthusiasts. In addition, he will welcome the interesting mix of social occasions the year can bring. Some months could be particularly lively, and for the unattached, a chance meeting could lead to a potentially significant romance. Socially, April, June, August and December could be particularly interesting times.

The Fire Dragon's home life will also see high levels of activity. With his own commitments as well as the activities of his family members, it will often be conducted at a hectic pace. Here the Fire Dragon's organizational abilities will be much appreciated, as will the help he offers at times of pressure. However, amid all the activity there will be treasured moments, and by sharing activities and setting aside time just to be with his loved ones, the Fire Dragon can achieve a good lifestyle balance both for himself and those close to him. His thoughtfulness can make a big difference this year.

If possible, he should also aim to take a holiday with his loved ones. Even if not travelling too far, he will find that a rest and change of scene can benefit everyone. Spring and late summer could see good travel possibilities.

The Fire Dragon's progress this year may not meet his expectations, but to compensate this can be a personally significant time. At work, consolidating his position can be very much to his future benefit, while personal interests and improvements to his lifestyle will be pleasing and his home and social life busy but rewarding. Overall, a satisfying year.

Tip for the Year
Focus on the present. What you do now can prove significant in the future. Cultivate your interests and value your relations with those who are close to you.

The Earth Dragon

The last few years will have been busy and eventful for the Earth Dragon and this year will bring the chance to consolidate. Used constructively, it can have important long-term significance.

With the Earth element reinforcing the practical side of the Dragon's nature, the Earth Dragon is realistic and acknowledges that some of his aims and aspirations are still some way off. However, by continuing to work towards these, he can make useful progress this year.

In work, many Earth Dragons will have established themselves in a particular career and made good headway of late. This year they should continue to build on their position. Some may have the opportunity to deputize for others, and if new initiatives are proposed, indicating their willingness to be involved can be a good way for these Earth Dragons to enhance their prospects. Throughout the year they should also work closely with their colleagues and seize any chances to network. By being active and raising their profile they will not only be demonstrating their potential but also placing themselves in a strong position for when promotion opportunities arise or they decide to move on elsewhere.

For Earth Dragons who are seeking a change, as well as those looking for work, the Goat year can be significant. Obtaining a position will involve great effort, but during their search these Earth Dragons will have the chance to think about what they would like to do next and other ways in which they can use their strengths. Sometimes talking to employment advisers, close friends and other contacts could alert them to possibilities they had not previously considered. Some could also take advantage of retraining opportunities. For many, this can be a year to reappraise their working life and possibly set their career on a new track. April, July, September and November are likely to see important developments.

Although often busy, the Earth Dragon should allow time for his interests and other recreational pursuits. If an idea occurs to him or he learns of a new subject that intrigues him, he should follow it up. The Goat year encourages personal growth and the broadening of skills and interests. There can often be a pleasing social element to the Earth Dragon's interests and over the year he may be encouraged by the feed-back he receives, the camaraderie some activities bring and perhaps the new friendships he forges. Setting aside time for personal interests can also be an excellent way to maintain a good lifestyle balance and it is essential that any Earth Dragons leading stressful existences allow them-selves regular 'me time' over the year.

Travel is also likely to feature on the agenda and the Earth Dragon could find it helpful to make early provision for a holiday and other trips during the year. Even if he has to conduct these on a tight budget, he will enjoy visiting new places and benefit from a break from his usual routine. Spring, late summer and the closing weeks of the year could bring good travel possibilities.

However, with travel plans, plus his other activities and expenses, the Earth Dragon will need to be disciplined in financial matters. He also needs to check the terms and conditions of any new commitment he takes on and, if tempted by anything speculative, exercise care. This is *not* a year for risk.

The genial Earth Dragon enjoys good relations with many people and will particularly appreciate the variety of social opportunities the Goat year will bring. Whether sharing interests, meeting friends or accepting invitations to various functions, many Earth Dragons will find themselves in demand, with friends valuing their company and sometimes their advice too. April, June, August and December could be particularly active months socially, and for the unattached, romance may suddenly be found in an often fortuitous and even bizarre way.

For Earth Dragons with a partner this can be an eventful year. Many will be keen to go ahead with home improvements and perhaps even moving to a more convenient location. However, while the Earth Dragon may know what he wants, events in the Goat year can take a curious course. Goat years can be changeable and bring uncertainty as new alternatives arise and plans evolve. Accordingly, the Earth Dragon will need to be flexible. A lot of his hopes can be realized over the year, but sometimes in ways that are quite different from what he originally envisaged. Throughout the year it is therefore important he talks openly about his activities, aims and concerns. This way those close to him, including more senior relations, can alert him to ideas worth considering or give additional support. Dragons may have their independent tendencies, but the Goat year rewards openness and a joint approach.

Overall, by using his abilities to advantage and seizing his opportunities, the Earth Dragon can add to his skills and experience this year and help both his present and future prospects. By further establishing himself in his work and building up contacts, he can again do himself much good, and his accomplishments can be something he can build upon, especially next year. He will also be encouraged by the good relations he enjoys with many of those around him, and his home and social life will be busy, with many special times to both share and enjoy.

Tip for the Year

Be alert and mindful of changing situations. By adapting, you can ultimately benefit. Also, value your relations with others. Whether family, friends or colleagues, their support and sometimes advice can be significant. Consult them and listen to what they have to say.

Famous Dragons

Adele, Maya Angelou, Jeffrey Archer, Joan Armatrading, Joan Baez, Count Basie, Maeve Binchy, Sandra Bullock, Michael Cera, Courteney Cox, Bing Crosby, Russell Crowe, Benedict Cumberbatch, Roald Dahl, Salvador Dali, Charles Darwin, Neil Diamond, Bo Diddley, Matt Dillon, Christian Dior, Placido Domingo, Fats Domino, Kirk Douglas, Faye Dunaway, Nigel Farage, Dan Fogler, Sir Bruce Forsyth, Sigmund Freud, Rupert Grint, Che Guevara, James Herriot, Paul Hogan, Joan of Arc, Boris Johnson, Sir Tom Jones, Immanuel Kant, Martin Luther King, John Lennon, Abraham Lincoln, Elle MacPherson, Michael McIntyre, Hilary Mantel, Queen Margrethe II of Denmark, Liam Neeson, Florence Nightingale, Nick Nolte, Sharon Osbourne, Al Pacino, Gregory Peck, Pelé, Edgar Allan Poe, Vladimir Putin, Nikki Reed, Keanu Reeves, Ryan Reynolds, Sir Cliff Richard, Rihanna, Shakira, George Bernard Shaw, Martin Sheen, Alicia Silverstone, Ringo Starr, Karlheinz Stockhausen, Emma Stone, Shirley Temple, Maria von Trapp, Louis Walsh, Andy Warhol, Mark Webber, Raquel Welch, the Earl of Wessex, Mae West, Sam Worthington.

23 January 1917 to 10 February 1918 — *Fire Snake*

10 February 1929 to 29 January 1930 — *Earth Snake*

27 January 1941 to 14 February 1942 — *Metal Snake*

14 February 1953 to 2 February 1954 — *Water Snake*

2 February 1965 to 20 January 1966 — *Wood Snake*

18 February 1977 to 6 February 1978 — *Fire Snake*

6 February 1989 to 26 January 1990 — *Earth Snake*

24 January 2001 to 11 February 2002 — *Metal Snake*

10 February 2013 to 30 January 2014 — *Water Snake*

The Snake

The Personality of the Snake

I think
And think some more.
About what is,
About what can be,
About what may be.
And when I am ready,
Then I act.

The Snake is born under the sign of wisdom. He is highly intelligent and his mind is forever active. He is always planning and always looking for ways in which he can use his considerable skills. He is a deep thinker and likes to meditate and reflect.

Many times during his life he will shed one of his famous Snake skins and take up new interests or start a completely different job. The Snake enjoys a challenge and he rarely makes mistakes. He is a skilful organizer, has considerable business acumen and is usually lucky in money matters. Most Snakes are financially secure in their later years, provided they do not gamble – the Snake has the distinction of being the worst gambler in the whole of the Chinese zodiac!

The Snake generally has a calm and placid nature and prefers the quieter things in life. He does not like to be in a frenzied atmosphere and hates being hurried into making a quick decision. He also does not like interference in his affairs and tends to rely on his own judgement rather than listen to advice.

At times the Snake can appear solitary. He is quiet, reserved and sometimes has difficulty in communicating with others. He has little time for idle gossip and will certainly not suffer fools gladly. He does, however, have a good sense of humour and this is particularly appreciated in times of crisis.

The Snake is certainly not afraid of hard work and is thorough in all that he does. He is very determined and can occasionally be ruthless in order to achieve his aims. His confidence, willpower and quick thinking usually ensure his success, but should he fail it will often take a long time for him to recover. He cannot bear failure and is a very bad loser.

The Snake can also be evasive and does not willingly let people into his confidence. This secrecy and distrust can sometimes work against him and these are traits that all Snakes should try to overcome.

Another characteristic of the Snake is his tendency to rest after any sudden or prolonged bout of activity. He burns up so much nervous energy that he can, if he is not careful, be susceptible to high blood pressure and nervous disorders.

It has sometimes been said that the Snake is a late starter in life and this is mainly because it often takes him a while to find a job in which he is genuinely happy. However, he will usually do well in any position that involves research and writing and where he is given sufficient freedom to develop his own ideas and plans. He makes a good teacher, politician, personnel manager and social adviser.

The Snake chooses his friends carefully and while he keeps a tight control over his finances, he can be particularly generous to those he likes. He will think nothing of buying expensive gifts or treating his friends or loved ones to the best theatre seats in town. In return he demands loyalty. The Snake is very possessive and can become extremely jealous and hurt if he finds his trust has been abused.

The Snake is also renowned for his good looks and is never short of admirers. The female Snake in particular is most alluring. She has style, grace and excellent (and usually expensive) taste in clothes. A keen socializer, she is likely to have a wide range of friends and the happy knack of impressing those who matter. She has numerous interests and her opinions are often highly valued. She is generally a calm person and while she involves herself in many activities, she likes to retain a certain amount of privacy in her undertakings.

Affairs of the heart are very important to the Snake and he will often have many romances before he finally settles down. He will find that he is particularly well suited to those born under the signs of the Ox, Dragon, Rabbit and Rooster. Provided he is allowed sufficient freedom to pursue his own interests, he can also build up a very satisfactory relationship with the Rat, Horse, Goat, Monkey and Dog, but he should try to steer clear of another Snake as they could very easily become jealous of each other. The Snake will also have difficulty in getting on with the honest and down-to-earth Pig, and will find the Tiger far too much of a disruptive influence on his quiet and peace-loving ways.

The Snake certainly appreciates the finer things in life. He enjoys good food and often takes a keen interest in the arts. He also enjoys reading and is invariably drawn to subjects such as philosophy, political thought, religion or the occult. He is fascinated by the unknown and his enquiring mind is always looking for answers. Some of the world's most original thinkers have been Snakes, and although he may not readily admit it, the Snake is often psychic and relies a lot on intuition.

The Snake is certainly not the most energetic member of the Chinese zodiac. He prefers to proceed at his own pace and to do what he wants. He is very much his own master and throughout his life he will try his hand at many things. He is something of a dabbler, but at some time – usually when he least expects it – his hard work and efforts will be recognized and he will invariably meet with the success and the financial security he so desires.

The Five Different Types of Snake

In addition to the 12 signs of the Chinese zodiac there are five elements and these have a strengthening or moderating influence on the signs. The effects of the five elements on the Snake are described below, together with the years in which they were exercising their influence. Therefore Snakes born in 1941 and 2001 are Metal Snakes, Snakes born in 1953 and 2013 are Water Snakes, and so on.

Metal Snake: 1941, 2001

This Snake is quiet, confident and fiercely independent. He often prefers to work on his own and will only let a privileged few into his confidence. He is quick to spot opportunities and will set about achieving his objectives with an awesome determination. He is astute in financial matters and will often invest his money well. He has a liking for the finer things in life and a good appreciation of the arts, literature, music and food. He usually has a small group of extremely good friends and can be generous to his loved ones.

Water Snake: 1953, 2013

This Snake has a wide variety of interests. He enjoys studying all manner of subjects and is capable of undertaking quite detailed research and becoming a specialist in his chosen area. He is highly intelligent, has a good memory and is particularly astute when dealing with business and financial matters. He tends to be quietly spoken and a little reserved, but he does have sufficient strength of character to make his views known and attain his ambitions. He is very loyal to his family and friends.

Wood Snake: 1965

The Wood Snake has a friendly temperament and a good understanding of human nature. He is able to communicate well and often has many friends and admirers. He is witty, intelligent and ambitious. He has numerous interests and prefers to live in a quiet, stable environment where he can work without too much interference. He enjoys the arts and usually derives much pleasure from collecting paintings and other items that appeal. His advice is often highly valued, particularly on social and domestic matters.

Fire Snake: 1917, 1977

The Fire Snake tends to be more forceful, outgoing and energetic than some of the other types of Snake. He is ambitious, confident and never slow in voicing his opinions, and he can be very abrasive to those he does not like. He does, however, have many leadership qualities and can win the respect and support of many with his firm and resolute manner. He usually has a good sense of humour, a wide circle of friends and a very active social life. He is also a keen traveller.

Earth Snake: 1929, 1989

The Earth Snake is charming, amusing and has a very amiable manner. He is conscientious and reliable in his work and approaches everything he does in a level-headed and sensible way. He can, however, tend to err on the cautious side and never likes to be hassled into making a decision. He is adept in dealing with financial matters and is a shrewd investor. He has many friends and is very supportive towards the members of his family.

Prospects for the Snake in 2015

The Horse year (31 January 2014–18 February 2015) will have been a demanding one for the Snake and there will be no let-up in the closing months. At times the Snake may despair of the pressure – he does like to do things at his own pace – but amid all the activity there will be benefits and some good personal times to be had.

With so much going on, the Snake will need to keep alert, stay on top of developments and be aware of the views of those around him. This is no time to be too independent. When in company, he should be attentive to others. Appearing preoccupied or distracted could lead to differences of opinion.

In work, pressures are likely to increase and there may be difficult decisions for the Snake to make. However, by using good judgement, he can obtain some useful results and may even find his efforts leading to further progress. October and November could be particularly busy and eventful months.

The closing months of the Horse year can also give rise to some additional social opportunities (October again being a notable month) and there will also be much to attend to domestically. To help ease later pressures, the earlier some plans are made, the better. For many Snakes there could be interesting family news or a special occasion to mark later on in the year.

Overall, the Horse year will have been demanding, but the Snake will have gained valuable experience that he can build on in the next Chinese year.

The Year of the Goat starts on 19 February and will be a pleasing one for the Snake. During it he will have a greater chance to do what *he* wants, and some good results will follow on. Also, Goat years favour creative thought and this will suit many a Snake. However, Goat years are notoriously fickle and at times the Snake will need to modify his actions to fit in with changing circumstances. Here his wide-ranging skills can serve him well.

This will be especially the case in his work. Although many Snakes will be content to focus on their duties, developments can occur which alter current approaches and procedures. Some Snakes may also be affected by internal reorganization or the need to cover for absent colleagues, and it will be a case of rising to challenges as they present themselves. Although some weeks could be unsettling, there will be scope for many Snakes to take on a greater role. Also, the Snake's experience can have an impact, and whenever he has ideas or can suggest possible solutions to problems, he should put these forward. This is very much a year for involvement.

The majority of Snakes can make important progress with their present employer, but there will be some who decide to capitalize on their experience and seek a position elsewhere. For these Snakes, as well as those looking for work, the Goat year can have significant developments. By virtue of their knowledge and reputation, some may easily move to another position and, in the process, successfully take their career to a new level. For others, the Goat year can also open up interesting possibilities. By keeping alert to what is available, these Snakes may well have the chance to use their skills in fresh ways. What happens over the year may also allow some to discover their forte and introduce them to a company or industry they will remain with for some time. March, June, September and November could be significant months, but throughout the year the Snake should remain alert for opportunities.

Progress at work can also help financially, and by managing his money well, the Snake will be able to proceed with many of his plans, including some satisfying purchases for himself and his home. If he is able, setting amounts aside for specific projects or the long term could be helpful. With care and diligence, he can fare well this year.

With his enquiring mind, he will also enjoy spending time on his interests. He could have some particularly engrossing and novel ideas and be encouraged by what develops. Goat years favour personal development and this can be a richly rewarding time for many Snakes. Some could become attracted by a new recreational activity and welcome the chance to try something different. Goat years offer possibility.

The Snake would also do well to give some consideration to his own well-being and if his diet tends not to be sufficiently balanced or he lacks regular exercise, he should seek advice on measures he could take. Some extra care could make a real difference.

The Snake has a tendency to be quieter than some signs and, valuing his privacy, he chooses his friends with care. However, in the Goat year he would find it helpful to be more forthcoming. To be alone or on the periphery of events could deny him opportunities. Whether in his work, personal interests or other activities, he will find that more can be achieved by liaising with others and getting support.

The Goat year can also see an increase in social opportunities. March, April, August and September could be particularly busy and pleasing months, but to make the most of the year the Snake needs to be involved.

For the unattached, romance can add considerable sparkle to the year, but new relationships should be allowed to evolve (and strengthen) over time.

The Snake's home life can also see pleasing developments. Not only will loved ones be keen to share in his progress, but they could enjoy some deserving triumphs of their own. However, as with any year there could be difficult moments too, as delays or setbacks occur or changes to arrangements are needed. Here the Snake's incisiveness and ability to think round problems will prove of great value. Practical plans in particular will sometimes need to be rescheduled. Domestically, a lot can be achieved this year, but the Snake does need to be aware of what is going on, mindful of others and, importantly, flexible with arrangements.

Overall, the Snake can accomplish a lot in the Goat year and will have the chance to put his strengths to effective use. In his work, his experience and approach will allow him to progress, and his interests can give him the chance to enjoy his creativity and try out new activities. He can also be greatly encouraged by the support he receives, but this *is* a year calling for involvement and putting himself forward. For the shy and reticent Snake (and there are some), it *is* worth making the effort, for luck and opportunity await those who are ready and willing to make the most of what this interesting year brings.

The Metal Snake

'The plan of the day is made in the morning', as the Chinese proverb reminds us. This equally applies to the year, for how it shapes up can very often be determined in its early months. With this in mind, it would benefit both the senior and junior Metal Snake to make plans and set objectives early on this year and to resolve that they will *make things happen.*

For the Metal Snake born in 1941, the Goat year will bring excellent opportunities to put his ideas into practice. However, he needs to act in true Metal Snake style and *seize the moment*. When an opportunity arises, an idea strikes or an offer is made, he should be quick to take advantage of it before the momentum is lost. Indeed, a feature of the Goat year is the suddenness with which events occur and the Metal Snake needs to be alert.

One area which will occupy many Metal Snakes will be their interests. Creative activities are particularly well aspected. Many Metal Snakes will also be interested in delving into the past and some will spend time researching local or family history or recording reminiscences. Purposeful pursuits can make this a rewarding time. Sometimes the acquisition of new equipment can open up new possibilities too. Interestwise, the Goat year is certainly encouraging for the Metal Snake.

Although some interests can be carried out independently, the Metal Snake could also be helped by making contact with other enthusiasts. In addition, with many events being held during the year, if he sees any which appeal to him, he should try to attend.

He will also enjoy the travel opportunities the year brings, and if there is a particular destination or attraction he is keen to visit, early planning will lead to more going ahead. In addition, some tempting offers or invitations could arise with little warning, including the chance to visit others, although sometimes existing arrangements may need to be changed to take advantage of the opportunity.

Quite a few Metal Snakes will also involve themselves in activities in their area. As joint activity is favourably aspected in the Goat year, those belonging to a group will enjoy some particularly pleasurable times. Even though some Metal Snakes prefer to be solitary, going out and involving themselves in what is happening can do all Snakes a lot of good this year. March to early May and August to early October could be interesting months.

Domestically, the Metal Snake will often content himself with projects around the house. Here his ideas and creative touches can bring him (and others) considerable pleasure. Metal Snakes who enjoy gardening, whether indoors or out, will once more delight in tending to their plants and find gardening an absorbing (and often therapeutic) activity.

Throughout the year the Metal Snake will closely follow the activities of family members and give what can be valuable support. However, at some point there could be an issue which greatly concerns him. If applicable, he could be helped by seeking an expert opinion rather than dealing with this single-handed. Metal Snakes, if worried, remember you are not alone. For the most part, though, the Metal Snake's home life will go well.

In view of some of the purchases the Metal Snake has in mind for the year, he will again find early planning leading to more becoming possible. Financially, this is a year for good control. However, the Metal Snake may enjoy some luck. Whether receiving a gift, taking advantage of an offer, enjoying success with an interest or even celebrating a competition win, he could experience some exciting moments of good fortune this year.

For Metal Snakes born in 2001, the Goat year offers a great many possibilities, but these Metal Snakes do need to make the most of what is on offer.

Many young Metal Snakes will find pressure increasing as they study subjects in greater depth. At times there could be a bewildering amount to do. However, by showing interest and commitment, the Metal Snake can not only make good progress but also find new abilities emerging. For quite a few Metal Snakes this can be a time of self-discovery, with as yet unseen talents coming to the fore.

Whenever possible, the young Metal Snake should also take advantage of the facilities available to him. Joining after-school activities or special interest groups or undertaking extra tuition (including in recreational pursuits) can all be to his benefit.

While in general this will be a constructive year for him, no year is ever free of problems and at times there will be issues that concern him. At such times it is important that the young Metal Snake speaks to others. He may be strong and independent, but support over certain matters can reassure him. Young Metal Snakes, take note and ask at times of need.

Generally, however, whether born in 1941 or 2001, the Metal Snake can find this a satisfying year. Setting himself specific objectives and adapting to situations will lead to more being realized. At times of pressure he does need to seek support, but overall this can be an interesting year laced with fine opportunities – and some lucky moments too.

Tip for the Year
Be focused. Work towards your aims and objectives and enjoy what you do. Also, don't do too much in isolation. With support and encouragement, far more will become possible.

The Water Snake

One of the strengths of the Water Snake is his creativity. He is good at thinking up ideas, considering different approaches and undertaking research. And his enquiring nature and personal talents can make this a special and interesting year.

Water Snakes whose work or personal interests allow self-expression or creative input will find their skills can have quite an impact this year. They could see several of their ideas being taken up and, in the process, opening potentially important doors for them.

In view of the expertise many Water Snakes will now have in their place of work, they may have the opportunity of greater involvement this year. This can include taking on specific objectives or, if in a large organization, moving to another sector. The good relations the Water Snake enjoys with many of his colleagues can also be to his advantage, with some influential people encouraging his progress.

The majority of Water Snakes can move forward in their current place of work, but for those who decide on change or are seeking work, the Goat year can have encouraging developments. Some people who know the Water Snake well can be helpful in making suggestions or alerting him to openings worth considering. He could also find it helpful to talk to employment officials as well as seek advice from relevant organizations. By following up possibilities, many Water Snakes will be successful in securing a new opening this year. Though it may be offered initially on a temporary basis only, it can often be a platform on which to build a career that is a refreshing change from what they have done before. March, June, September and November could see important work developments.

Progress at work may lead to an increase in income and some Water Snakes may also receive a bonus or gift or benefit from a maturing policy. To make the most of any improvement the Water Snake could find it helpful to set amounts aside for specific plans and, if possible, the longer term. With travel opportunities arising several times during the year, he should also make allowance for this.

The aspects are also encouraging for the Water Snake's personal interests. This is an excellent year for him to develop his ideas and, where applicable, promote what he does. Some Water Snakes, including those who are newly retired, may be tempted to take their interests in new directions. Whatever he chooses to do, the Water Snake can derive much pleasure from his activities. For a few Water Snakes, financial benefits may follow on too.

The Water Snake should also give some thought to his well-being. If he does not take regular exercise, it may be worth seeking advice on suitable activities he could pursue. In some cases swimming, walking or practices such as *t'ai chi*, yoga and Pilates could be of benefit.

Throughout the year the Water Snake will also value the support of others. Particularly when toying with ideas or grappling with a dilemma, he will find that if he talks to those with relevant experience, he can be reassured and assisted. To fully benefit, though, he does need to be forthcoming. Also, where his personal interests, and sometimes career aspirations, are concerned, people he knows can be important in terms of the opportunities that emerge. March to early May and August to early October could see some fine social opportunities.

The Water Snake's home life will also see a lot happen. The Water Snake himself will have quite a few ideas he is keen to implement and will take genuine pleasure in what is achieved over the year. Ideally, activities should not be rushed and everyone in the household should share in what is done.

The Water Snake will also spend time assisting close relations. However, while this will generally be a positive year, there could be a difficult matter to address. Fortunately, the Water Snake's kindness and support will help the situation move towards a satisfying resolution. If appropriate, he could find it helpful to get professional advice. In general, he will be very much at the heart of family life over the year.

Overall, the Goat year can be a special one for the Water Snake. Whether he is developing his ideas or using his skills to greater advantage, this is a time of scope and potential. And the keen and enthusiastic Water Snake can fare well.

Tip for the Year

Don't underestimate your abilities or what is possible. Believe in yourself and put yourself forward. You have much to offer and this is a favourable year for you. Use it well.

The Wood Snake

This year the Wood Snake enters a new decade in his life and he will be keen to realize certain hopes and improve specific aspects of his lifestyle. With determination, he can make this a constructive year. However, while an encouraging time, it is not necessarily a straightforward one, and the Wood Snake will need to remain alert and adjust as required.

As he sets about his various activities, it is important that he talks them over with those around him, including those with relevant experience. With the good advice they are able to offer, he will find more opening up for him. This is no time for him to go it alone.

In his home life this can be a full and interesting year. The Wood Snake will have plans he is keen to carry through and the Goat year has a strongly practical element. As a result, quite a few Wood Snakes will make major improvements to their home as well as attend to matters that have been problematic in the past. Also, where home purchases are concerned, if all members of the family consider the choices together, some excellent buys can be secured, and often on advantageous terms.

The year will also see some special occasions. Not only will loved ones be keen to celebrate the Wood Snake's fiftieth birthday in style, and with possible surprises in store, but there could also be other family achievements to mark.

During the year the Wood Snake will play a pivotal role in the lives of those around him, including assisting some more senior. He may also decide to mark his fiftieth year by going somewhere special. By discussing possible destinations, he will find some exciting ideas can quickly take shape. However, the Goat year also has a certain spontaneity about it and some additional travel possibilities could arise quite suddenly. Whenever possible, the Wood Snake should try to take advantage of them.

He could also derive considerable pleasure from making more use of the amenities in his area. These can include sporting and recreational facilities as well as events being held locally. By keeping himself informed, the Wood Snake can enjoy some fun times.

Another important aspect of the year will be the contact the Wood Snake has with his friends. Once more, he will be glad to talk over mutual concerns as well as share interests. Some of his contacts could offer him good advice this year.

For Wood Snakes who have had some recent personal difficulty, the year can be a significant one. By pursuing their interests, becoming more involved in their community and taking up any invitations they receive, these Wood Snakes can find pleasure coming back into their lives. Some will have the chance to start a new social circle, and romantic prospects are in store for quite a few Wood Snakes who start the year unattached. March, April and late July to early October could see the most social opportunities.

The Goat year also favours personal development and the Wood Snake should consider ways in which he can take certain interests further, perhaps by studying, setting himself new challenges or exploring ideas. Some Wood Snakes may also be keen to introduce more exercise into their lives. This would be a good time to do so, as it is very much a year for purposeful action and new ideas.

There will also be important developments in the Wood Snake's work situation. Sometimes due to restructuring or the introduction of new procedures or products, there will be scope for him to advance his career. His in-depth knowledge and reputation can be very much to his advantage and when openings arise and offers are made, he should respond quickly. Sometimes he could be surprised at the speed with which developments take place.

While the majority of Wood Snakes will remain with their present employer this year, some will feel ready for a new challenge. For these Wood Snakes, and those seeking employment, the Goat year can be an important juncture in their working lives. By keeping alert for openings and contacting large employers in their area, they may well be able to secure a position in which they can develop their skills in new ways.

128 YOUR CHINESE HOROSCOPE 2015

March, June, September and November could see significant developments.

The Wood Snake's progress at work can help financially, but with travel and some of the ambitious plans he has in mind, he will need to budget carefully. The Goat year rewards good planning and discipline. Also, when making large purchases, the Wood Snake should investigate options and seek expert opinion. By avoiding rush, he will find his decisions are better informed and his purchases often secured on more favourable terms.

Overall, the Goat year will be a busy one for the Wood Snake and by the end of it he may well be astonished by all that has happened. The year will have brought surprises and special times with others, and it will also have given many Wood Snakes the chance to put their ideas into practice. This can be a personally satisfying time, but the Wood Snake does need to be receptive to opportunities.

Tip for the Year

Your fiftieth year is a time for furthering plans. Seize the moment and be flexible and willing. What opens up now can be significant in both the present and the future. Also, enjoy your relations with others. Their support and affection can help you in so many ways.

The Fire Snake

The Fire Snake is ambitious and keen to make the most of his opportunities. In 2015 he will have a lot in his favour although to fully benefit he will need to liaise well with others and take careful note of developing situations. To act too independently or seem inflexible could undermine his prospects. Fire Snakes, take note. Much is possible this year, but it does call for increased awareness.

This is especially the case in the Fire Snake's home life. With his own commitments and others in his household similarly busy, there needs to be good co-operation. It would also be helpful if major plans were made early on rather than left in limbo or to a late stage. This way, everyone can work towards them.

The Fire Snake will do a lot to assist close family members, and if a parent, he will find the encouragement he gives to his children will lead to some treasured moments. Some Fire Snakes will also have occasion to assist more senior relations and his support will be significant. However, should any tricky matter arise, the Fire Snake would find it helpful to get professional advice. He may mean well, but in some delicate matters the expertise of another person can make an important difference.

A pleasing aspect of the year will be the many activities that the Fire Snake can become involved in. There could be interesting events taking place locally, attractions to visit or tempting travel opportunities. The Goat year does have an element of fun and variety to it. The Fire Snake should also aim to keep in regular contact with his friends. This is not a year for being independent, and some friends he has known for many years will be keen to assist him if necessary.

For unattached Fire Snakes, the Goat year can have surprising developments in store. Although some may like their independent lifestyle, a chance meeting can quickly develop into a possible romance. Also, Fire Snakes who have experienced recent personal difficulties will find that people they meet or interests they take up over the year can bring energy and joy back into their lives. Goat years are personally encouraging for the Fire Snake, but he does need to assist the process by being willing to reach out. March to mid-May and August to early October could see the most social activity.

This is also an excellent year for personal interests, especially any that allow the Fire Snake to use the creativity and knowledge he has built up. For Fire Snakes who are interested in the arts, this can be an inspiring year, while those who enjoy outdoor pursuits can enjoy some lively times. The Fire Snake can also derive considerable pleasure from visiting attractions related to his interests.

He could also find it helpful to give some thought to his general well-being over the year and if his diet is deficient or he does not take regular exercise, he should seek advice on improvements he could introduce. Some personal care and a good lifestyle balance can benefit him considerably.

The Fire Snake's work situation can also see important developments. Fire Snakes following a specific career will often be encouraged to take on further responsibilities. Those who work in creative environments can see their ideas making a real impact. This year can mark an important stage in the Fire Snake's ongoing career development.

For Fire Snakes who are seeking to better themselves by looking for a new position, as well as those looking for work, the Goat year can have important developments in store. By widening the scope of his search, the Fire Snake could discover a position which is different from what he has done before but has potential for the future. Here again, he needs to keep alert this year and be prepared to adapt. Headway made now can be built on over the next few years. March, June, September and November could see important work developments.

Many Fire Snakes will enjoy an improvement in income during the year and some will also benefit from a gift or extra payment. However, with many outgoings likely, the Fire Snake will need to keep a close watch on spending and, when considering major purchases, allow himself time. This will not only enable him to assess suitability but sometimes benefit from attractive offers.

Overall, the Goat year holds encouraging prospects for the Fire Snake. It will be a busy time. Important new opportunities can arise at work, personal interests are favourably aspected and some attention to lifestyle will be of benefit. The Fire Snake's home and social life will also offer special times, though he would do well to be mindful of the views of others. Throughout the year, he will need to liaise with those around him and be aware of emerging situations. If he does, what he achieves this year can have far-reaching consequences.

Tip for the Year
Keep your lifestyle in balance at this busy time and enjoy what the year offers. It has both scope and promise. Use it well, for its rewards can come in many ways.

The Earth Snake

While quietly ambitious (a key Snake trait), the Earth Snake is also a realist and works steadily towards the things he wants. His approach will serve him well this year.

In his personal life this can be a busy and potentially exciting year. Earth Snakes with a partner will often have exciting plans to carry through. However, these should not be rushed. Ideally, time should be set aside for discussion and thought and, where outlay is involved, comparing costs and ranges. Taking some time can also allow other ideas to occur and offers to become available. During the year many Earth Snakes can look forward to timely strokes of good fortune.

Much of the Earth Snake's attention will centre on accommodation matters. Earth Snakes who move will enjoy settling into their new home. But there will also be other exciting plans, including, for a few, marriage. Goat years favour coming together and many Earth Snakes will value the special relationship they have with another person. Quite a few Earth Snakes who are currently alone, including those who have experienced recent personal hurt, can see a transformation in their situation. A chance meeting can quickly develop into something special and some Earth Snakes will meet their life partner. Goat years can be personally significant and see events happening as if decreed by fate.

In view of the Earth Snake's many plans for the year, it is also important that he draws on the support of those around him. More senior relations could assist in a sometimes surprising way. However, to fully benefit from the help that is available to him, the Earth Snake does need to be forthcoming. This is no year to hold back.

As well as support, the Earth Snake can also look forward to some lively times in his social life. Whether going to parties, celebrating special occasions (of which there can be quite a few this year) or meeting his friends, he will often have an interesting mix of things to do. Earth Snakes who move to a new area will find themselves forming a new social circle, and friendships (existing or new), contact with others and, for so many, love will be important ingredients of the year. Late February to early May, August and September could see the most social activity.

The Earth Snake's work prospects are also encouraging. Duties he has been engaged in recently will have given him practical experience he can now build on. As a result, when opportunities become available, either in his existing place of work or elsewhere, he should put himself forward. His ability to gauge when and what is right for him can lead to some notable achievements. Many Earth Snakes will successfully take their career to a new level during the year.

For Earth Snakes who would like to move to a new position, as well as those seeking work, the Goat year again has possibilities. By keeping alert and following up ideas and hunches, they may secure an interesting position, possibly in a new capacity or industry, but with potential for the future. March, June, September and November could see important developments, but of chief importance this year will be the Earth Snake's ability to read situations and sense what is right for him at this stage in his career.

Progress made at work can help financially and here again the Earth Snake's judgement will serve him well. When considering important purchases, if he allows time and seeks advice, he could benefit from some attractive propositions. Also, while he will be keen to go ahead with many plans, he should try to make provision for travel. Time away can do him a lot of good.

The Earth Snake can also derive considerable pleasure from his personal interests over the year and creative activities will prove particularly satisfying. For Earth Snakes who lead pressured lifestyles, it is also important to allow time to unwind. This can be a rewarding year, but the Earth Snake, especially when busy, does need to keep his lifestyle in balance and enjoy the fruits of his efforts.

Overall, this can be a fine year for the Earth Snake, with some excellent and well-deserved opportunities, some of which he has been working towards for some time. The Goat year can highlight his qualities and this too will help as he looks to move forward. In addition, he may benefit from the workings of chance. With effort and self-belief, he can make this an enjoyable and constructive year.

Tip for the Year
Build on your strengths. This is no time to stand still, for your ideas and abilities can lead to a lot happening for you. Also, value your relations with those around you, for they can contribute a lot to your year. A time for action and enjoyment!

Famous Snakes

Jason Aldean, Muhammad Ali, Ann-Margret, Avicii, Kim Basinger, Ben Bernanke, Björk, Tony Blair, Michael Bloomberg, Michael Bolton, Brahms, Pierce Brosnan, Casanova, Jackie Collins, Tom Conti, Cecil B. de Mille, Robert Downey Jr, Bob Dylan, Elgar, Michael Fassbender, Sir Alexander Fleming, Mahatma Gandhi, Greta Garbo, Art Garfunkel, J. Paul Getty, W. E. Gladstone, Johann Wolfgang von Goethe, Princess Grace of Monaco, Tom Hardy, Stephen Hawking, Audrey Hepburn, Jack Higgins, Elizabeth Hurley, James Joyce, Stacy Keach, Ronan Keating, J. F. Kennedy, Chaka Khan, Carole King, Courtney Love, Rory McIlroy, Mao Tse-tung, Chris Martin, Henri Matisse, Piers Morgan, Alfred Nobel, Mike Oldfield, Hayden Panettiere, Sarah Jessica Parker, Pablo Picasso, Mary Pickford, Daniel Radcliffe, Franklin D. Roosevelt, J. K. Rowling, Jean-Paul Sartre, Franz Schubert, Charlie Sheen, Paul Simon, Delia Smith, Ben Stiller, Taylor Swift, Madame Tussaud, Shania Twain, Dionne Warwick, Mia Wasikowska, Charlie Watts, Kanye West, Oprah Winfrey, Virginia Woolf.

11 February 1918 to 31 January 1919 — *Earth Horse*

30 January 1930 to 16 February 1931 — *Metal Horse*

15 February 1942 to 4 February 1943 — *Water Horse*

3 February 1954 to 23 January 1955 — *Wood Horse*

21 January 1966 to 8 February 1967 — *Fire Horse*

7 February 1978 to 27 January 1979 — *Earth Horse*

27 January 1990 to 14 February 1991 — *Metal Horse*

12 February 2002 to 31 January 2003 — *Water Horse*

31 January 2014 to 18 February 2015 — *Wood Horse*

The Horse

The Personality of the Horse

There are many worn paths,
but the most rewarding
is the one you decide on and forge yourself.

The Horse is born under the signs of elegance and ardour. He has a most engaging and charming manner and is usually very popular. He loves meeting people and likes attending parties and other large social gatherings.

The Horse is a lively character and enjoys being the centre of attention. He has many leadership qualities and is much admired for his honest and straightforward manner. He is an eloquent and persuasive speaker and has a great love of discussion and debate. He also has a particularly agile mind and can assimilate facts remarkably quickly.

He does, however, have a fiery temper and although his outbursts are usually short-lived, he can often say things that he will later regret. He is also not particularly good at keeping secrets.

The Horse has many interests and involves himself in a wide variety of activities. He can, however, get involved in so much that he can often waste his energies on projects that he never has time to complete. He also has a tendency to change his interests rather frequently and will often get caught up in the latest craze or 'in thing' until something more exciting turns up.

The Horse also likes to have a certain amount of freedom and independence. He hates being bound by petty rules and regulations and as far as possible likes to feel that he is answerable to no one but himself. But despite this spirit of freedom, he still likes to have the support and encouragement of others in his various enterprises.

Due to his many talents and likeable nature, the Horse will often go far in life. He enjoys challenges and is a methodical and tireless worker. However, should things go against him and he fail in any of his enterprises, it will take a long time for him to recover and pick up the pieces again. Success to the Horse means everything. To fail is a disaster and a humiliation.

The Horse likes to have variety in life and will try his hand at many different things before he settles down to one particular job. Even then, he will probably remain alert to see whether there are any better opportunities for him to take up. He has a restless nature and can easily get bored. He does, however, excel in any position that allows him sufficient freedom to act on his own initiative or brings him into contact with a lot of people.

Although the Horse is not particularly bothered about accumulating great wealth, he handles his finances with care and will rarely experience any serious financial problems.

The Horse also enjoys travel and loves visiting new and faraway places. At some stage during his life he may be tempted to live abroad for a short period of time and due to his adaptable nature will find that he will fit in well wherever he goes.

The Horse pays a great deal of attention to his appearance and usually likes to wear smart, colourful and rather distinctive clothes. He is very attractive to others and will often have many romances before he settles down. He is loyal and protective to his partner, but despite his family commitments he still likes to retain a certain measure of independence and have the freedom to carry on with his own interests and hobbies. He will find that he is especially well suited to those born under the signs of the Tiger, Goat, Rooster and Dog. He can also get on well with the Rabbit, Dragon, Snake, Pig and another Horse, but he will find the Ox too serious and intolerant for his liking. He will also have difficulty in getting on with the Monkey and the Rat – the Monkey is very inquisitive and the Rat seeks security, and both will resent the Horse's rather independent ways.

The female Horse is usually most attractive and has a friendly, outgoing personality. She is highly intelligent, has many interests and is alert to everything that is going on around her. She particularly enjoys outdoor pursuits and often likes to take part in sport and keep-fit activities. She also enjoys travel, literature and the arts, and is a very good conversationalist.

Although the Horse can be stubborn and rather self-centred, he does have a considerate nature and is often willing to help others. He has a good sense of humour and will usually make a favourable impression wherever he goes. Provided he can curb his slightly restless nature and keep tight control over his temper, he will go through life making friends, taking part in a multitude of different activities and generally achieving many of his objectives. His life will rarely be dull.

The Five Different Types of Horse

In addition to the 12 signs of the Chinese zodiac there are five elements and these have a strengthening or moderating influence on the signs. The effects of the five elements on the Horse are described below, together with the years in which they were exercising their influence. Therefore Horses born in 1930 and 1990 are Metal Horses, Horses born in 1942 and 2002 are Water Horses, and so on.

Metal Horse: 1930, 1990

This Horse is bold, confident and forthright. He is ambitious and a great innovator. He loves challenges and takes great delight in sorting out complicated problems. He likes to have a certain amount of independence and resents any outside interference in his affairs. He has charm and a certain charisma, but he can also be very stubborn and rather impulsive. He usually has many friends and enjoys an active social life.

Water Horse: 1942, 2002

The Water Horse has a friendly nature and a good sense of humour and is able to talk intelligently on a wide range of topics. He is astute in business matters and quick to take advantage of any opportunities that arise. He does, however, have a tendency to get easily distracted and can change his interests – and indeed his mind – rather frequently, and this can often work to his detriment. He is nevertheless very talented and can often go far in life. He pays a great deal of attention to his appearance and is usually smart and well turned out. He loves to travel and also enjoys sport and other outdoor activities.

Wood Horse: 1954, 2014

The Wood Horse has a most agreeable and amiable nature. He communicates well with others and is able to talk intelligently on many different subjects. He is a hard and conscientious worker and is held in high esteem by his friends and colleagues. His opinions are often sought and, given his imaginative nature, he can often come up with some very original and practical ideas. He is usually widely read and likes to lead a busy social life. He can also be most generous and often holds high moral views.

Fire Horse: 1966

The element of Fire combined with the temperament of the Horse creates one of the most powerful forces in the Chinese zodiac. The Fire Horse is destined to lead an exciting and eventful life and to make his mark in his chosen profession. He has a forceful personality and his intelligence and resolute manner bring him the support and admiration of many. He loves action and excitement and his life will rarely be quiet. He can, however, be rather blunt and forthright in his views and does not take kindly to interference in his own affairs or to obeying orders. He is a flamboyant character, has a good sense of humour and will lead a very active social life.

Earth Horse: 1918, 1978

This Horse is considerate and caring. He is more cautious than some of the other types of Horse, but is wise, perceptive and extremely capable. Although he can be rather indecisive at times, he has considerable business acumen and is very astute in financial matters. He has a quiet, friendly nature and is well thought of by his family and friends.

Prospects for the Horse in 2015

In the Horse's own year (31 January 2014–18 February 2015) he is very much the architect of his own fortune. Horse years have the potential for great undertakings and pleasing personal successes, but they can also bring disaster. In his own year, the Horse needs to be careful he doesn't overreach himself or misjudge things due to haste. While it can be a promising year for him, it is still one to tread carefully.

In the remaining months of the year, the Horse needs to remain aware. Should he have uncertainties over any situation or be in an uncharacteristic dilemma over what to do, he should talk to those around him and take note of their views. With greater input from others, some actions can have more assured outcomes.

In his work the Horse should again liaise closely with others. By being part of a team rather than acting too independently, he can deal with his workload more effectively and achieve some key targets. He should also make the most of any chances to network, especially towards the year's end. Horses who are seeking change or work may benefit from an unexpected opportunity at this time and will need to act quickly. September could be a significant month for work matters.

With increased outgoings likely towards the end of the year, the Horse should keep a close watch on spending and be wary of making more substantial purchases too hastily.

The closing months of the year will also see an increase in social and domestic activity, and the Horse needs to keep well organized and spread out his commitments. Although busy, he can look forward to some special occasions and some Horses will have exciting news to share with loved ones near the end of the year.

The Goat year starts on 19 February and will be a constructive one for the Horse. Coming after all the activity of his own year, it is a time when he will be better able to focus on his objectives. Rather than having his attention drawn in many directions, he will feel in control of his destiny.

To help, as the Goat year starts the Horse would do well to decide on what *he* would like to see happen over the next 12 months. Having clear thoughts in mind will not only give him something to work towards but also make him more aware of what he needs to do. With focus and effort, he will find that much can become possible this year. For any Horse who is starting the year at a low ebb (for some, their own year could have brought difficulties), this is a time to draw a line under what has gone before and treat the Goat year as a new chapter.

At work, the aspects are especially encouraging. Horses who have been nurturing hopes of advancing their career or making more of certain skills will find the Goat year can present them with the chance they have been seeking. It could be that they are offered training and/or given the opportunity to extend their duties. What opens up for the Horse this year can strengthen both his current position and future prospects.

Many Horses will make good headway in their present place of work, but there will also be those who are feeling staid or stuck. If these Horses take the initiative and explore possibilities, they could find opportunities elsewhere. Goat years encourage progress and the enterprising Horse can fare well.

For Horses who are seeking work, the Goat year can again open up good possibilities. In their quest, these Horses should stress their strengths and relevant experience. With determination, they can find important doors opening for them. For all Horses, March, April, July and September could see particularly encouraging work developments.

Progress made at work can lead to many Horses enjoying a rise in income over the year. However, the Goat year can be an expensive time for the Horse. A move is possible for some, with all the extra expense this entails, and travel is also strongly indicated, possibly for family or work reasons. The Horse could therefore find himself spending considerably more than usual. In view of this, he needs to be disciplined and, whenever possible, budget ahead.

Domestically, this can be a particularly busy year. Horses who have been considering moving could now be inclined to go ahead. It could be a lengthy process, with many finding their eventual choice by chance. Horses who remain where they are will also have ambitious (and sometimes expensive) plans to carry through which can be both time-consuming and disruptive. In view of the often major decisions needing to be made, the Horse and other family members need to be open and honest and aware of each other's viewpoints. A lot can happen this year, but it very much favours collective effort.

With so much happening, it is important that the Horse makes sure more pleasurable activities do not get sidelined. If he sets time aside for others and perhaps suggests an occasional treat, his thoughtfulness will be much appreciated. With travel strongly indicated, a holiday could do everyone good. August and September could be particularly interesting months in many a Horse household.

With his alert and engaging nature, the Horse will also welcome the variety of social opportunities that arise over the year. Often these will be related to his interests. For the sport and music enthusiast in particular, the Goat year will hold some special delights. The Horse will also enjoy meeting up with his friends. Some of them could give pertinent advice on an issue of concern. However, to benefit, the Horse does need to listen to others and take on board what is said. March, June, July and September could see the most social activity.

For Horses who find romance, exciting times are in store. Time and attention will cement many a relationship this year.

With his busy lifestyle, it is also important that the Horse gives some consideration to his own well-being. With some tiring days and sometimes long nights, he does need to allow himself time to catch up and unwind. If reliant on fast foods, he will find that a more balanced diet will help. Horses, take note. Do look after yourselves and seek advice if feeling under par.

Overall, however, the Goat year can be a satisfying one for the Horse. He will be able to go ahead with many of his plans and by the year's end could be astonished by all that has happened. In his work and personal interests he will have the chance to put his strengths to good use and enjoy some significant results, while domestically he will set about some ambitious undertakings. The Goat year has great possibilities for him, and with good planning, purpose and use of his time, he can accomplish a great deal. As Virgil noted, 'Fortune favours the bold,' and in 2015 fortune will certainly favour the bold and enterprising Horse.

The Metal Horse

The Metal Horse sets about his activities with great resolve and this can be a constructive and personally exciting time for him. The aspects are on his side, but the Metal Horse is self-willed and can be stubborn and to be obtuse or too independent in his actions could lead to him not doing as well as he otherwise might. During the year it is important that the Metal Horse consults others, *listens to them* and is prepared to adapt.

His work situation can see some particularly important developments. Metal Horses who are relatively new in their current position should aim to establish themselves. By working well with their colleagues and being an active member of any team, many will quickly impress and could find themselves with the opportunity to widen their experience and, in the process, substantially help their future prospects. A strength of many Metal Horses is their ability to express themselves, and those whose work involves presentations or brings them into contact with others could enjoy a particularly pleasing measure of success. For all Metal Horses, joining a professional organization (if applicable) and attending staff and industry events can also raise their profile and lead to useful connections being made. This is very much a year favouring active participation and by the end of it many Metal Horses will have substantially improved their position.

Some Metal Horses will, however, feel their prospects could be bettered by looking for a position elsewhere. For these Metal Horses, as well as those currently seeking work, the Goat year could have significant developments in store. To benefit fully from the encouraging aspects, these Metal Horses should explore their options, including any training they may be eligible for. With initiative and the willingness to learn, many could secure a position with good prospects for future development. Once in a new position, by seizing their opportunities and showing commitment, these Metal Horses can quickly demonstrate their potential and many will be able to make further progress as the year continues. March, April, July and September to mid-October could be particularly important months.

Although the Metal Horse will be kept busy this year, he should also give himself some time to enjoy personal interests. These cannot only give him a chance to unwind but also be satisfying to carry out. Creative activities are particularly well aspected and some recreational activities have a good social element which will add to the fun.

While the Metal Horse may well be active over the year, it could also be helpful for him to give some consideration to his general level of exercise and the quality of his diet. If he feels either is deficient, he should seek medical advice on appropriate measures he could take. If he ignores his own well-being or drives himself relentlessly, there could be times this year when he is not at his best.

The Goat year can give rise to some good travel opportunities, some occurring at short notice. On some occasions the Metal Horse may be able to combine travel with a particular event or interest, and he will thoroughly enjoy many of his trips.

With travel, personal aspirations and possibly some ambitious accommodation plans, he will need to be disciplined in money matters, however. If considering large transactions or entering into agreements at any time, he would also find it prudent to seek an expert opinion. Financially, this is a year for thoroughness and control.

Domestically, the year promises to be busy, especially with some Metal Horses moving house. With so much happening, it is again important that the Metal Horse draws on the support of those around him and talks over any concerns. He may like to make his own decisions, but additional input can make an important difference. A further feature of this year is that once action is taken, plans can very quickly gather momentum and be moved along by unforeseen developments.

For Metal Horses with a partner, time spent together can be very special this year. Many Metal Horses will also have cause to celebrate, perhaps due to a joint decision, new accommodation or a personal event.

The Metal Horse has a wide social circle and once again this year his personality can impress and he can make new friends and important contacts. For the unattached, serious romance can beckon, while Metal Horses who move will find the Goat year offering excellent chances to involve themselves in their new area. All Metal Horses should do their best to attend events that appeal to them, as their social life can do them a lot of good. March, mid-May to the end of July and September will see the most social activity.

In so many ways, this is an encouraging time for the Metal Horse, but a lot hinges upon his own approach. To get the most from the year he needs to seize his chances, promote himself and set his plans in motion. It is also important that he involves others and is mindful of their advice and of changing situations. The Metal Horse has an exciting future ahead of him and what he can accomplish this year can be very significant in the longer term.

Tip for the Year

You put a lot of energy into your activities. However, with this being a full year, you must be careful not to let your lifestyle get out of balance. Too much attention in one area can impact on others. Be mindful of this and use your time well. This includes allowing time for recreation and those who are special to you. A good lifestyle balance can make an important difference to you personally as well as to how you fare.

The Water Horse

Goat years encourage activity and participation, and with a willing attitude, the Water Horse can do a lot in this one and enjoy himself in the process.

For the Water Horse born in 1942 this can be an especially pleasing year. He will often have specific plans he will be keen to get underway, but, as he will quickly find, Goat years can have curious twists and turns and while some projects are accomplished easily, others may stall and need reconsideration. Provided the Metal Horse remains mindful of this and makes allowances for it, however, he can accomplish a great deal.

And some thwarted plans may even turn out to be blessings in disguise.

Whatever is happening, it is important that the Water Horse involves others. Not only can this help with decisions that need taking, but should he have reservations or doubts about any matter, those around him can often allay concerns or provide assistance. The Water Horse may like to take responsibility, but if he draws on the help of others this year, so much more will happen for him. Water Horses who live alone should not hold back from asking relatives or close friends for assistance or even contacting helplines. Support during the Goat year can make an importance difference.

Some matters that the Water Horse will be keen to attend to will concern home maintenance. It could be that equipment needs replacing, faults correcting or items installed to make certain tasks easier or more efficient. To get the best results, the Water Horse again needs to seek advice, consider his options and think through the implications of his choices. Decisions should not be rushed. Also, with his eye for style, the Water Horse could have had a few niggles of late. Perhaps, in his view, some rooms have become shabby or stale. Over the year he may well take great pride in making alterations. In some instances, the actual changes may be small but make a noticeable difference.

In addition to practical activities, the Goat year will contain an interesting mix of things to do. For many Water Horses there could be a special family occasion to look forward to, often in early summer. The Water Horse may also be tempted by local events or keen to take advantage of travel opportunities. Late May to the end of July, September and December could be particularly full and interesting months.

Another positive element of the year will concern the Water Horse's personal interests. Many Water Horses will be inspired to start new projects or follow up specific ideas and can look forward to some absorbing times. A few may also take advantage of courses in their area and will find the Goat year satisfying their enquiring nature.

For Water Horses who would welcome additional company, their interests – including any courses started during the year – can bring them into contact with others. Local activities or community groups could also be of benefit. Goat years reward participation.

With all the activity of the year, however, the Water Horse will need to keep a watchful eye on spending and try to make early provision for more expensive outlay. When entering into new agreements or dealing with potentially important correspondence, he should check the details carefully and seek advice if necessary. Extra attention, including drawing on support if required, can lead to better outcomes.

For the Water Horse born in 2002, the Goat year will also open up important possibilities. As the young Water Horse advances in his education, he will have the chance to do more, including having greater use of facilities and equipment. By making the most of these opportunities, these Water Horses will not only enjoy trying different things out but also learn more about their capabilities. This is not a year to be resistant or hold back – Goat years favour those who are prepared to give things a go *and take part*. Young Water Horses, take note!

Also, while the Water Horse may have subject areas he prefers, he should not close his mind to those which are not so attractive to him. These can not only have a bearing on his overall education but, with greater effort on the Water Horse's part, may not prove as difficult or unappealing as he originally thought.

The young Water Horse will enjoy pursuing his personal interests this year, especially those he can share with friends, and again, new knowledge and equipment will often lead to him doing more. For Water Horses who are sporting and musically inclined, extra tuition can take them to new levels.

It is also important that the young Water Horse is forthcoming with those at home. This way, others will be better able to appreciate what he does, wants or is working towards and he can benefit from their encouragement. Input from others can make a lot of difference to his year.

Whether born in 1942 or 2002, the Water Horse will find that this is a time to put his ideas into practice. Pleasing results can often follow on. The year can also give him the chance to enjoy his interests and benefit from his strengths. Overall, a satisfying and constructive time.

Tip for the Year
Act upon your ideas, but be flexible as new opportunities arise. Also, share your thoughts and activities. The Goat year can bring special times with family, friends and other contacts. It is a time to be inspired, to act and to enjoy what you do.

The Wood Horse

This will be a positive year for the Wood Horse. He may enjoy a certain amount of luck in what he sets out to do and will often find that once plans are underway, new developments can move them forward. This is a year for action.

In particular, Wood Horses who have experienced recent problems (and there will be some) should look at how they can remedy the situation and, in some cases, be prepared to draw a line under what has gone before. The Goat year has considerable potential and it is important the Wood Horse does not feel fettered by past difficulties. For the active and enterprising Wood Horse, this is a year of considerable possibility.

At work, many Wood Horses will experience a change in their responsibilities and, rather than having to cope with a large and diverse workload, will have the chance to concentrate on their area of expertise. This could happen through being given specific objectives or moving to a different position or sector in their organization. With their in-depth knowledge, they will also have more chance to contribute and influence decisions. Colleagues will often value the Wood Horse's considered approach and he may play a significant role in his workplace.

The majority of Wood Horses will make important headway where they are, but there will be some who are feeling stale and would welcome the chance to do something different. If they work in a large organization, there could be the opportunity to take on responsibilities elsewhere, possibly involving relocating. For those who are keen to switch employer or are seeking work, this can be a time of intriguing possibilities. By not being too restrictive in the type of work they are considering, these Wood Horses could benefit from large companies recruiting in their area or secure an interesting (and often different) position elsewhere. Some may consider self-employment or going freelance and will promote a specific skill they have. The Goat year is generally encouraging and March, April, July and September will see important developments.

Progress made at work may assist the Wood Horse financially, but, as he is likely to have some ambitious plans, he will need to manage his finances carefully. When considering large purchases, he should allow the time to assess suitability, and if taking on any new commitment, he should check the terms. To rush, take risks or be lax could disadvantage him in some way. Wood Horses, do take note.

An area which can bring the Wood Horse great satisfaction this year is his personal interests. There will be some subject areas in which he has extensive knowledge and over the year he will be keen to make greater usc of this, perhaps by setting himself a specific project or developing an idea. Wood Horses who enjoy writing may decide to write about a topic that appeals to them. And any Wood Horse who finds himself with more spare time this year and/or has let his interests lapse will discover that a new recreational pursuit could both engage and absorb him.

The Goat year also has interesting travel possibilities in store, and if he is able, the Wood Horse should make provision for a holiday. He may combine this with a personal interest or special event and, with the Goat year being a culturally rich time, visiting places of interest could appeal to him, as could some events held locally.

Throughout the year the Wood Horse will also be encouraged by the support of others. Many will be rooting for him and even if he doesn't want to bother some, he will find that if he asks for an opinion or possibly for help, the assistance given can make a real difference to his situation. Wood Horses, do take note. You do so much for others – give them the chance to reciprocate.

The Goat year can also see an increase in social activity. The Wood Horse may decide to attend several occasions related to his interests and if he is a member of a society or group, or joins one, he will appreciate the contact this opens up. Many people will warm to his friendly, practical manner, and any Wood Horses who have been feeling lonely or had recent problems to contend with will find that involving themselves in local activities can brighten their situation. March, June to early August and September could see the most social activity.

The Wood Horse's home life can also bring him much contentment this year. In addition to some personal successes, there could be special family occasions to mark and opportunities to see, or perhaps visit, relations the Wood Horse has not seen for some while. The summer and the closing weeks of the year could be particularly active times.

The Wood Horse will also be keen to go ahead with several ambitious home projects. A few Wood Horses will even move house. However, whatever the Wood Horse chooses to do, his plans should not be rushed.

The Wood Horse has a keen and determined nature and should make good use of his strengths this year, as they will help him move forward. The Goat year can also have its lucky moments, with plans benefiting from helpful developments. Overall, this is a time of possibility for the Wood Horse and he can achieve – and enjoy – a great deal.

Tip for the Year
Value your relations with others. Talk to those around you, get to know them and seek support. It will help in many of your activities. Also, set time aside for your own interests. These can benefit you and develop in encouraging ways.

The Fire Horse

The element of Fire and the Horse personality are a dynamic combination and this year the Fire Horse will have the chance to put it to good use. This is an encouraging time for him and if he reads situations well and seizes his opportunities, he can enjoy considerable success.

At work many Fire Horses will have ambitions they are keen to realize. And although quite a few will have experienced change in recent times, there will still be many who feel unfulfilled. Pleasingly, the Goat year can bring some fine opportunities. A further factor in the Fire Horse's favour will be the excellent relations he enjoys with his colleagues, and some senior personnel may put in recommendations on his behalf. At times the Fire Horse may not know everything that is going on behind the scenes, but his commitment will not have gone unnoticed. Accordingly, quite a few Fire Horses will secure promotion over the year. Those who work in large organizations may also have the chance to relocate.

Fire Horses who feel the time is right to move to another employer will find their reputation and background can make them strong candidates, and by putting in that extra effort both on application and at interview, many will make the move they have been hoping for.

Fire Horses seeking work may also find openings of interest as well as benefit from training initiatives. Opportunities do need to be seized quickly this year, but March, April, July and September could see encouraging developments.

Another important aspect of the year will be the way the Fire Horse develops his ideas. Being a creative thinker, he will often have schemes to pursue, and by taking these forward, whether in his work, personal interests or home life, he will often see positive developments following on.

With personal interests in particular, this can be a satisfying year. Practical and creative pursuits are well aspected, and Fire Horses who are keen on outdoor pursuits can look forward to some memorable (and in some cases exciting) times.

The Fire Horse will also see an increase in social activity over the year. There will be many convivial occasions and he will enjoy having the chance to extend his social network. Once again his engaging manner and conversational skills will impress those around him and some of the people he meets will have specialist knowledge that can be helpful to him. March, June, July and September could be particularly active and interesting months.

The Fire Horse's home life will also be busy. A few Fire Horses may move this year, and even those who stay where they are will find some alterations to domestic routines may be needed due to work and other changes. Here the Fire Horse's organizational skills can be especially useful and, despite some chaotic weeks, new patterns can quickly emerge and some of the changes prove to have unforeseen benefits. This is, though, a time when everyone in the Fire Horse's household needs to pull together. Goat years can be eventful, and with this in mind, the Fire Horse should ensure that quality time with his loved ones does not get sidelined. There could be a special family occasion to mark in the middle of the year and September and December could be busy months. Throughout the year, the Fire Horse will be very much at the heart of family life and his attentiveness will be valued.

In view of the active nature of the year, he will, however, need to manage his finances with care. The more he can plan ahead, the more he will ultimately benefit, including sometimes from advantageous offers. Fire Horses who move will need to keep an especially close watch on the costs incurred.

All Fire Horses may be tempted by travel this year and if they are able to make provision for a holiday, or even just a short break away, they will appreciate the chance to experience something different from their usual routine.

Overall, the Goat year is one of possibility for the Fire Horse, but to fully benefit he needs to seize his opportunities. This is no time to be idle. Also, events can work in curious ways in the Goat year and the Fire Horse should be prepared to adapt to take advantage of what occurs. By being active and aware, though, he can make good headway. Personally, the year will be pleasing and the Fire Horse's domestic and social life will keep him busy and reward him well.

Tip for the Year
Be watchful and alert. A lot is set to happen and speed and initiative will be of the essence. This is a year rich in possibility. Act well so you may do well.

The Earth Horse

Being conscientious, the Earth Horse puts a lot of energy into his activities and takes his responsibilities seriously. He also has wide interests and likes to keep well informed. Over the year his tenacity and skills will lead to a great deal opening up for him. It is very much a time for setting out to achieve his ambitions.

Almost all areas of the Earth Horse's life will see considerable activity over the year. In his home life in particular, he will have several ideas he is keen to implement. Whether smartening up rooms, replacing outmoded equipment or adjusting household routines for greater efficiency, he will instigate many changes this year. Where home purchases are concerned, his sense of style and suitability will lead to particularly good choices being made. However, to obtain the best results, openness and good liaison between everyone in the household will be required. In this busy year, the Earth Horse's ability to empathize and offer good advice will also be particularly appreciated. By setting time aside to share with his loved ones and indulging in some fun activities, he can make his home life special.

In addition, there could be the opportunity to travel and even just a short break can lead to some interesting times and the chance to try out new activities.

The genial and outgoing Earth Horse can also look forward to some lively social occasions and some celebratory events during the year. March, June, July and September could be particularly busy months, although at most times of the year the Earth Horse will have opportunities to meet his friends and attend interesting events. His advice will once more be in demand, with a close friend likely to seek his views on what could be a delicate matter. The Earth Horse may not always appreciate how highly he is regarded by those around him, but many depend on him for advice and support.

For Earth Horses who are feeling lonely, including those who have had some recent personal problems, the Goat year can see an increase in activity. Some of the work changes that occur over the year or an interest they follow or take up can lead to some significant new friendships being made. For some, there are prospects of romance too. The year is rich in possibility.

Although the Earth Horse leads a busy lifestyle, it is also important that he allows himself time to pursue his personal interests this year. Often he will have ideas he is keen to try out. Some Earth Horses will also become involved in a new activity, sometimes with a keep fit or outdoor element. Whatever he does, by developing his ideas and seizing his opportunities, the Earth Horse can derive great pleasure from his interests this year.

He will also see significant developments in his work. Earth Horses pursuing a particular career could now be given the opportunity to focus on more specific tasks, while Earth Horses who are keen to further their career in new ways or are looking for work can benefit from important possibilities. To help their quest move forward, these Earth Horses should keep in regular contact with employment officials, seek information from relevant organizations and consider any training or refresher courses for which they are eligible. Their initiative and resolve can be rewarded by the offer they have been seeking. March, April, July and September could see important developments, but the key importance of this year will be the chance many Earth Horses will have to display and develop their strengths. A lot can follow on, particularly in the auspicious Monkey year that follows.

Progress made at work can also lead to an increase in income for many Earth Horses and some may benefit from an additional sum, possibly arising from an enterprising idea. However, the Earth Horse will need to watch his spending and carefully consider the implications of any new obligation he takes on. Financially, this is a year to be thorough and vigilant.

With Earth as his element, the Earth Horse has great commitment and this will serve him well during the Goat year. With purpose and initiative, he can accomplish a great deal and build on his success in following years. Also, he will often find himself in the right place at the right time. With self-belief and resolve, he can make this a significant time.

Tip for the Year
Look ahead and develop your ideas. Much can follow on from what you undertake now. Also, value your relations with others. Their support can spur you on. Enjoy this positive year which can bring you well-deserved success.

Famous Horses

Roman Abramovich, Neil Armstrong, Rowan Atkinson, Samuel Beckett, Ingmar Bergman, Leonard Bernstein, Joe Biden, Helena Bonham Carter, David Cameron, James Cameron, Jackie Chan, Ray Charles, Chopin, Nick Clegg, Sir Sean Connery, Billy Connolly, Catherine Cookson, Elvis Costello, Kevin Costner, James Dean, Clint Eastwood, Thomas Alva Edison, Harrison Ford, Aretha Franklin, Bob Geldof, Samuel Goldwyn, Billy Graham, Rita Hayworth, Jimi Hendrix, François Hollande, Janet Jackson, R. Kelly, Calvin Klein, Ashton Kutcher, Jennifer Lawrence, Lenin, Annie Lennox, Pixie Lott, Sir Paul McCartney, Nelson Mandela, Angela Merkel, Ben Murphy, Sir Isaac Newton, Louis Pasteur, Dennis Quaid, Gordon Ramsay, Rembrandt, Ruth Rendell, Jean Renoir, Theodore Roosevelt, Helena Rubenstein, Alex Salmond, Adam Sandler, David Schwimmer, Martin Scorsese, Kristen Stewart, Barbra Streisand, Kiefer Sutherland, Patrick Swayze, John Travolta, Usher, Vivaldi, Robert Wagner, Emma Watson, Billy Wilder, Brian Wilson, the Duke of Windsor, Caroline Wozniacki, Jacob Zuma.

1 February 1919 to 19 February 1920 — *Earth Goat*

17 February 1931 to 5 February 1932 — *Metal Goat*

5 February 1943 to 24 January 1944 — *Water Goat*

24 January 1955 to 11 February 1956 — *Wood Goat*

9 February 1967 to 29 January 1968 — *Fire Goat*

28 January 1979 to 15 February 1980 — *Earth Goat*

15 February 1991 to 3 February 1992 — *Metal Goat*

1 February 2003 to 21 January 2004 — *Water Goat*

19 February 2015 to 7 February 2016 — *Wood Goat*

The Goat

The Personality of the Goat

Amid the complexities of life,
it is the ability to appreciate that is so special.

The Goat is born under the sign of art. He is imaginative, creative and has a good appreciation of the finer things in life. He has an easy-going nature and prefers to live in a relaxed and pressure-free environment. He hates any sort of discord or unpleasantness and does not like to be bound by a strict routine or rigid timetable. He is not one to be hurried against his will, but despite his seemingly relaxed approach to life, he is something of a perfectionist and when he starts work on a project he is certain to give his best.

The Goat usually prefers to work in a team rather than on his own. He likes to have the support and encouragement of others and if left to deal with matters on his own he can get very worried and tend to view things rather pessimistically. Wherever possible he will leave major decision-making to others while he concentrates on his own pursuits. If, however, he feels particularly strongly about a certain matter or has to defend his position in any way, he will act with great fortitude and precision.

The Goat has a very persuasive nature and often uses his considerable charm to get his own way. He can, however, be rather hesitant about letting his true feelings be known and if he were prepared to be more forthright he would do much better as a result.

The Goat tends to have a quiet, somewhat reserved nature, but when he is in company he likes he can often become the centre of attention. He can be highly amusing, a marvellous host at parties and a superb entertainer. Whenever the spotlight falls on him, his adrenaline starts to flow and he can be assured of giving a sparkling performance, particularly if he is allowed to use his creative skills in any way.

Of all the signs in the Chinese zodiac, the Goat is probably the most gifted artistically. Whether it is in the theatre, literature, music or art, he is certain to make a lasting impression. He is a born creator and is rarely happier than when occupied in some artistic pursuit. But even in this he does well to work with others rather than on his own. He needs inspiration and a guiding influence, but when he has found his true *métier*, he can often receive widespread acclaim and recognition.

In addition to his liking for the arts, the Goat is usually quite religious and often has a deep interest in nature, animals and the countryside. He is also fairly athletic and there are many Goats who have excelled in some form of sporting activity or who have a great interest in sport.

Although the Goat is not particularly materialistic or concerned about finance, he will find that he will usually be lucky in financial matters and will rarely be short of the necessary funds to tide himself over. He is, however, rather self-indulgent and tends to spend his money as soon as he receives it rather than make provision for the future.

The Goat usually leaves home when he is young but he will always maintain strong links with his parents and the other members of his family. He is also rather nostalgic and is well known for keeping mementoes of his childhood and souvenirs of places that he has visited. His home will not be particularly tidy, but he knows where everything is and it will be scrupulously clean.

Affairs of the heart are particularly important to the Goat and he will often have many romances before he finally settles down. Although he is fairly adaptable, he prefers to live in a secure and stable environment and he will find that he is best suited to those born under the signs of the Tiger, Horse, Monkey, Pig and Rabbit. He can also establish a good relationship with the Dragon, Snake, Rooster and another Goat, but he may find the Ox and Dog a little too serious for his liking. Neither will he care particularly for the Rat's rather thrifty ways.

The female Goat devotes all her time and energy to the needs of her family. She has excellent taste in home furnishings and often uses her considerable artistic skills to make clothes for herself and her children. She takes great care over her appearance and can be most attractive to others. Although she is not the most organized of people, her engaging manner and delightful sense of humour create a favourable impression wherever she goes. She is also a good cook and usually derives much pleasure from gardening and outdoor pursuits.

The Goat can win friends easily and people generally feel relaxed in his company. He has a kind and understanding nature and although he can occasionally be stubborn, he can, with the right support and encouragement, live a very satisfying life. And the more he can use his creative skills, the happier he will be.

The Five Different Types of Goat

In addition to the 12 signs of the Chinese zodiac there are five elements and these have a strengthening or moderating influence on the signs. The effects of the five elements on the Goat are described below, together with the years in which they were exercising their influence. Therefore Goats born in 1931 and 1991 are Metal Goats, Goats born in 1943 and 2003 are Water Goats, and so on.

Metal Goat: 1931, 1991

This Goat is thorough and conscientious in all that he does and is capable of doing very well in his chosen profession. Despite his confident manner, he can be a great worrier and he would find it helpful to discuss his concerns with others rather than keep them to himself. He is loyal to his family and employers and will have a small group of particularly close friends. He has good taste and is usually highly skilled in some of aspect of the arts. He is often a collector of antiques and his home will be very tastefully furnished.

Water Goat: 1943, 2003

The Water Goat is very popular and makes friends with remarkable ease. He is good at spotting opportunities but does not always have the necessary confidence to follow them through. He likes to have security both in his home life and work and does not take kindly to change. He is articulate, has a good sense of humour and is usually very good with children.

Wood Goat: 1955, 2015

This Goat is generous, kind-hearted and always eager to please. He usually has a large circle of friends and involves himself in a wide variety of activities. He has a very trusting nature but can sometimes give in to the demands of others a little too easily and it would be in his interests if he were to stand his ground more often. He is usually lucky in financial matters and, like the Water Goat, is very good with children.

Fire Goat: 1967

This Goat usually knows what he wants in life and often uses his considerable charm and persuasive personality to achieve his aims. He can sometimes let his imagination run away with him and has a tendency to ignore matters that are not to his liking. He is rather extravagant in his spending and would do well to exercise a little more care when dealing with financial matters. He has a lively personality, many friends, and loves attending parties and social occasions.

Earth Goat: 1919, 1979

This Goat has a considerate and caring nature. He is particularly loyal to his family and friends and invariably creates a favourable impression wherever he goes. He is reliable and conscientious in his work but sometimes finds it difficult to save and never likes to deprive himself of any little luxury he might fancy. He has numerous interests and is often very well read. He usually derives much pleasure from following the activities of the various members of his family.

Prospects for the Goat in 2015

With his wide interests and an engaging manner, the Goat will have had plenty to do during the Horse year (31 January 2014–18 February 2015) and the closing months will continue to see much activity.

On a personal level the Goat will be in increasing demand, with quite a few social occasions to look forward to. Goats who have found love over the year could find their relationship becoming more meaningful at this time. Whatever his situation, the Goat will often delight in the activity – and surprises – the closing months of the year can bring.

Domestically, a lot is set to happen, including some keynote decisions. There will need to be good liaison and some flexibility as options are discussed. However, what is agreed upon could delight many a Goat, and some ideas will move swiftly ahead.

The Horse year will have also brought its demands, however, and sometimes forced the Goat out of his comfort zone. Work-wise, many Goats will continue to have a considerable workload to deal with. If they concentrate on what needs to be done, their efforts and patience can bring some notable results, which they can successfully build on in their own year.

With the closing months of the year traditionally being an expensive time, the Goat will need to be disciplined in his spending. Without care, his outgoings could be greater than anticipated. Goats, take note and keep watch on the purse-strings.

Overall, the Horse year will have been a busy one for the Goat. However, while there will have been occasions when he will have despaired of the demands placed on him, he will be well prepared for what awaits in his own year.

On 19 February millions around the world will be celebrating the start of the Year of the Goat and the Goat himself will be excited and wondering what his own year has in store. He will be keen to make his own year special. And it can be. But there is a but. Although the Goat may start his own year with many hopes, he needs to be realistic and pace himself. Some of what he wants to see happen needs to be worked towards over time. Rush or hurry can lead to disappointment. This is year which favours a steady approach. Effort and patience will yield the best results.

With resolve, however, the Goat can see encouraging developments. Any Goat who starts the year despondent should focus on the present rather than feel held back by what has gone before. By taking positive action, he can start to make a difference to his situation. For quite a few Goats, their own year can mark a significant turning point.

Throughout the year the Goat will also be helped by the good relations he enjoys with many of those around him. He empathizes easily and relates well, and during the year his ability to make useful connections can help him personally, with his work, with his interests and in other spheres too.

At work, Goats who have been in the same position for some time may now have the opportunity to further their career. With staff changes likely to take place, promotion opportunities could arise and the Goat's in-depth knowledge make him a strong candidate. Unlike some times, when Goats may feel weighed down and that their talents are being stifled, their own year will give them the chance to move ahead. For those who work in a creative environment in particular, this can be an inspiring time.

The aspects are also encouraging for Goats who currently feel unfulfilled, consider their prospects are limited where they are and are seeking work. To help their situation, these Goats should talk to professionals and other contacts. They could be alerted to new possibilities. With assistance, backed by their own resolve, they may be able to obtain a significant opportunity and, once in a new position, will welcome the chance to prove themselves in a different capacity. Such are the aspects that possibilities can occur at almost any time of the year, but April, July, August and November could be significant, as will the early weeks of 2016.

The headway made by many Goats at work will also lead to an increase in income. However, this will be an expensive year for the Goat and to do all he wants (and more), he will need to be wary of too many impulse buys. Without care, spending levels could be higher than he had allowed for. Goats, take note and be disciplined in your finances.

The Goat invariably has a wide range of interests and these can bring him considerable pleasure during the year. For the many Goats who are creatively inclined, some interests will take on additional meaning. Many Goats will also enjoy sharing what they do with others.

The Goat will also delight in the year's social opportunities. For the keen partygoer and young at heart, this can be a fun-packed year. Existing friends can also introduce the Goat to new people. Many Goats will widen their social circle over the year. March, June, September and December will see the most social activity.

For affairs of the heart, the Goat's own year can be a special one for him. Some Goats who are newly in love will marry or settle down together, while quite a few who start the year unattached will meet someone, often in chance circumstances, who will quickly become important.

The Goat's home life will also see much activity and it will be very much a case of family members pulling together and helping each other out. In many households there may be a considerable change of routine, and adjustments will be needed. Several weeks, especially around May, could be particularly busy. With his eye for style, the Goat will also have some ideas for the home. However, these should not be rushed. The more time is spent pondering choices, the more satisfying the outcome.

Despite all the activity, if possible the Goat should take a holiday with his loved ones over the year. He will enjoy the chance to unwind and visit areas new.

Throughout the year the Goat will be kept busy and to keep on good form he should try to ensure he has a balanced diet and takes regular and appropriate exercise. To be neglectful of his own well-being, or to take risks, could leave him prone to minor ailments. This can be a good year, but some personal care and attention would not come amiss.

The Goat will have high expectations for his own year and during it he can fare well. However, he does need to be realistic in what he sets out to do. Rather than rush or expect quick results, he should work steadily towards his objectives and build upon his progress. This is a year that rewards persistent effort. As ideas occur to him, or opportunities open up, the Goat should, however, look to develop them. His special talents can lead to some pleasing results. He will also be helped by the good relations he enjoys with many of those around him and affairs of the heart are favourably aspected. The Goat year holds considerable promise for the Goat himself and with a willing attitude he can both enjoy himself and accomplish a great deal.

The Metal Goat

'Diligence leads to riches', as the Chinese proverb runs, and this year the Metal Goat will find much truth in it. With commitment and a keen, careful approach, he can make this a memorable and successful time.

Throughout the year the Metal Goat's relations with others are favourably aspected and he can look forward to a splendid mix of places to go and people to meet. In addition, often as a result of work, a change in location or his personal interests, he could find himself building a new network of friends. Late February, March, June, September and December could see the most social activity. Certain friends can be especially helpful this year, particularly as some may have first-hand knowledge which could be useful to the Metal Goat. No matter what he may want to do this year, he need not feel alone.

Unattached Metal Goats, including those who have recently experienced heartache or some personal difficulty, can see a transformation in their situation, with a meeting in chance circumstances suddenly blossoming into a wonderful romance. This Goat year can be personally important in many ways.

For Metal Goats with a partner, the year can give rise to some very special times. Both the Metal Goat and his partner will have ideas they will be keen to carry through, particularly concerning their home. By working towards objectives together, they will find that much can be accomplished and a lot of fun had in the process. In many instances, the Metal Goat's creative flair will be evident too.

Although he will be kept busy over the year, it is also important that the Metal Goat allows time to develop his own interests. If he wants to take particular talents further, it could be worth consulting experts on how to proceed. Input from others can open up a lot for the Metal Goat this year, but he does need to be forthcoming.

He can also see important developments in his work situation. Although many Metal Goats will have experienced changes of late, some will feel they are still not making the most of their potential. 'Diligence can lead to riches', however, and the Metal Goat's current efforts will in many cases be recognized and lead to the offer of extra responsibility. There will be good chances for many Metal Goats to move ahead this year.

While many will make headway with their present employer, there will also be some who feel their prospects could be helped by a move elsewhere or who are seeking work. These Metal Goats will find friends and contacts particularly helpful. If they talk to others, keep in regular contact with employment agencies and follow up openings they see, their resolve may well pay off. In many cases, a position secured now will also have scope for further development. April, July to early September and November could be significant months.

Progress made at work will lead to many Metal Goats increasing their income and several will also benefit from a gift, bonus or extra sum. Although welcome, with ambitious plans and the need to save towards certain requirements (including deposits), the Metal Goat should try to remain within his budget when socializing or shopping. If possible, he should also aim to set some funds aside for travel and other personal plans. With good financial control (and some restraint), he can fare well.

With his busy lifestyle, he should also pay attention to the quality of his diet as well as allow himself time to catch up if he has a succession of long days and late nights. To drive himself relentlessly could result in him not feeling his best. Metal Goats, take note and don't neglect your own welfare this year.

In general, the Year of the Goat can be an exciting one for the Metal Goat. It will give him the chance to put his talents to greater use as well as acquire experience he can build on in the future. His personal life can bring him great happiness and by working steadily towards his goals, he can end the year with accomplishments that are both worthy and considerable.

Tip for the Year
Believe in yourself. Go forward. Make your talents count. Many people believe in you and your actions can now have real significance. This can be a successful year and your achievements can form a platform on which you can build in following years.

The Water Goat

The Water Goat relies a lot on instinct and as the Goat year begins he will sense that it can be important for him. And his canny sense will not let him down.

Water Goats born in 1943 will often use this year to immerse themselves in particular projects. Personal interests can be especially gratifying and the Water Goat will enjoy seeing his thoughts take shape. Many Water Goats are blessed with an imaginative nature and for those who enjoy writing, art, photography or a similar form of self-expression, this can be an inspiring time. Creative activities are particularly well aspected this year and their individualistic approach can produce some interesting results.

Also, while many Water Goats will already have built up considerable knowledge in certain areas, they should look to take this further over the year. By reading about the latest developments and following up anything that interests them, they could have fresh ideas or become aware of other approaches. Some interest-related events could prove especially inspiring too. Some Water Goats may also discover courses that could be useful.

With his genial nature, the Water Goat will also enjoy the social opportunities of the year. There will be friends to meet and events to attend. Some Water Goats may also decide to help in their community or with a charitable cause and their involvement will add further meaning to their year.

In his home life the Water Goat will again carry out a great many plans – indeed, many Water Goats will view this year as one for action! There may be some ambitious undertakings and even a possible move. However, while the Water Goat may start certain projects in earnest, it would be best if he were to set about his activities at a steady pace rather than try to accomplish too much too quickly. By allowing time, he can carry out his plans more carefully and thoroughly and obtain better results. By the year's end, many Water Goats will be thrilled by what they have achieved, but activities do need to be spread out throughout the year.

The Water Goat will also do much to assist family members this year and younger relations in particular will be grateful for his time and attention. The bond he has with some of them will mean a lot to him. In addition, there could be some family news to celebrate. The summer can be an important time in many a Water Goat household, as will the closing weeks of 2015.

Water Goats who have gardens will also find that these can be a source of great pleasure. Spending time in the garden, or visiting parks and open spaces, can be both relaxing and therapeutic.

There will also be a lucky element to the year and if the Water Goat sees a competition that interests him, especially one related to a personal interest, he would do well to enter. In addition some may benefit from a gift or special payment, and those who enjoy travel should keep alert for special offers. For the more adventurous Water Goat, this year can open up some exciting possibilities.

However, while luck can play its part this year, the Water Goat cannot afford to be lax in financial matters. As well as watching spending levels, he should be thorough when attending to important paperwork. If anything concerns him, it would be worth seeking guidance.

For the Water Goat born in 2003, this is also a year of great possibility. Not only will more open up for the young Water Goat in his education, but his talents and interests could develop in encouraging ways. By taking advantage of the help, tuition and facilities available to him, he can make important strides this year and lay the foundations for the more advanced work to follow. Creative activities are particularly well aspected and many young Water Goats will delight in furthering their ideas and skills.

Throughout the year the Water Goat will also be encouraged by the support of those around him. If he shares his hopes and asks for help when necessary, assistance can be given and concerns often allayed. With his lively nature he will also enjoy the company of his friends and, as he undertakes more activities, will have the chance to make new ones. He will be involved in many things this year and delight in what he is able to achieve.

Overall, whether born in 1943 or 2003, the Water Goat can find this a satisfying time. Ideas can be advanced and skills used to good effect. However, it is a year for steady effort rather than rush. The Water Goat will value the support he receives and will in turn often play an important part in the lives of those who are dear to him. This is a year to take action, to seize opportunities and to make the most of personal strengths.

Tip for the Year
You are by nature creative – act upon your ideas! Your zest, instinct and personable nature will often ensure a pleasing outcome. Enjoy yourself!

The Wood Goat

This is the Year of the Wood Goat and it promises to be a special one for the Wood Goat himself. Not only does it mark the start of a new decade in his life but it is also a time of opportunity. A lot is set to happen, although to get the best from his year the Wood Goat will need to pace himself and be realistic in the amount of time needed for some undertakings. This is a time for steady, consistent effort. It is also one when the Wood Goat will be blessed with a certain amount of luck.

'Well begun is half done,' as the Chinese proverb reminds us, and during the year the Wood Goat would do well to bear this in mind. No matter what his hopes and plans, by attending to those all-important early stages, he can often ensure they develop well. In his thinking, he should not only consider what is needed, but also seek additional information and run his thoughts past others. He can set the agenda in many areas this year, but his plans do require both preparation and good follow-through.

At work there will be important decisions to make. Some Wood Goats may be offered the chance to retire and they should consider the terms with care. If they have uncertainties, they should ensure these are addressed before proceeding. Decisions should not be rushed this year.

Other Wood Goats may find the year presenting them with some unanticipated work choices. Although they may feel comfortable in their role, they could be affected by change. This could come through new working practices being introduced or, as the workforce changes, their area of responsibility changing too. Although some weeks will be challenging, good opportunities can follow on. As the year progresses, many Wood Goats will take on an increased role and have the chance to use their skills more effectively. The Year of the Wood Goat is an encouraging one for the Wood Goat himself, and particularly in terms of the opportunities it will bring.

There will also be some Wood Goats who are keen to move to another position, perhaps to alter their hours, reduce their commute or to fit in other commitments. For these Wood Goats, as well as those seeking a position, the year can again have interesting possibilities. Highlighting their experience in their application and at interview can help many to secure a new position over the year. April, July to early September and November could see important decisions being made.

The Goat year very much favours creativity and for Wood Goats who work or have interests in this area, this can be an inspiring time. Many Wood Goats will be keen to make more of their ideas and talents, and those who retire or have extra time available should also give thought to specific activities they could now take up. If they have had it in mind to learn more about a subject or add to a skill, this would be an excellent time to do so.

The Wood Goat would also do well to give some consideration to his well-being, including his diet and general level of exercise. If he feels either is deficient, he should seek medical advice. It is important for him to pay some attention to his own welfare in this active year.

He also needs to be careful in financial matters. Whenever possible, advance provision for more ambitious undertakings would be helpful and could make an important difference. Also, with some plans and activities having considerable financial implications, the Wood Goat should spend time checking details and questioning anything that is unclear. This is not a year for risk, rush or making assumptions.

One expense this year may be travel, especially as the Wood Goat may be tempted to celebrate his sixtieth birthday by taking a special holiday. For many Wood Goats, this can be a highlight of the year. Also, with this being a year rich in cultural pursuits, the Wood Goat could enjoy visiting exhibitions and special attractions.

This will also be an active time domestically, with loved ones often keen to celebrate the Wood Goat's sixtieth birthday in style, and some surprises too. Parts of the year will have a celebratory feel to them and there will be several special occasions for the Wood Goat to look forward to. Shared activities are favourably aspected and the Wood Goat will find that by combining ideas and efforts, a lot can be accomplished, including some useful acquisitions for the home. Where practical activities are concerned, good planning and the avoidance of rush will help.

During the year the Wood Goat will also have occasion to assist certain family members, including with decisions affecting the longer term. His views will carry much weight. Many of those around him do value his judgement.

Socially, the Wood Goat can look forward to some special occasions with his friends and could find himself being invited to some interesting gatherings. Quite a few Wood Goats will also welcome the chance to make contact with friends they have not seen for some time, and for the unattached, their own year is not without romantic possibilities. Late February, March, June, September and December could be particularly full and interesting months.

Overall, the Year of the Wood Goat can be a special and rewarding one for the Wood Goat himself, although he does need to seize his opportunities. With good planning and preparation, a lot will be possible for him this year. Luck and support will give added weight to his plans and he can greatly enjoy the pleasing developments his own year will bring.

Tip for the Year

This is your year. Act. Make things happen. With good planning and a positive 'can do' approach, you can achieve a great deal. Also, enjoy your own interests and your relations with those around you. These can help make your year special.

The Fire Goat

The Fire Goat has a great many qualities and is often noted for his engaging manner, wide interests and inventive mind. In the Goat year his strengths can serve him well, but there is a but. The Fire Goat may like to see the results of his efforts coming through quickly, but this is no year for rush or risk. His gains this year will come through good planning and steady effort.

Throughout the year the Fire Goat will, however, be assisted by the good relations he enjoys with many of those around him and can not only benefit from their encouragement but also their expertise. Also, it could be to his advantage to raise his profile, perhaps by joining a professional organization or a society connected with a key interest. By being active and involved, he will not only be helping his current situation but also benefit personally.

This also applies to Fire Goats who find themselves in a new environment or location this year or are feeling lonely due to a recent change in circumstances. This is a year to go out *and be a part of life*. Goat years reward effort and the Fire Goat's quick and vibrant personality can impress many people this year. March, June, September and December could see the most social activity, and for the unattached, a meeting in sometimes unusual circumstances could suddenly blossom into serious romance. In so many ways, the Goat year can be special and often lucky for the Fire Goat.

The Fire Goat enjoys a variety of interests and over the year certain activities could take on additional meaning. Fire Goats who favour creative pursuits in particular could enjoy some well-deserved success.

In addition to the pleasure personal interests can bring, this is also an excellent year for self-development. If there is a skill the Fire Goat feels may be useful, an additional qualification that could help his prospects or a subject that catches his attention, he should follow it up. This year he can make an investment in himself.

To be at his best and maintain his energy levels, he should also give some consideration to his general well-being, including having a balanced diet and taking regular exercise. Extra attention can make a real difference.

The Fire Goat's domestic life will be abuzz with activity this year and it is important that there is both good communication and flexibility over arrangements. While the Fire Goat (or another) may be keen to go ahead with certain home projects, haste can lead to oversights or add to existing pressures. Major activities need to be spread out over the year. Amid the activity there can, though, be special times. Younger relations could enjoy academic or personal success and there will also be family occasions which the Fire Goat will often both instigate and greatly enjoy. The summer and the closing weeks of the year could be particularly full and lively times.

In the Fire Goat's work, too, this will be an eventful year. In view of the experience many Fire Goats now have, they could find themselves being given more challenging tasks to deal with. Some parts of the year will be daunting, but the Fire Goat will have the chance to prove himself and add to his skills. What occurs now can be good preparation for the next stage in his career. April, July, August and November could see important work developments.

With this being the Goat year, some Fire Goats may regard it as a good time to embark on a major change in their career. Particularly if they are feeling unfulfilled or seeking work, they should consider other ways in which they could use their skills and seek advice. Many could be alerted to other types of work which will suit them well. Some of what arises this year can have far-reaching significance for the Fire Goat.

Progress made at work can help financially, but with commitments, home improvements and an often active lifestyle, the Fire Goat's outgoings can be considerable. As a result, he will need to keep track of spending and make early provision for some of his plans. And, as with so much this year, he should be wary of rush.

The Year of the Goat has great potential for the Fire Goat, but he does need to proceed steadily. With application, however, he can see many of his plans developing well. He will also be encouraged by the support of those around him and his personal qualities will not only help his progress but be especially valued by those close to him. He will have a lot in his favour this year and a lot to enjoy.

Tip for the Year
Be bold. Be active. Be involved. Make the most of your strengths and personality. This is a year of possibility for you and with belief in yourself, you can emerge from it with some pleasing progress to your credit.

The Earth Goat

This will be an encouraging year for the Earth Goat. A lot is set to happen and he will generally fare well, although he does need to be realistic in his expectations and avoid unnecessary rush. By putting in the effort and working steadily, however, he can benefit from some fortunate developments.

In his work the aspects are especially encouraging. Earth Goats who have been with their present employer for some time will find their in-house knowledge and desire to move their career forward may well lead to the offer of new responsibilities or training that will enable them to do more. Another positive factor will be the good relations the Earth Goat has with many of those around him. Not only will he be an appreciated member of many a team this year but will also find that more senior colleagues encourage his career development. He should also make good use of his chances to network. By being active and visible he will not only be helping his present situation but also his future prospects.

Many Earth Goats will be able to further their career where they are, but there will be some who feel they can improve their situation by moving elsewhere. For these Earth Goats, as well as those who are feeling staid or unfulfilled by their work, this is a year for action. By looking for positions elsewhere and considering other ways in which they could use their skills, many will be successful in moving to something more suitable and remunerative. Similarly, Earth Goats seeking work will find that by widening the nature of their search, they too can set their career off on an interesting new track. Admittedly, considerable adjustment may be needed, but the Goat year can give many Earth Goats the opportunity they have been seeking for so long. Mid-March to the end of April, July, August and November could see important developments.

Progress made at work will enable many Earth Goats to increase their income, but with existing commitments, together with the plans the Earth Goat will have in mind, he will need to manage his resources carefully. In addition, when entering into any important agreement, he should check the terms and consider the implications. Risk or haste could work to his disadvantage. Earth Goats, take note.

Born under the sign of art, the Earth Goat often has a creative streak and he will enjoy developing his ideas over the year, including sharing some of what he does with others. Earth Goats who have let interests lapse or would welcome a new activity will find that by keeping informed about what is available in their area, they could discover a new recreational pursuit that suits them well. Some may also join an activity or community group, and their involvement can do them a lot of good.

The Earth Goat will also delight in the social opportunities of the year and will find himself in demand. In view of some of the decisions he will have to take, he could find the support (and expertise) of a long-standing friend of particular help and should listen carefully to their views. The increased social activity will also give him the chance to meet new people, and for the unattached, Cupid's arrow could suddenly strike. March, June, September and December could see the most social opportunities.

The Earth Goat's home life will also see a lot of activity. Routines may be liable to change and at particularly hectic times, the Earth Goat's ability to communicate, organize and determine priorities will be much appreciated. Also, the more everyone can share in decisions, the better. However, while some weeks may be pressured, a lot can still be achieved and many Earth Goats will enjoy the benefits some domestic changes and purchases (especially new equipment) bring. Over the year there will also be achievements to mark, including a possible special birthday, anniversary or family occasion, with the Earth Goat very much involved and enjoying what takes place.

If possible, he should also try to take a holiday with his loved ones over the year. All concerned will appreciate the rest this brings and the chance to visit interesting places.

Overall, the Year of the Goat will be a busy one for the Earth Goat and there will be times of pressure and uncertainty. The Earth Goat may sometimes wish for a let-up in all the activity, but this can also be a year of great possibility. In both his work and interests, he will have the chance to develop his skills and make good progress. His home and social life will also see a lot happen and he will value the special relationships he has with many of those around him. The Earth Goat has great personal skills and much to offer, and this fine year will give him the chance to do more. An encouraging and constructive time.

Tip for the Year
This is a year to move forward and make more of yourself. To drift could deny you some fine opportunities. Also, build on your skills and seize your chances to meet others. Your efforts can reward you well. Enjoy your interests, too, and your relations with those who are special to you. You have much in your favour this year. Use it well.

Famous Goats

Pamela Anderson, Jane Austen, Lord Byron, Vince Cable, Coco Chanel, Nat 'King' Cole, Jamie Cullum, Robert de Niro, Catherine Deneuve, Charles Dickens, Vin Diesel, Ken Dodd, Sir Arthur Conan Doyle, Douglas Fairbanks, Will Ferrell, Jamie Foxx, Noel Gallagher, Bill Gates, Robert Gates, Mel Gibson, Whoopi Goldberg, Mikhail Gorbachev, John Grisham, Oscar Hammerstein, George Harrison, Billy Idol, Julio Iglesias, Sir Mick Jagger, Steve Jobs, Norah Jones, Nicole Kidman, Sir Ben Kingsley, Christine Lagarde, John le Carré, Matt LeBlanc, Franz Liszt, James McAvoy, Sir John Major, Michelangelo, Joni Mitchell, Rupert

Murdoch, Randy Newman, Sinead O'Connor, Michael Palin, Aaron Paul, Eva Peron, Pink, Marcel Proust, Keith Richards, Flo Rida, Julia Roberts, William Shatner, Queen Silvia of Sweden, Gary Sinise, Jerry Springer, Lana Turner, Mark Twain, Rudolph Valentino, Vangelis, Barbara Walters, John Wayne, Justin Welby, King Willem-Alexander of the Netherlands, Bruce Willis.

20 February 1920 to 7 February 1921 — *Metal Monkey*

6 February 1932 to 25 January 1933 — *Water Monkey*

25 January 1944 to 12 February 1945 — *Wood Monkey*

12 February 1956 to 30 January 1957 — *Fire Monkey*

30 January 1968 to 16 February 1969 — *Earth Monkey*

16 February 1980 to 4 February 1981 — *Metal Monkey*

4 February 1992 to 22 January 1993 — *Water Monkey*

22 January 2004 to 8 February 2005 — *Wood Monkey*

The Monkey

The Personality of the Monkey

The more open to possibility,
the more possibilities open.

The Monkey is born under the sign of fantasy. He is imaginative, inquisitive and loves to keep an eye on everything that is going on around him. He is never backward in offering an opinion or trying to sort out the problems of others. He likes to be helpful and his advice is invariably sensible and reliable.

The Monkey is intelligent, well read and always eager to learn. He has an extremely good memory and there are many Monkeys who have made particularly good linguists. The Monkey is also a convincing talker and enjoys taking part in discussions and debates. His friendly, self-assured manner can be very persuasive and he usually has little trouble in winning people round to his way of thinking. It is for this reason that he often excels in politics and public speaking. He is also particularly adept in PR work, teaching and any job that involves selling.

The Monkey can, however, be crafty, cunning and occasionally dishonest, and he will seize any opportunity to make a quick profit or outsmart his opponents. He has so much charm and guile that people often don't realize what he is up to until it is too late. But despite his resourceful nature, he does run the risk of outsmarting even himself. He has so much confidence in his abilities that he rarely listens to advice or is prepared to accept help from anyone. He likes to help others, but prefers to rely on his own judgement when dealing with his own affairs.

Another characteristic of the Monkey is that he is extremely good at solving problems and has a happy knack of extricating himself (and others) from the most hopeless of positions. He is the master of self-preservation.

With so many diverse talents, the Monkey is usually able to make considerable sums of money, but he does like to enjoy life and will think nothing of spending his money on some exotic holiday or luxury he has had his eye on. He can, however, become very envious if someone else has what he wants.

The Monkey is an original thinker and despite his love of company, he cherishes his independence. He has to have the freedom to act as he wants and any Monkey who feels hemmed in or bound by too many restrictions will soon become unhappy. Likewise, if anything becomes too boring or monotonous, the Monkey will soon lose interest and turn his attention to something else. He lacks persistence and this can often hamper his progress. He is also easily distracted, a tendency that he should try to overcome. By concentrating on one thing at a time, he will almost certainly achieve more in the long run.

The Monkey is a good organizer and even though he may behave slightly erratically at times, he will invariably have a plan at the back of his mind. On the odd occasion when his plans do not work out, he is usually quite happy to shrug his shoulders and put it down to experience. He will rarely make the same mistake twice and throughout his life he will try his hand at many different things.

The Monkey likes to impress and is rarely without followers or admirers. Many are attracted by his good looks, his sense of humour, or simply because he instils so much confidence in those around him.

Monkeys usually marry young and for it to be a success their partner must allow them time to pursue their many interests and indulge their love of travel. The Monkey has to have variety in his life and is especially well suited to those born under the sociable and outgoing signs of the Rat, Dragon, Pig and Goat. The Ox, Rabbit, Snake and Dog will also be enchanted by his resourceful and outgoing nature, but he is likely to exasperate the Rooster and Horse, and the Tiger will have little patience with his tricks. A relationship between two Monkeys will work well – they will understand each other and be able to assist each other in their various enterprises.

The female Monkey is intelligent, extremely observant and a shrewd judge of character. Her opinions are often highly valued and, having such a persuasive nature, she invariably gets her own way. She has many interests and involves herself in a wide variety of activities. She pays great attention to her appearance, is an elegant dresser and likes to take particular care over her hair. She can be a doting parent and will have many good and loyal friends.

Provided the Monkey can curb his desire to take part in everything that is going on around him and concentrate on one thing at a time, he can usually achieve what he wants in life. Should he suffer any disappointment, he is bound to bounce back. He is a survivor and his life is usually both colourful and eventful.

The Five Different Types of Monkey

In addition to the 12 signs of the Chinese zodiac there are five elements and these have a strengthening or moderating influence on the signs. The effects of the five elements on the Monkey are described below, together with the years in which they were exercising their influence. Therefore Monkeys born in 1920 and 1980 are Metal Monkeys, Monkeys born in 1932 and 1992 are Water Monkeys, and so on.

Metal Monkey: 1920, 1980

The Metal Monkey is very strong-willed. He sets about everything he does with dogged determination and often prefers to work independently rather than with others. He is ambitious, wise and confident, and is certainly not afraid of hard work. He is very astute in financial matters and usually chooses his investments well. Despite his somewhat independent nature, he enjoys attending parties and social occasions and is particularly warm and caring towards his loved ones.

Water Monkey: 1932, 1992

The Water Monkey is versatile, determined and perceptive. He also has more discipline than some of the other Monkeys and is prepared to work towards a particular goal rather than be distracted by something else. He is not always open about his true intentions and when questioned can be particularly evasive. He can be sensitive to criticism but also very persuasive and usually has little trouble in getting others to fall in with his plans. He has a very good understanding of human nature and relates well to others.

Wood Monkey: 1944, 2004

This Monkey is efficient, methodical and extremely conscientious. He is also highly imaginative and is always trying to capitalize on new ideas or learn new skills. Occasionally his enthusiasm can get the better of him and he can get very agitated when things do not quite work out as he had hoped. He does, however, have a very adventurous streak and is not afraid of taking risks. He also loves travel. He is usually held in great esteem by his friends and colleagues.

Fire Monkey: 1956

The Fire Monkey is intelligent, full of vitality and has no trouble in commanding the respect of others. He is imaginative and has wide interests, although sometimes these can distract him from more useful and profitable work. He is very competitive and always likes to be involved in everything that is going on. He can be stubborn if he does not get his own way and he sometimes tries to indoctrinate those who are less strong-willed than himself. He is a lively character, attractive to others and loyal to his partner.

Earth Monkey: 1968

The Earth Monkey tends to be studious and well read, and can become quite distinguished in his chosen line of work. He is less outgoing than some of the other types of Monkey and prefers quieter and more solid pursuits. He has high principles, a very caring nature and can be most generous to those less fortunate than himself. He is usually successful in handling financial matters and can become very wealthy in old age. He has a calming influence on those around him and is respected and well liked. He is, however, especially careful about whom he lets into his confidence.

Prospects for the Monkey in 2015

The Horse year (31 January 2014–18 February 2015) often proceeds at a heady pace and during it the Monkey will have been involved in a great many activities. There will have been dreams to pursue, decisions to make and ideas to implement. The closing months will see little let-up, with many a Monkey fully occupied.

While he can generally do well at this time, the Monkey needs to ensure he does not overreach himself. While his judgement is usually sound, misreading a situation or taking a risk could rebound on him. Monkeys, do bear this in mind.

At work there will be much to attend to and again the Monkey needs to be thorough and take the time to think through his actions. Impulsiveness could be to his disadvantage. However, with care, much can be accomplished.

In money matters the Monkey could enjoy some luck, including receiving extra funds or a special gift. He could be particularly thrilled with a purchase he makes, often on advantageous terms.

The closing months of the Horse year will also see a flurry of social activity, with the last six weeks particularly busy. In the Monkey's home life a lot is set to happen, possibly including travel later on in the year. With a lot to arrange, he does need to be forthcoming and take note of the views of others. With care, however, he will find the final months of the year constructive and generally pleasing.

The Year of the Goat begins on 19 February and will be a variable one for the Monkey. In some areas of his life he is set to do particularly well, but in others, care and caution are advised. However, by being aware of the trickier aspects, many Monkeys will be able to steer their way successfully around them and emerge with some important gains to their credit.

One area which will need particularly close attention is finance. Although usually adept when dealing with money matters, the Monkey will need to remain disciplined and keep a close watch on his spending levels. Without care, these could become greater than anticipated. Similarly, when making costly purchases or entering into new agreements, he should check the terms and consider the implications. Taking risks or making assumptions may lead to difficulties later. Monkeys, *do* take note.

However, travel is favourably aspected and if possible the Monkey should try to make provision for a holiday or break at some time during the year. In addition some Monkeys could have the chance to visit family or friends living some distance away. Over the year, many will enjoy visiting new places and some impressive attractions.

A feature of the Goat year is that it encourages creativity, and the Monkey, with his inventive nature, is never short of ideas. Over the year it is important he allows himself the time to develop his personal interests. Not only will he take pleasure in putting his ideas into practice but will very often find that one thought can broaden out into something much bigger.

He should also pay some attention to his own well-being this year. If he tends to be sedentary for much of the day or is reliant on convenience foods, he should consider ways he could exercise more and make improvements to his diet. Also, if feeling below par, he should seek advice. Extra care and attention can make a difference.

With his genial nature, the Monkey enjoys company and can look forward to an interesting mix of social occasions, with April to early June, August and September seeing the most activity. However, while many agreeable times can be had, the aspects advise care. It could be that a minor difference of opinion escalates, a casual remark is misconstrued or someone lets the Monkey down. In the Goat year he does need to be on his guard, and if he detects difficult undercurrents or potential problems with friends, he should be attentive and careful. Monkeys are generally adept in handling personal relations, but the diplomatic skills of quite a few could be tested this year.

The Monkey's home life is set to be busy and here again there could be issues that are of concern to him. It could be that problems facing a loved one cause him some anxiety or a clash of interests arises. The fortitude – and ingenuity – of the Monkey will prove a great asset and when difficulties appear (as they will in any year), he will find that by talking these through and reaching consensus, he and those around him will often be able to resolve them satisfactorily.

Although during parts of the year decisions, activities and commitments may seem to need the Monkey's attention all at once, there will also be many pleasing occasions for him to look forward to. Joint projects can be especially satisfying. With travel favourably aspected, a holiday, or just some time away, can do everyone a lot of good. May and August could be particularly interesting and lively months in many a Monkey household.

Work prospects can be encouraging this year and there will be the opportunity for many Monkeys to make more of specific strengths and take on greater (and more remunerative) responsibilities. The majority of Monkeys will remain with their present employer, but some could be attracted by opportunities elsewhere. The Goat year will open up some interesting possibilities.

Monkeys who are looking for work will find that by making enquiries, including to companies which are active and expanding in their area, they can make their initiative count. Many of these Monkeys will impress prospective employers this year and be offered the chance they have been seeking. It will take time, but Goat years, despite their difficult moments, do recognize the Monkey's enterprise and can bring him some good opportunities. March, June, July and November could see particularly interesting developments, but throughout the year the Monkey should act quickly if an opportunity comes his way. With next year being his own year, what he accomplishes now can often prepare him for the more substantial progress that lies ahead.

In general, the Year of the Goat will be a full and interesting one for the Monkey. It will contain its difficult moments, and financially and in his relations with others the Monkey needs to take extra care. But he is astute and can often counter or avoid the year's more awkward aspects. More positively, this is an excellent year for travel, for developing ideas and for moving ahead at work. Goat years may not be the easiest for the

Monkey, but there are still personal gains to be had in this one, along with some well-deserved successes.

The Metal Monkey

With a strong will and engaging style, the Metal Monkey sets about his activities with considerable resolve. Over the year he can look forward to some pleasing results. However, he will need to proceed carefully. Goat years can pose hazards for the unwary.

At work, many Metal Monkeys will feel they are ready to move forward in their career. These Metal Monkeys should not only keep alert for openings in their present place of work but make soundings elsewhere. Whether through talking to contacts, making enquiries to prospective employers or following up vacancies, their initiative will lead to many taking on greater responsibilities during the year and, in some cases, alert them to other ways in which they could use their skills. Late February, March, June, July and November could see important developments and whether the Metal Monkey chooses to stay with his present employer or move elsewhere, the Goat year can bring a considerable shift in responsibilities.

The aspects are also encouraging for Metal Monkeys seeking work. Again, they should actively pursue the openings they see as well as consider how they could adapt their skills. Some may find themselves eligible for retraining or decide to update their knowledge through personal study. The initiative of many will lead to chances being given and what happens now can be a significant factor in the Metal Monkey's future success.

Another encouraging feature of this year is the way in which the Metal Monkey will be able to build on his ideas. This not only applies to his work situation but his personal interests too. By following through his thoughts, he will not only take pleasure in how his ideas and projects evolve, but also be inspired to add to his skills. Some Metal Monkeys may become attracted by new interests, too. The Goat year can certainly open up the Metal Monkey's mind to some interesting possibilities.

It would also be to his advantage to give some thought to his well-being, including considering the quality of his diet and making sure he has regular exercise. To neglect his own welfare could leave him prone to minor ailments.

He should also take care in financial matters. Although he may enjoy an increase in income, his outgoings are likely to be considerable. If he enters into a new agreement or makes a large purchase, he should give himself time to check the terms and consider other options. Rush, risk or assumptions could all be to his disadvantage. Metal Monkeys, take note.

Travel, though, is well aspected and if possible the Metal Monkey should make provision for a holiday. A rest can do him good. Some Metal Monkeys will also appreciate the chance to combine a holiday with a special interest or event.

With his wide interests and outgoing nature, the Metal Monkey knows a great many people and enjoys socializing. However, this year he will need to keep his wits about him. A friend could take umbrage over a certain matter or someone the Metal Monkey trusts may let him down. A friendship issue could be of concern and if the Metal Monkey detects a possible disagreement arising, he should try to address this before it escalates. The diplomatic skills of many Metal Monkeys will be tested this year.

For the unattached Metal Monkey who finds love this year, romance also needs to be nurtured. A new relationship should be built up steadily, rather than rushed.

However, while the Metal Monkey will need to be mindful of others this year, he will enjoy the variety of events on offer. April to early June and August to early October could see the most social activity.

The Metal Monkey's diplomatic talents will again be needed, however, in his home life. This will be a busy year and in view of the pressures some family members will be facing, there will need to be good communication and co-operation. It is also important that quality time is not lost. The Metal Monkey should strive for a good lifestyle balance this year.

Although home life will be busy, the Goat year can give rise to some enjoyable occasions, including the celebration of individual successes.

Visits to local events and attractions can also provide some lively moments. The Metal Monkey should keep alert for events that he and others may enjoy.

In general, the Goat year is one of considerable possibility for the Metal Monkey. In his work and personal interests, it is a time to develop skills and promote ideas. Good progress can be made, although the Metal Monkey will need to exercise care in his relations with others and may be troubled by a friendship issue. Domestically, too, he needs to remain mindful and aware. With care, he will be able to successfully steer his way around the year's more awkward aspects, however, and his current efforts will be something he can build on next year.

Tip for the Year

Pay close attention to your relations with others. Give time to those who are important to you and be aware of their points of view. In addition, look to further your skills. This can be a rewarding year and good achievements are possible.

The Water Monkey

The Water Monkey is ambitious and resourceful. He not only works hard, but always tries to make the most of his situation. And this year he can make important headway.

Some Water Monkeys will be in education, and as their courses draw to a close and exams approach, the pressures may be considerable, but by working consistently and keeping the end result in mind, they will often be pleased with their results. For the Water Monkey, an important feature of this Goat year is that what is achieved during it can be a springboard to some wonderful opportunities, either late in 2015 or in 2016, the auspicious Year of the Monkey.

For Water Monkeys in work, again the Goat year can be significant. If they are active and involved in their place of work, their talents will often be recognized and they may have the chance to take on greater responsibility. It is well worth them putting in the effort.

The aspects are also encouraging for Water Monkeys seeking work. Although the job-seeking process can be wearying, deep down the Water Monkey knows he can achieve a great deal, and by having self-belief and persisting, he may be successful in his quest. Admittedly, what is offered may not be exactly what he was looking for, but the Water Monkey has a talent for making the best of his situation and some of what the Goat year makes possible, unexpected though it may be, can be to his longer-term advantage. Late February to early April, June, July and November could see important developments.

The Water Monkey can derive considerable pleasure from his personal interests this year and should again look to build on his skills. By endeavouring to do more, he will not only be pleased with how his activities progress but enjoy himself in the process.

He will also delight in the travel opportunities that arise, including chances to attend special events and visit well-known attractions. Even though he may be on a tight budget and some trips may be arranged at short notice, the Goat year can give rise to some interesting times.

In money matters, however, the Water Monkey will need to be careful. He will often have many demands on sometimes limited resources and will need to be disciplined. Should he enter into any new agreement, he would do well to check the terms and conditions. This is a year for care, control and vigilance.

It is also a good time to consider his well-being. With his busy life-style and often long days, the Water Monkey needs to allow himself time to catch up rather than drive himself relentlessly. He should also take care with his diet and not skimp on healthy, nutritious food. With the considerable energy he uses and the many demands that will be placed upon him this year, some extra care and attention will help him to keep on good form. If at any time he feels under par, he should seek advice.

With his enquiring and lively nature, the Water Monkey sets great store by his social life and this will again be both busy and significant. Water Monkeys who move to a new location will have the chance to build a new social circle, and April to early June, August and September could see a whirl of social activity. The Water Monkey's social life can generally go well, but there is a but. Without care, a friendship could sour and it is also possible that someone may let the Water Monkey down. The paths of friendship are not always smooth. Water Monkeys, take note and do be aware.

Affairs of the heart can, however, make this a thrilling time, with some Water Monkeys finding love in unlikely ways. For Water Monkeys with a partner this can be an exciting year. While many will have specific plans, especially accommodation-wise, these should not necessarily be regarded as final. Goat years can spring surprises. Much will be achieved this year, but not always in the way or on the timescale originally envisaged. Also, as routines and commitments alter, adjustments will be required, and flexibility and good communication will be of benefit.

Family-wise, it is important that all Water Monkeys are aware that support is available from more senior relations. If ever the Water Monkey is in a dilemma, would welcome advice or has an important decision to make, he should be forthcoming. With the experience that some senior relations have, their advice can be of great worth. Water Monkeys, in this good but sometimes demanding year, do bear this in mind.

The Water Monkey has many strengths and the effort he makes this year is an investment in himself *and* his future. He can make important headway, but the Goat year does have its trickier aspects and the Water Monkey will need to manage his financial situation well and tread carefully in any potentially awkward friendship matter. He is alert, adept and keen, though, and over the year he can lay the foundation for future success.

Tip for the Year
Be active and involved. What you achieve now prove significant. Also, develop your personal interests. These can bring you pleasure and often be a good outlet for your talents as well.

The Wood Monkey

The Wood Monkey enjoys a wide variety of activities and this can be an interesting and satisfying year for him.

As the Goat year starts, the Wood Monkey born in 1944 will have plans he is keen to get underway. Whether these are domestic projects, personal interests or other activities, early 2015 will see many Wood Monkeys giving thought to what they would like to see happen in the year ahead. However, Goat years can proceed in curious ways and the Wood Monkey will need to be flexible. He will also need to talk through plans and projects with those around him, listen closely to their points of view and, when appropriate, seek an expert opinion. The more input and advice he receives, the better his results will be. This especially applies to new equipment he may be considering or improvements he would like to make to his home.

Wood Monkeys who have gardens will also have ideas they will be keen to implement, including buying new stock and adding additional features. As in so many areas this year, the Wood Monkey's mind will be abuzz with possibility.

In addition to the practical activities of the year, the Wood Monkey will give valuable support to family members. With some younger relations facing difficult choices, his empathy and expertise will be greatly valued. There could also be a matter which causes concern and if the Wood Monkey feels it appropriate, he should consider getting professional advice. He is caring and wants to do his best, but in some instances the guidance of an expert can make an important difference.

Although there may be some worrying moments during the year (and no year is ever problem-free), there will be much to delight the Wood Monkey too. Some Wood Monkey households could celebrate a special anniversary or family milestone and some younger relations could enjoy an academic or professional achievement. The Goat year will certainly give rise to some special occasions.

Travel, too, is favourably aspected, with the Wood Monkey having the opportunity to visit some impressive places. In some instances, these may not be too far away but in areas the Wood Monkey hasn't properly seen or appreciated before. In addition, if he receives an invitation to visit others or is attracted by a last-minute travel offer, he should follow it up. There is a spontaneity to the Goat year and by being flexible the Wood Monkey can get far more out of it.

He will also spend a lot of time on his interests and here surprises are in store. Sometimes an idea will develop in an unanticipated way or the Wood Monkey will decide to experiment with new approaches or techniques or try something different altogether. Goat years can enthuse the Wood Monkey.

He will also value his social opportunities, and late March to early June, August and September could see a lot of activity. However, while many social occasions will be agreeable, the Wood Monkey does need to ensure that a minor disagreement does not escalate. Fortunately, he is adept at picking up signals, and if he senses problems emerging, he may be able to defuse them before they cause any upset. Wood Monkeys, do take note and be aware.

The Wood Monkey will also need to be careful in financial matters. In view of his overall spending and the plans he may have for his home, he should take his time when making substantial purchases and check his requirements are being met. The more care (and advice) he takes, the better his decisions will be. Also, when dealing with financial paperwork, he should check the details and query anything that concerns him. This is a year for increased vigilance.

Although the Wood Monkey usually keeps himself active, if he feels changes to his diet or starting an exercise discipline would be useful, he should seek medical guidance on how best to proceed. Similarly, if he has concerns at any time, he should get these checked out.

For the Wood Monkey born in 2004, this is also a year of interesting possibility. In his place of education, especially if he changes school this year, there will be additional facilities and resources to use, and many young Wood Monkeys will enjoy the chance to do more. For the active and enquiring, this can be an exciting and illuminating time.

However, at times the Wood Monkey may feel daunted by the changes taking place and what is being asked of him. Rather than keep his concerns to himself, it is important that he seeks advice. That way, his worries can be eased. The young Wood Monkey should not suffer in silence this year.

His personal interests can develop well and he may be taught a new skill which he can put to good use over the next few years. The Goat year can open up some rewarding possibilities.

Overall, this can be a satisfying year for the Wood Monkey. Whether born in 1944 or 2004, he will find his ideas developing well, sometimes in unexpected ways. By being willing and open-minded, he can also benefit from new opportunities. Admittedly, the year will have its problems, and when in company the Wood Monkey will need to be his mindful self. However, forewarned and forearmed, many Wood Monkeys will be able to steer their way around these awkward aspects and take pleasure in what they achieve.

Tip for the Year

Be alert to changing situations. By making the most of what arises, you can achieve a lot and have some good times too. Also, value your relations with others and be mindful of their views. Although this is a positive year for you, extra care and attention will help in so much.

The Fire Monkey

The Fire Monkey has a great capacity to give. Whether in his home, his work or his personal interests, he commits himself and gives his all. Being conscientious, he also sets high standards. While he often meets these, in the Goat year problems can arise and some activities prove more challenging than anticipated. This can be a testing time, although true to form, the Fire Monkey can still accomplish a great deal.

This will be especially the case in his work. During the year many Fire Monkeys will experience change, including working with new personnel and new procedures. What arises will test the abilities (and patience) of the Fire Monkey, but he is experienced and his in-depth knowledge will help him deal with – and influence – many a situation. The challenges will also underline his strengths and he may emerge with credit after what could be some pressured weeks.

There will also be opportunities for Fire Monkeys who are keen to move on in their career or switch roles to make the change they have been seeking. These openings can arise suddenly and may be different or more extensive than the Fire Monkey expected, but he will need to make the best of what is offered. Next year is his own year and progress made now can often be taken further then.

For Fire Monkeys seeking work, the process can be wearying, but they should remain persistent. By keeping alert for openings, staying in regular contact with employment agencies and approaching companies directly, they may well find a new position, even if (again) in a unexpected capacity. Goat years can move in curious but potentially advantageous ways. March, June to early August and November could see important developments.

Progress made at work can also lead to an increase in income, but the Fire Monkey will need to manage his finances carefully. Many Fire Monkeys could have additional family expenses this year and home maintenance may be needed too. Where major outlay is involved, the Fire Monkey should check the terms of any deal and ensure it covers his needs. Financial care is very much advised this year.

Despite the many outgoings the Fire Monkey is likely to have, if possible he should make provision for a holiday. Travel is favourably aspected and by choosing his destination carefully (and it need not be too far away), he will not only enjoy his time away but also benefit from a much-needed rest. There could be further travel opportunities later on in the year.

In view of his many commitments, it is also important that the Fire Monkey gives himself some 'me time'. His own interests can not only be satisfying, but with the Goat year encouraging creativity and self-expression, many Fire Monkeys will be tempted to take their ideas further or even try out a new activity.

In addition, the Fire Monkey should pay some attention to his own well-being, including his diet and level of exercise. Not taking sufficient care of himself could leave him lacking his usual energy. Should he have concerns at any time, he should get these checked out.

Socially, there will be a good mix of occasions for the Fire Monkey to enjoy. He will appreciate his chances to go out, often to do something different, and his keen and genial nature will make him popular company. His work and interests can lead to him meeting new people over the year and April to early June and August to early October could see the most social activity. However, if he detects a disagreement arising with one of his friends, he should try to prevent it escalating. He should also be wary of making unguarded remarks. An uncharacteristic *faux pas* could cause upset. Fire Monkeys, be alert!

The Fire Monkey's home life will be busy and his advice and support will be appreciated, particularly by his partner or younger relations, and in some cases help steer them through difficult decisions. Once again the Fire Monkey's care and resourcefulness will be valued assets. This Goat year also has an element of the unexpected and it could be that plans need altering to fit in with changed circumstances or repairs are required when something breaks. However, with flexibility and co-operation from all concerned, many difficulties and niggles can be successfully overcome and the solutions – in some instances, updated equipment – appreciated by all.

Overall, the Year of the Goat may not be the easiest for the Fire Monkey, but it can be a valuable one. Its sometimes difficult situations can open up new opportunities for him as well as highlight his personal qualities and strengths. In his work, progress can be made and with personal interests this is a year to broaden his ideas and skills. Domestically and socially, the Fire Monkey will be in demand, although he will need to be aware of what is going on around him and mindful of the views of others. A minor difference of opinion or awkward moment could cause difficulties. However, the Fire Monkey is adept and resourceful and, with care, can gain much from the year and sow the seeds of next year's notable success.

Tip for the Year
Keep your wits about you and act quickly when necessary. That way you can make the most of what opens up for you this year. Also, give time to those who are important to you *as well as to yourself*. This can be a busy time and you need to strive for a good lifestyle balance.

The Earth Monkey

The Earth Monkey is careful and thorough and rarely takes on more than he can handle at any one time. He also chooses his moments well, sensing when the time is right for action or when it is best to hold back. In the Goat year his perceptiveness will serve him well.

In his work the Earth Monkey could find himself affected by change. New staff and initiatives could alter his role and he may have the chance to take on new responsibilities. His experience could even place him at the forefront of change, with his views being frequently sought by his colleagues. Some weeks could be pressured, but by concentrating on what needs to be done, the Earth Monkey will often have the chance to make a notable contribution to his workplace.

The majority of Earth Monkeys will advance their career with their present employer, but for those keen to make a change, as well as those seeking work, the Goat year can be significant. Although the job-seeking process may be difficult, by looking at other ways in which they could use their skills (here employment advisers could make important suggestions), many could secure a position which is different from what they have done before but has potential for the future. March, June to early August and November could see encouraging developments and what is achieved now can often be the springboard to some notable successes next year.

Progress at work can bring an increase in income, but it will be an expensive year and the Earth Monkey will need to control his budget. Some Earth Monkeys could face repair costs as well as decide to replace outdated equipment. More positively, travel may be particularly appealing this year and if possible the Earth Monkey should make provision for a holiday and other breaks.

Although he will have many commitments, he also values his interests, and these will continue to bring him great pleasure. Goat years favour the arts and many an Earth Monkey will be inspired to develop his talents. Some may even take their interests in new directions or start a new activity entirely. The Goat year is an encouraging one in this respect.

The Earth Monkey would also do well to give some attention to his own well-being. If reliant on convenience foods or tending not to get much regular exercise, he could consider some modifications to his diet and routine. Some self-care can make a real difference this year. Should he have concerns at any time, he should get these checked out.

With his genial nature, the Earth Monkey enjoys going out and the Goat year can contain an interesting mix of things to do. Some Earth Monkeys may enjoy becoming more involved in local activities or participating in an interest group. This can become more meaningful over the year. Late March to early June, August and September could be particularly active and interesting months. However, while a lot will go well, should the Earth Monkey detect a disagreement arising between himself and another person or find himself in a volatile situation, he should exercise caution. A friendship issue may prove troublesome this year. Earth Monkeys, take note.

The Earth Monkey's home life will see considerable activity and there will need to be good liaison and co-operation between all. In addition, some flexibility will be required as plans and requirements change or need a rethink. Goat years can bring uncertainty, but amid the pressures the Earth Monkey's thoughtfulness and organizational abilities will yet again prove of real value. Busy though the year will be, there will also be special family times to enjoy, with individual successes bringing some proud moments. In addition, the help some Earth Monkeys give to more senior relations could be more appreciated than they may realize. Domestically, May and August could be particularly busy and fulfilling months.

The Goat year will be a full and varied one for the Earth Monkey and he will need to be aware of what is going on around him and adapt as situations require. Plans may change, but the Earth Monkey will have the chance to build on his skills and prepare the way for greater achievements next year. Throughout the year he will need to be cautious in financial matters and his mindful self when in company, but he reads people and situations well and his perceptiveness will help in this sometimes complex year. Overall, a year for care, but with interesting and potentially significant opportunities.

Tip for the Year

Use any chances to further your knowledge and skills. What you learn now can open up important opportunities. Also, be attentive when in company and, as far as you can, keep your lifestyle in balance. The year may at times be demanding, but its benefits can be far-reaching.

Famous Monkeys

Gillian Anderson, Jennifer Aniston, Christina Aguilera, Patricia Arquette, Lady Ashton, J. M. Barrie, José Manuel Barroso, Kenny Chesney, Colette, John Constable, Patricia Cornwell, Daniel Craig, Joan Crawford, Miley Cyrus, Leonardo da Vinci, Timothy Dalton, Bette Davis, Danny De Vito, Celine Dion, Michael Douglas, Mia Farrow, Carrie Fisher, F. Scott Fitzgerald, Ian Fleming, Paul Gauguin, Ryan Gosling, Jake Gyllenhaal, Jerry Hall, Tom Hanks, Harry Houdini, Charlie Hunnam, Hugh Jackman, P. D. James, Katherine Jenkins, Julius Caesar, Buster Keaton, Alicia Keys, Gladys Knight, Taylor Lautner, George Lucas, Bob Marley, Kylie Minogue, V. S. Naipaul, Lisa Marie Presley, Debbie Reynolds, Little Richard, Mickey Rooney, Diana Ross, Tom Selleck, Wilbur Smith, Rod Stewart, Jacques Tati, Elizabeth Taylor, Dame Kiri Te Kanawa, Justin Timberlake, Harry Truman, Venus Williams.

8 February 1921 to 27 January 1922 — *Metal Rooster*

26 January 1933 to 13 February 1934 — *Water Rooster*

13 February 1945 to 1 February 1946 — *Wood Rooster*

31 January 1957 to 17 February 1958 — *Fire Rooster*

17 February 1969 to 5 February 1970 — *Earth Rooster*

5 February 1981 to 24 January 1982 — *Metal Rooster*

23 January 1993 to 9 February 1994 — *Water Rooster*

9 February 2005 to 28 January 2006 — *Wood Rooster*

The Rooster

The Personality of the Rooster

With a clear destination
and firm will,
I raise my sails
to the winds of fortune.

The Rooster is born under the sign of candour. He has a flamboyant and colourful personality and is meticulous in all that he does. He is an excellent organizer and wherever possible likes to plan his various activities well in advance.

The Rooster is usually highly intelligent and very well read. He has a good sense of humour and is an effective and persuasive speaker. He loves discussion and enjoys taking part in any sort of debate. He has no hesitation in speaking his mind and is forthright in his views. He does, however, lack tact and can easily damage his reputation or cause offence by some thoughtless remark or action. He has a very volatile nature and should always try to avoid acting on the spur of the moment.

He is usually very dignified in his manner and conducts himself with an air of confidence and authority. He is adept at handling financial matters and organizes his financial affairs with considerable skill. He chooses his investments well and is capable of achieving great wealth. Most Roosters use their money wisely, but there are a few who are the reverse and are notorious spendthrifts. Fortunately, the Rooster has great earning capacity and is rarely without sufficient funds to tide himself over.

Another characteristic of the Rooster is that he invariably carries a notebook or scraps of paper around with him. He is constantly writing himself reminders or noting down important facts lest he forgets – the Rooster cannot abide inefficiency and conducts all his activities in an orderly, precise and methodical manner.

The Rooster is usually very ambitious, but can be unrealistic in some of what he hopes to achieve. He occasionally lets his imagination run away with him and while he does not like any interference from others, it would be in his own interests to listen to their views a little more often. He also does not like criticism, and if he feels anybody is doubting his judgement or prying too closely into his affairs, he is certain to let his feelings be known. He can also be rather self-centred and stubborn over relatively trivial matters, but to compensate for this he is reliable, honest and trustworthy, and this is appreciated by all who come into contact with him.

Roosters born between the hours of five and seven, both at dawn and sundown, tend to be the most extrovert of their sign, but all Roosters like to lead an active social life and enjoy attending parties and big functions. The Rooster usually has a wide circle of friends and is able to build up influential contacts with remarkable ease. He often belongs to several clubs and societies and involves himself in a variety of different activities. He is particularly interested in the environment, humanitarian affairs and anything affecting the welfare of others. He has a very caring nature and will do much to help those less fortunate than himself.

He also gets much pleasure from gardening, and while he may not spend as much time in the garden as he would like, his garden is invariably well kept and productive.

The Rooster is generally very distinguished in his appearance and if his job permits he will wear an official uniform with great pride and dignity. He is not averse to publicity and takes great delight in being the centre of attention. He often does well at PR work or any job which brings him into contact with the media. He also makes a very good teacher.

The female Rooster leads a varied and interesting life. She involves herself in many different activities and there are some who wonder how she can achieve so much. She often holds very strong views and, like her male counterpart, has no hesitation in speaking her mind or telling others how she thinks things should be done. She is supremely efficient and well organized and her home is usually very neat and tidy. She has good taste in clothes and usually wears smart but very practical outfits.

The Rooster usually has a large family and takes a particularly active interest in the education of his children. He is very loyal to his partner and will find that he is especially well suited to those born under the signs of the Snake, Horse, Ox and Dragon. Provided they do not interfere too much in his various activities, the Rat, Tiger, Goat and Pig can also establish a good relationship with him, but two Roosters together are likely to squabble and irritate each other. The rather sensitive Rabbit will find the Rooster a bit too blunt for his liking, and the Rooster will quickly become exasperated by the ever-inquisitive and artful Monkey. He will also find it difficult to get on with the anxious Dog.

If the Rooster can overcome his volatile nature and exercise tact, he will go far in life. He is capable and talented and will make a lasting – and usually favourable – impression almost everywhere he goes.

The Five Different Types of Rooster

In addition to the 12 signs of the Chinese zodiac there are five elements and these have a strengthening or moderating influence on the signs. The effects of the five elements on the Rooster are described below, together with the years in which they were exercising their influence. Therefore Roosters born in 1921 and 1981 are Metal Roosters, Roosters born in 1933 and 1993 are Water Roosters, and so on.

Metal Rooster: 1921, 1981

The Metal Rooster is a hard and conscientious worker. He knows exactly what he wants in life and sets about everything in a positive and determined manner. He can at times appear abrasive and he would almost certainly do better if he were willing to reach a compromise with others rather than hold so rigidly to his beliefs. He is very articulate and most astute when dealing with financial matters. He is loyal to his friends and often devotes much energy to working for the common good.

Water Rooster: 1933, 1993

This Rooster has a very persuasive manner and can easily gain the co-operation of others. He is intelligent, well read and enjoys taking part in discussions and debates. He has a seemingly inexhaustible amount of energy and is prepared to work long hours in order to secure what he wants. He can, however, waste a lot of valuable time worrying over minor and inconsequential details. He is approachable, has a good sense of humour and is highly regarded by others.

Wood Rooster: 1945, 2005

The Wood Rooster is honest, reliable and often sets himself high standards. He is ambitious, but also more prepared to work in a team than some of the other types of Rooster. He usually succeeds in life but does have a tendency to get caught up in bureaucratic matters and attempt too many things at the same time. He has wide interests, likes to travel and is very caring and considerate towards his family and friends.

Fire Rooster: 1957

This Rooster is extremely strong-willed. He has many leadership qualities, is an excellent organizer and is most efficient in his work. Through sheer force of character he often secures his objectives, but he does have a tendency to be very forthright and not always consider the feelings of others. If he can learn to be more tactful he can often succeed beyond his wildest dreams.

Earth Rooster: 1969

This Rooster has a deep and penetrating mind. He is efficient, perceptive and particularly astute in business and financial matters. He is also persistent and once he has set himself an objective, he will rarely allow himself to be deflected from achieving his aim. He works hard and is held in great esteem by his friends and colleagues. He usually enjoys the arts and takes a keen interest in the activities of the various members of his family.

Prospects for the Rooster in 2015

The Horse year (31 January 2014–18 February 2015) is characterized by its energy and vitality and during it the Rooster will have been involved in many activities.

In his work a lot will have happened, and staff movements and new initiatives will have had an impact. However, from pressure opportunity can emerge, and in the remaining months of the Horse year not only will many Roosters have a good chance to demonstrate their strengths but also to benefit from new opportunities. November could be particularly active for work matters.

In view of the general activity of the closing months of the Horse year, it is also important that the Rooster remains mindful of the opinions of others and liaises with those around him over his projects and plans. Being strong-minded, he may like his own views to hold sway, but more consultation will lead to more going ahead, particularly with the many arrangements that will need making towards the year's end.

The closing months of the year can also see a flurry of social activity. While the Rooster will enjoy most of what takes place, a petty matter or difference of opinion could overshadow a particular occasion or friend-ship. All Roosters need to be aware and watch their sometimes candid tendencies.

With this being an expensive time of year, the Rooster's watchfulness needs to extend to finance. He should take his time when considering more expensive purchases as well as avoid unnecessary risk.

In general, the Horse year will have been a busy and sometimes demanding one for the Rooster, but it will have also opened up some good opportunities.

The Year of the Goat starts on 19 February and will be a constructive one for the Rooster. Rather than being continually busy pursuing umpteen different activities, he will have more chance to take stock and enjoy a better lifestyle balance. The Rooster likes to plan and be well prepared, but this is very much a time for living in the present and enjoying the spontaneous nature of the Goat year. Admittedly, this may not always sit comfortably with the Rooster (he does like to be organized and in control), but by embracing the spirit of the year he can benefit from what it will bring.

In view of the changes the majority of Roosters will have experienced recently in their work, many will welcome the opportunity to focus on specific duties and make more of their expertise. In addition, by involving themselves in their workplace and liaising well with their colleagues, they will not only find that their influence will carry more weight but that they can strengthen their position and ultimately their prospects.

Most Roosters will choose to stay with their present employer this year and will enjoy a good level of job satisfaction. There will, though, be some who start the year frustrated by a lack of opportunity or uninspired by what they are currently doing. For these Roosters, and those seeking work, the Goat year can be encouraging. However, to benefit, these Roosters should not only consider what it is they want to do, but also be active in making enquiries. The Rooster has style and verve, and if he takes the initiative, it can lead to an important opportunity being presented. Also, as many Roosters will find, events can sometimes take a surprising course this year. Some Roosters will be offered a position that is very different from what they have done before but uses *and* furthers their skills. Work-wise, this can be a satisfying year, with March, May, July, September and January 2016 seeing particularly encouraging developments.

Another positive area concerns the Rooster's personal interests. Although he likes to be involved in a great many activities, it is important that he sets aside some regular 'me time' to spend on pursuits he enjoys. For Roosters who have let their personal interests lapse recently, this would be a good time to consider taking up something new. Not only can time set aside for interests do the Rooster much personal good, including helping him unwind and giving greater balance to his lifestyle, but new ideas and talents can emerge as a result. Many Roosters will take real pleasure in their recreational activities this year. Some may also benefit from the chance of additional exercise and the social opportunities their interests can bring. The Goat year is an excellent one for the Rooster to reconnect with himself and enjoy his talents rather than be continually driving himself on.

If possible, he should also consider making provision for a holiday this year. Some Roosters may also choose to combine travel with a special event. The Goat year will offer some tempting possibilities, including some very late on.

With the possibility of travel and all his other activities, the Rooster will need to be disciplined with spending and make advance provision for forthcoming plans and commitments. With good budgeting he will be able to do most of what he wants, but this is a year which favours good control over the purse-strings. The more spendthrift Rooster, take note.

The Rooster will welcome the social opportunities of the year and there will be an excellent chance for him to extend his social network. His style and conversational skills will impress others, and for the unattached, including those who have had recent personal difficulties, the Goat year can see a great improvement, with exciting romantic opportunities on the horizon. March, June to August and December could see the most social activity, although at most times of the year there will be events to attend.

The Rooster will also be keen to keep his home life organized, but with loved ones sometimes changing routine and his own various commitments, he will need to show some flexibility. In some instances the timing of certain plans may need to be altered and the Rooster may also have to deal with sudden developments (including some home maintenance issues) that need attention as well as supporting another person with a key decision. However, by concentrating on what needs to be done, he can satisfactorily accomplish a great deal and his efforts will be appreciated by those around him.

In addition, the Goat year can see the realization of some important ambitions. If there are ideas the Rooster has been keen to implement or home improvements he has long wanted to carry out, this would be an excellent year to proceed. Again, he will need to be accommodating and flexible, but many of his plans can be successfully carried through.

Overall, the Goat year can be a rewarding one for the Rooster. If he focuses on what is happening at any given moment and uses his time well, rather than aiming to do too much, he will be satisfied by what he is able to achieve. Work-wise, he will often have a chance to make more of his skills and experience greater fulfilment in his role. Time set aside for personal interests can be of great benefit, and the gregarious Rooster will also enjoy the increased social opportunities of the year. He has much in his favour and, rather than drive himself on, can enjoy being himself and enjoy what is happening around him.

The Metal Rooster

The Metal Rooster possesses great resolve and is good at spotting opportunities. In the Goat year his skills will serve him well, especially as the year will contain several curious twists and turns.

In work many Metal Roosters will have built up considerable experience by now and have good knowledge of a particular industry. In the Goat year they will have the chance to build on this, although not always as originally envisaged. Some could be asked to take on a new role or, if in a large organization, alerted to a position in another department or sector. What opens up this year will allow many Metal Roosters to add to their capabilities and, in the process, increase their options for later.

The majority of Metal Rooters will make important headway with their current employer, but some could benefit from the year's curious workings in other ways. It could be that they learn of a vacancy that is quite different from what they have done before but very appealing to them. By pursuing it, they could find significant wheels are set in motion.

Similarly, Metal Roosters seeking work should not be restrictive in the type of position they are seeking. By making enquiries, many could enjoy taking on something totally new. Such are the workings of the year that a fresh opportunity can quickly lead on to other responsibilities. For the swift and enthusiastic Metal Rooster, the Goat year has exciting potential. March, May, July and September and January 2016 could see particularly important developments, but throughout the year all Metal Roosters need to be alert and to act swiftly when necessary.

With the emphasis on self-development this year, the Metal Rooster will also find interesting opportunities arising in his recreational pursuits. Again, those expert in a particular field could have the chance to use their knowledge in new ways or set themselves a rewarding challenge. Some Metal Roosters may be attracted by a new interest, perhaps one with an outdoor or keep-fit element. Whatever the Metal Rooster chooses to do, this can be an encouraging time for him.

A further pleasure of the year will be the travel opportunities it brings, sometimes at short notice. A last-minute offer, the chance to enjoy a long weekend away or a sudden invitation can all lead to some lively times and often be enjoyed all the more because they are unexpected. In addition, with the Goat year favouring culture, the Metal Rooster should take advantage of the special events and exhibitions being held over the year. Some could be particularly inspiring.

The variety of activities he does over the year can, though, impact on the Metal Rooster's financial situation. Not only will some expenses not have been budgeted for, but he (or another) could have accommodation or other plans which entail considerable outlay. The Metal Rooster will need to watch his spending and, in some instances, cut back on less essential outgoings. He can take pleasure in many things this year, but it will require good financial management.

In his home life, a lot can happen at a speedy pace and the Metal Rooster will not always be able to plan and prepare as much as he would like. Routines could suddenly change, ideas, decisions and repairs could need prompt action and where home purchases are concerned, offers could arise which need to be taken advantage of before the chance is lost. Some weeks could be particularly busy, but the Metal Rooster will be pleased with a lot of what happens, including some of the choices which may initially seem to have been foisted upon him.

Over the year several practical projects will also take place in the home, and shared activities, including trips away, will bring considerable pleasure. If a parent, the Metal Rooster will give important encouragement to his children and help instil qualities he particularly values. Caring and conscientious, the Metal Rooster enjoys a special bond with some close relations and this can be especially meaningful this year.

For many Metal Roosters, the Goat year will also contain an interesting mix of social occasions. In some instances, friends or other contacts could prove especially helpful too. March, June to August and the last six weeks of the year could see the most social activity and for the unattached, romance could suddenly yet gloriously be found. The Goat year is one of surprising yet satisfying developments.

Overall, the Year of the Goat will be a full and interesting one for the Metal Rooster. As a deliberator, he may not welcome some of its volatility, but the opportunities it brings can further his career, add to his knowledge and open up possibilities for both now and the near future. The Metal Rooster will often benefit from the support of those around him and his home life and personal interests will bring him much contentment. All in all, a busy and often surprising year, but an instructive one, with some important personal and professional benefits.

Tip for the Year
Make the most of the moment. What you do now can have important consequences. Also, value your relations with those around you. Loved ones can help make your year special *and* more successful.

The Water Rooster

This will be an important and often special year for the Water Rooster. Although it will contain its pressures, what the Water Rooster decides upon during it can have far-reaching significance.

One particular feature of the year is that it encourages involvement, and no matter what the Water Rooster's current position, whether in education, in work or actively pursuing his interests, there will be a good chance for him to participate in what is going on around him. Being with like-minded others of similar age can add meaning (and fun) to many activities as well as create a synergy and buzz.

With his outgoing nature, the Water Rooster will welcome many of the year's social opportunities and have an often interesting mix of things to do. With the Goat year being a culturally rich one, many Water Roosters will be tempted to attend events being held – perhaps concerts, festivals or sporting events – and will often delight in going to these with friends. There will be a lot happening this year and a lot for the Water Rooster to enjoy.

Affairs of the heart can also make this a special time. Water Roosters who start the year alone may find that an interest they have can bring them into contact with a person with whom they quickly form a special bond. For those currently enjoying courtship, this lively year can bring many special moments. Some Water Roosters will decide to settle down with their loved one and here again decisions made during the year can have long-term significance. March and June to early September are times that could see the most social activity and the year's end will also be lively.

In addition to the great personal value of the Water Rooster's friendships, he will be considerably helped over the year by those around him. More senior relations will be keen to assist with decision-making or to help ease some of the pressures he may be under, although to fully benefit the Water Rooster does need to speak out about the choices in front of him and any matters on his mind. If he does so, others will be better able to understand and assist.

A large number of Water Roosters will be in education this year, and with much riding on their exams and the work they are currently engaged in, these Water Roosters should remain focused. Determined effort will enable many to secure pleasing results. With the Goat year being capable of surprises, some Water Roosters may review what they are intending to do after their studying and decide on a new career option. Goat years can open up an array of interesting possibilities.

This also applies to Water Roosters in work. In order to broaden their experience and learn more about their industry, many of these Water Roosters could be encouraged to take on new duties as well as be offered additional training. By making the most of such chances, they can acquire the skills necessary for further progress. Some will also be inspired by the synergy created by working with those of similar age and this will add impetus to what they do.

For Water Roosters seeking work, the Goat year can also open up interesting possibilities. Although the job-seeking process may be disheartening and some Water Roosters may be uncertain about the direction they wish to pursue, by keeping alert for opportunities and talking to professional advisers (here the Water Rooster's enthusiastic manner can impress), many could secure a position and then demonstrate the commitment that can lead to other duties being given. March, May, July, September and January 2016 could see particularly encouraging developments. The Goat year can spring surprises, however, and some Water Roosters will take on work in a very different capacity from what they envisaged. Nevertheless, this can still be an important springboard to later success.

With all the different interests and activities the Water Rooster pursues, together with an active social life, he will have many demands on his resources and will need to keep a close watch on spending levels. Many Water Roosters will be tempted to travel, too, and making early provision for this will enable them to do more while away. In addition, while usually careful, the Water Rooster does need to look after his belongings this year. A loss could inconvenience him. Water Roosters, take note.

The Year of the Goat can be significant for the Water Rooster in many ways. Whether obtaining qualifications, gaining valuable work experience and/or securing a new position, he can, with effort, make important headway. The year can have curious twists, but much that unfolds can be to the Water Rooster's present *and* long-term advantage. He will also enjoy the support of many and not only be encouraged by the advice given but also value the interests, hopes and activities he can share. For many Water Roosters, love and romance can make this time even more special. In so many ways, this can be a significant year.

Tip for the Year

Put in the effort, for the rewards that follow can be substantial. Also, don't be too restrictive in outlook. New and exciting possibilities can open up for you. Enjoy your relations with others – many believe in you and can help you to make more of your potential.

The Wood Rooster

This year marks the Wood Rooster's either tenth or seventieth birthday and for both it can hold surprises and encouraging developments.

As it begins, many senior Wood Roosters will have given thought to what they would like to do this year and, as always, will be keen to be organized and plan ahead. However, Goat years are notoriously fickle and at times the Wood Rooster will find himself having to revise his plans to fit in with changing circumstances. Although this can frustrate him (the Wood Rooster does not like delay), what arises can often lead to more satisfying outcomes. This can be especially the case with more substantial home purchases, as the Wood Rooster reassesses the suitability of what he is considering.

Some of the Wood Rooster's plans will involve tackling matters in his home, some of which may have been niggling him for some time. Whether sorting out untidy storage areas, updating equipment or smartening living areas, the Wood Rooster will be satisfied with what he gets to do over the year. In some instances, tasks can yield surprises – the Wood Rooster may rediscover a forgotten family treasure or something of personal value.

With this being his seventieth year, his family may also have some surprises in store, with a possible celebration or treat demonstrating their affection. Certain occasions will bring the Wood Rooster into contact with people he hasn't seen for a considerable while, which will please him greatly. At times during the year he will find himself very much the centre of attention and delighting in the special arrangements that have been made for him.

Travel, too, could feature on the agenda, and if there is a special holiday or destination that appeals to the Wood Rooster, he should make early enquiries. Over the year many Wood Roosters can look forward to some special times away. July could be a particularly active and enjoyable month.

A further pleasure for many Wood Roosters will be their personal interests. With the knowledge that many have now built up, they may be keen to share their ideas and gifts with others. Those who enjoy writing may consider writing up their thoughts and experiences for publication. Many a Wood Rooster has a talent for words, and for those who are tempted, writing could be a satisfying and sometimes therapeutic activity. Some new equipment the Wood Rooster acquires may also help advance an interest, and some Wood Roosters could be inspired by ideas or techniques they read about. Developments over the year can whet the interest of many Wood Roosters and encourage them to do more.

Socially, many Wood Roosters will take advantage of activities, groups and events in their area, and with the Goat year often culturally rich, there could also be special occasions or exhibitions to attend. March, June to early September and December could see the most social activity, but at most times of the year there will be interesting things for the Wood Rooster to do.

He will also find himself dispensing advice to others, with both a younger relation and long-standing friend especially grateful for his understanding and thoughtful words. His empathy and perceptiveness are qualities that many appreciate.

With travel, home purchases, personal interests and other commitments, his outgoings will be extensive, however, and he will need to keep a close watch on budget. When considering major purchases, he needs to fully explore his options. Also, should a financial or bureaucratic matter concern him during the year, especially relating to pensions or benefits, he should seek advice. Extra care can prevent mistakes or the Wood Rooster being disadvantaged in some way. Wood Roosters, take note and do manage your finances carefully.

Younger Wood Roosters will find their tenth year can be a full and varied one. In addition to adding to their skills and knowledge, there will be the chance to take some activities further as well as start new ones. By keeping an open mind, they can benefit from some exciting possibilities and many a young Wood Rooster will grow in confidence over the year.

A feature of the Goat year is that it is an expansive time, with a lot available to participate in and enjoy. Both the younger and more senior Wood Rooster can see considerable activity and will need to be flexible as situations change, but they can enjoy an interesting year with some memorable personal highlights.

Tip for the Year

Be open to possibility. With assistance, a lot can happen this year. Plans may have to be altered as new opportunities arise, but a lot can be accomplished. Enjoy yourself in this full and satisfying year.

The Fire Rooster

The Fire Rooster prides himself on efficiency. With carefully considered ideas and the ability to use his time well, he invariably packs a lot into a year. By the end of this one, he could be astonished by the amount he has been able to do – and the curious developments that have taken place. The Fire Rooster may like to set his own course, but in the Goat year he may need to adjust his plans.

Work-wise, there may be important developments. Many a workplace will be affected by change, sometimes quite suddenly. New personnel, new ideas, new technology, new working practices – all these could impact on the Fire Rooster's role and some weeks will be unsettling. However, at such times the Fire Rooster's long years of experience can be helpful and by focusing on what needs to be done, he will be able to make the most of what occurs. Situations will settle and some Fire Roosters will benefit from sudden offers. Few will remain untouched by the changeable influences that prevail in the Goat year, but many will have the chance to put their strengths to greater use.

Fire Roosters who feel the time is right for change, perhaps in order to make more of certain skills or avoid a long commute, as well as those seeking work, will find that by actively exploring options, they may be presented with an often ideal position which offers the challenge they may feel has been lacking in recent years. Again, opportunities can arise suddenly, and sometimes on the back of disappointment. March, May, July, September and January 2016 could be key months work-wise, but throughout the year the Fire Rooster needs to watch developing situations and act quickly when he sees something worth following up.

In his home life this will be a busy year and at various times both he and other family members will have important decisions to make, changes to adjust to and commitments to meet. To help, it is important that the Fire Rooster is prepared to talk about his thoughts and activities. That way, those around him can not only better understand how he feels but also help.

The Fire Rooster will also be keen to carry out various projects on his home. Initial thoughts can develop in unexpected ways this year and he may benefit from a fortuitous offer, or perhaps just the mention of an idea (and its potential advantages) may be enough to get plans underway. Goat years favour shared activity, so the more that is undertaken jointly, the more successful the results. Several home improvements could delight both the Fire Rooster and his loved ones this year.

Amid all the activity, it is also important that the Fire Rooster spends some quality time with those who are important to him. Shared interests, trips and, if possible, a holiday would all bring valuable lifestyle balance to this busy year.

With this in mind, the Fire Rooster can also derive considerable satisfaction from recreational activities. With his wide interests, there will be much to stimulate his imagination this year. Whether setting himself a new project, testing out ideas or enjoying some of the cultural events being held, he should make the most of what occurs.

With some of the decisions the Fire Rooster will face over the year he will also value the support and sometimes first-hand experience of close friends. If he is in a dilemma or has a particular concern, it is important that he is forthcoming. Some of his interests can have a good social element and he will welcome the chance to meet other enthusiasts and, in some cases, attend special occasions. Any Fire Rooster who is feeling lonely and/or moves to a new area would find it worth joining an interest or social group. This will give him an excellent chance to meet like-minded people and make new friends. March, June to early September and December could see the most social activity and some of the Fire Rooster's travels will also lead to some lively times.

Although many Fire Roosters will enjoy a modest increase in income over the year, this can be an expensive time. With increased spending on home, family commitments, transport and travel, the Fire Rooster will need to watch his outgoings and make early allowance for more expensive plans. This is a year for good financial housekeeping.

Overall, however, the Year of the Goat will be an encouraging one for the Fire Rooster and he will see many plans come to fruition. In both his work and personal interests, this is a time of opportunity, but the Fire Rooster will need to adapt as situations change. Goat years favour quick, decisive action rather than forward-planning. However, the Fire Rooster will be encouraged by the support he receives and both domestically and socially this can be a rewarding year. Efficient, keen and determined, the Fire Rooster puts a lot of effort into his activities and while the Goat year will have its pressures, he can still gain some good results.

Tip for the Year
You have a lot to offer, but don't try to do everything by yourself! By consulting others and working together, you can accomplish more. Also, keep your lifestyle in balance – do enjoy quality time with your loved ones and set some aside for your own interests.

The Earth Rooster

The Earth Rooster is forward-looking and as the Goat year starts he will have several key objectives he is keen to realize. These could relate to advancing his career, improving his home or developing his personal interests. With a certain amount of effort, he may see a lot come to pass.

To help him in his endeavours, it is important that he liaises well with those around him. Whether family, friends, colleagues or experts, they can all offer assistance that will help the Earth Rooster move his plans forward. Although he may like to set his own course, if he is willing to consult others and share his goals, his year can be made far more agreeable *and* successful.

One area which can be the subject of considerable change is his work. Although many Earth Roosters will have made progress of late, there will be quite a few who do not feel fulfilled. For these Earth Roosters, as well as those seeking work, the Goat year can give rise to some interesting and sometimes surprising developments. By giving careful thought to what they would now like to do, some of these Earth Roosters could find an opening which offers them more scope as well as the chance to make greater use of their strengths. Opportunities can arise suddenly this year and need to be seized before the moment is lost. March, May, July, September and January 2016 could see encouraging developments.

For Earth Roosters who decide to remain where they are, there will also be good opportunities to advance their career. Sometimes new initiatives or an increased workload will give these Earth Roosters the chance to widen their role. Some may also benefit from promotion opportunities or an offer that is put to them. Events can happen quickly and the Earth Rooster needs to seize his chances. For the enterprising, the rewards can be considerable.

One of the Earth Rooster's strengths is his ability to enjoy good relations with many of his colleagues, and throughout the year he should continue to liaise closely with those around him and use any chances to network more widely. The more involved and visible he is, the more he can benefit. Earth Roosters who work in innovative and creative environments should also promote their ideas. In the Goat year, their special talents can lead to impressive results.

Although the Earth Rooster will have many demands on his time, he should also give himself the chance to enjoy personal interests. The creative nature of this Goat year can inspire him. Earth Roosters who have let interests lapse should consider taking up something new, perhaps with an outdoor or keep-fit element. The summer could be an especially pleasing time for taking interests further.

In many of his activities this year the Earth Rooster will enjoy the company of others and will be encouraged by the support and camaraderie they bring. For the unattached, a chance meeting, often connected with an interest, could prove significant. March, June to August, December and early January 2016 will see the most social activity.

The Earth Rooster's home life will also see a lot happen, but while the Earth Rooster may have specific projects lined up for the year, he should not be too rigid in his planning. With the busy schedules he and others may have, arrangements will need frequent review, with all in the household adapting and helping out as required. In addition, work decisions need to be talked through and the implications carefully considered. If the Earth Rooster is flexible and liaises well with those around him, however, he can carry out many of his plans and enjoy many gratifying outcomes.

The Goat year can also give rise to some lively family occasions. With ideas to follow through, interests to share and attractions to visit, some excellent times can be had. When possible, the Earth Rooster should also take a holiday with his loved ones. Travel can lead to some treasured times. Some travel opportunities will arise quite suddenly, as there is quite a bit of spontaneity to the year.

With some expensive home plans and purchases in mind, travel possibilities and his existing commitments, the Earth Rooster will have many outgoings, however, and needs to keep a close watch on his financial position. He should also attend to important paperwork carefully and promptly, and keep receipts and guarantees safe. While usually thorough, he could find an oversight, misplaced document or rushed purchase leading to problems. Earth Roosters, take careful note.

In general, the Year of the Goat will be busy and often surprising for the Earth Rooster. At work, he may have the opportunity to further his career and make fuller use of his strengths. To benefit, though, he will need to be adaptable and make the most of opportunities *as they arise*. His personal interests can bring him pleasure and carrying out new projects can sometimes open up fresh possibilities. However, with so much happening this year, it is important that the Earth Rooster discusses his thoughts and options with those around him and listens to their advice. With support and synergy, he can make this a progressive and pleasing year.

Tip for the Year
Build on your ideas and strengths. You have much to offer and by looking to do more, you can have an impact. Fortune will favour the active and enterprising this year and there will also be some good (even if sometimes unanticipated) opportunities. Make the most of this interesting and rewarding time.

Famous Roosters

Tony Abbott, Fernando Alonso, Beyoncé, Cate Blanchett, Barbara Taylor Bradford, Gerard Butler, Sir Michael Caine, the Duchess of Cambridge, Enrico Caruso, Eric Clapton, Joan Collins, Rita Coolidge, Daniel Day-Lewis, Minnie Driver, the Duke of Edinburgh, Gloria Estefan, Paloma Faith, Roger Federer, Errol Flynn, Benjamin Franklin, Dawn French, Stephen Fry, Joseph Gordon-Levitt, Melanie Griffith, Josh Groban, Goldie Hawn, Katherine Hepburn, Paris Hilton, Jay-Z, Catherine Zeta Jones, Quincy Jones, Diane Keaton, Søren Kierkegaard, D. H. Lawrence, David Livingstone, Steve McQueen, Jayne Mansfield, Steve Martin, James Mason, W. Somerset Maugham, Paul Merton, Bette Midler, Ed Miliband, Van Morrison, Willie Nelson, Kim Novak, Yoko Ono, Dolly Parton, Matthew Perry, Michelle Pfeiffer, Natalie Portman, Priscilla Presley, Joan Rivers, Kelly Rowland, Paul Ryan, Jenny Seagrove, George Segal, Carly Simon, Britney Spears, Johann Strauss, Verdi, Richard Wagner, Serena Williams, Neil Young, Renée Zellweger.

28 January 1922 to 15 February 1923 — *Water Dog*

14 February 1934 to 3 February 1935 — *Wood Dog*

2 February 1946 to 21 January 1947 — *Fire Dog*

18 February 1958 to 7 February 1959 — *Earth Dog*

6 February 1970 to 26 January 1971 — *Metal Dog*

25 January 1982 to 12 February 1983 — *Water Dog*

10 February 1994 to 30 January 1995 — *Wood Dog*

29 January 2006 to 17 February 2007 — *Fire Dog*

The Dog

The Personality of the Dog

I have my values
and beliefs.
These are my beacon
in an ever-changing world.

The Dog is born under the signs of loyalty and anxiety. He usually holds very firm views and beliefs and is the champion of good causes. He hates any sort of injustice or unfair treatment and will do all in his power to help those less fortunate than himself. He has a strong sense of fair play and will be honourable and open in all his dealings.

The Dog is very direct and straightforward. He is never one to skirt round issues and speaks frankly and to the point. He can be stubborn, but he is prepared to listen to the views of others and will try to be as fair as possible in coming to his decisions. He will readily give advice where it is needed and will be the first to offer assistance when things go wrong.

The Dog instils confidence wherever he goes and there are many who admire him for his integrity and resolute manner. He is a very good judge of character and can often form an accurate impression of some-one very shortly after meeting them. He is also very intuitive and can frequently sense how things are going to work out long in advance.

Despite his friendly and amiable manner, the Dog is not a big social-izer. He dislikes having to attend large functions or parties and much prefers a quiet meal with friends or a chat by the fire. He is an excellent conversationalist and is often a marvellous raconteur of amusing stories and anecdotes.

The Dog is also quick-witted and his mind is always alert. He can keep calm in a crisis and although he does have a temper, his outbursts tend to be short-lived. He is loyal and trustworthy, but if he ever feels badly let down or rejected by someone, he will rarely forgive or forget.

The Dog usually has very set interests. He prefers to specialize and become an expert in a chosen area rather than dabble in a variety of different activities. He usually does well in jobs where he feels that he is being of service to others and is often suited to careers in the social services, the medical and legal professions and teaching. He does, however, need to feel motivated in his work. He has to have a sense of purpose and if ever this is lacking he can quite often drift through life without ever achieving very much. Once he has the motivation, however, very little can prevent him from securing his objective.

Another characteristic of the Dog is his tendency to worry and to view things rather pessimistically. Quite often his worries are totally unnecessary and are of his own making. Although it may be difficult, worrying is a habit that all Dogs should try to overcome.

The Dog is not materialistic or particularly bothered about accumu-lating great wealth. As long as he has the money necessary to support his family and to spend on the occasional luxury, he is more than happy. However, when he does have any spare money he tends to be rather a spendthrift and does not always put it to its best use. He is also not a very good speculator and would be advised to get professional advice before entering into any major long-term investment.

The Dog will rarely be short of admirers, but he is not an easy person to live with. His moods are changeable and his standards high, but he will be loyal and protective to his partner and will do all in his power to provide a comfortable home. He can get on extremely well with those born under the signs of the Horse, Pig, Tiger and Monkey, and can also establish a sound and stable relationship with the Rat, Ox, Rabbit, Snake and another Dog, but will find the Dragon a bit too flamboyant for his liking. He will also find it difficult to understand the imaginative Goat and is likely to be highly irritated by the candid Rooster.

The female Dog is renowned for her beauty. She has a warm and caring nature, although until she knows someone well she can be both secretive and very guarded. She is highly intelligent and despite her calm and tranquil appearance can be extremely ambitious. She enjoys sport and other outdoor activities and has a happy knack of finding bargains in the most unlikely of places. She can also get rather impatient when things do not work out as she would like.

The Dog usually has a very good way with children and can be a doting parent. He will rarely be happier than when he is helping someone or doing something that will benefit others. Providing he can cure himself of his tendency to worry, he will lead a very full and active life, and in that life he will make many friends and do a tremendous amount of good.

The Five Different Types of Dog

In addition to the 12 signs of the Chinese zodiac there are five elements and these have a strengthening or moderating influence on the signs. The effects of the five elements on the Dog are described below, together with the years in which they were exercising their influence. Therefore Dogs born in 1970 are Metal Dogs, Dogs born in 1922 and 1982 are Water Dogs, and so on.

Metal Dog: 1970

The Metal Dog is bold, confident and forthright and sets about everything he does in a resolute and determined manner. He has a great belief in his abilities and no hesitation about speaking his mind or devoting himself to some just cause. He can be rather serious at times and can become anxious and irritable when things are not going according to plan. He tends to have very specific interests and it would certainly help him if he were to broaden his outlook and become more involved in group activities. He is loyal and faithful to his friends.

Water Dog: 1922, 1982

The Water Dog has a very direct and outgoing personality. He is an excellent communicator and has little trouble in persuading others to fall in with his plans. He does, however, have a somewhat carefree nature and is not as disciplined or as thorough as he should be in certain matters. Neither does he keep as much control over his finances as he should, but he can be most generous to his family and friends and will make sure that they want for nothing. He is usually very good with children and has a wide circle of friends.

Wood Dog: 1934, 1994

This Dog is a hard and conscientious worker and will usually make a favourable impression wherever he goes. He is less independent than some of the other types of Dog and prefers to work in a group rather than on his own. He is popular, has a good sense of humour and takes a keen interest in the activities of the various members of his family. He is often attracted to the finer things in life and can obtain much pleasure from items of interest, beauty or antiquity. He prefers to live in the country rather than the town.

Fire Dog: 1946, 2006

This Dog has a lively, outgoing personality and is able to establish friendships with remarkable ease. He is an honest and conscientious worker and likes to take an active part in all that is going on around him. He also likes to explore new ideas and providing he can get the necessary support and advice, he can often succeed where others have failed. He does, however, have a tendency to be stubborn. Providing he can overcome this, he can often achieve considerable fame and fortune.

Earth Dog: 1958

The Earth Dog is very talented and astute. He is methodical and efficient and is capable of going far in his chosen profession. He tends to be rather quiet and reserved, but has a very persuasive manner and usually secures his objectives without too much opposition. He is generous and kind and always ready to lend a helping hand when it is needed. He is also held in very high esteem by his friends and colleagues and is usually most dignified in his appearance.

Prospects for the Dog in 2015

The Dog is determined and redoubtable and in the Horse year (31 January 2014–18 February 2015), his fine qualities will have served him well. This will have been a busy time for him and the closing months will continue to be fast paced and bring good opportunities.

On a personal level the Dog will find himself in demand. His home life will be busy and he will give important assistance to someone close to him. There will also be interesting times to share and the year's end can bring the chance to travel as well as meet some people he does not often see. Socially, too, there will be an increase in activity and, with Horse years favouring affairs of the heart, there could be romantic opportunities for the unattached. September and December could be two full and lively months.

The Dog could also make some pleasing purchases both for himself and his home at this time and his judgement will be excellent. However, he will need to look after his possessions. A lost or mislaid item could be upsetting.

Work-wise, many Dogs will experience an upturn in activity, with changes in their workplace. Although demanding, this will give rise to some interesting opportunities, and for those keen to progress or looking for a position, the closing months of the year, especially around November, could see important developments.

Overall, the Horse year will have brought its pressures but enabled the Dog to accomplish a great deal.

The Year of the Goat starts on 19 February and will be a challenging one for the Dog. Dogs appreciate order and method, but Goat years can be volatile, with sudden changes and plans subject to alteration. Some parts of the year may exasperate the Dog, but the Goat year can also have its positive side and the Dog's personal life can be particularly rewarding.

One of the values of Chinese horoscopes is that they can forewarn, and early knowledge can alert us to more awkwardly aspected areas as well as allow us to counter these to some extent. In the Goat year the Dog will need to accept that there will be challenges ahead and some of his plans will be affected by change and delay. In view of this, he will need to show flexibility and watch his sometimes stubborn tendencies. To be wedded to just one approach or idea could limit his progress. Dogs, do take note.

At work, many Dogs will be affected by change. There may be a plethora of new ideas, schemes and working practices. The Dog, who favours tradition, will often view the developments with some misgiving. However, by exercising patience and concentrating on his duties, he will find that things *will* settle down and new opportunities can open up for him. In the meantime he needs to be watchful, alert and prepared to adapt as required. Should he be intransigent or inflexible, there is a risk he could undermine his prospects.

For Dogs who are keen to move ahead in their career, interesting opportunities can arise in the wake of change, and by being quick to show interest, many of these Dogs can successfully advance their position. Speed and initiative are of the essence this year.

For Dogs who decide the time is right to move elsewhere, as well as those seeking work, the Goat year can be tricky but significant. These Dogs should not be too restrictive in the type of position they now pursue. By considering alternatives, quite a few could be offered an opportunity to develop their skills in different ways. Goat years are times of reappraisal and adjustment and those who embrace their spirit can do well. April, June, July and October could see interesting work developments.

Progress made at work can lead to a rise in income and over the year many Dogs may also benefit from a bonus payment or some extra funds from another source. However, this will be an expensive year, especially as quite a few Dogs will move or carry out major projects on their home, and the Dog will need to manage his finances carefully, seeking professional help when necessary. Also, as is the way with Goat years, delays and snags can slow down certain transactions, but if the Dog has patience, he will often be satisfied with the eventual results.

With large-scale projects featuring prominently this year, the Dog's home life is likely to be full and busy. However, these can be exciting times and by ensuring that all in his household are involved in what is going on, the Dog can give the plans added impetus. Goat years favour a collective approach. In addition to the often considerable practical activity, there could be some family highlights this year. Whether celebrating an addition to his family, an academic achievement, a personal success, an anniversary or a housewarming, the Dog will have milestones to mark. This will be a busy, eventful and often special time for him.

When in company, the Dog can be guarded and it can often take him some time before he is comfortable with another person. This year can introduce him to quite a few new people and while he may initially be wary, in time some of these can become firm friends. His relations with others can be important this year and others will value his presence and dependable qualities. March, April, August and December could see the most social activity.

Dogs enjoying newfound romance will enjoy the way their relationship becomes more meaningful over the year, while the unattached or those who have had recent personal upset could see a special person entering their life almost by chance.

The Dog has a talent for using his time well and, although he will often find himself with more than enough to do this year, it is important that he gives himself the chance to unwind. To drive himself relentlessly could take its toll. With creative activities favourably aspected, pursuits that allow some form of self-expression, including art, writing and photography, could inspire him. In addition, if sedentary for much of the day, he will find additional exercise of benefit. Any time and attention the Dog can give to himself will be of value and bring some balance in this busy year.

Overall, the Goat year will demand a lot of the Dog but nevertheless bring opportunities. At work, he may be uncomfortable with overall developments, but out of the changes will come the chance for him to further his career. Accommodation decisions can give rise to pressure and uncertainty, but the benefits gained can be considerable. But one of the most significant factors of this year will be the Dog's relations with those around him. Their support and encouragement can bring him times of personal joy.

The Metal Dog

This can be an interesting year for the Metal Dog. While it may contain times of uncertainty, what transpires will allow many Metal Dogs to improve their position, extend their skills and enjoy pleasing developments in their personal life.

At work, however, the Goat year can be demanding. Although many Metal Dogs will by now have considerable expertise in what they do, changes could be introduced which will affect their role. Some of what arises will worry the Dog, but will be a case of knuckling down and adapting as required. New developments can also have their advantages, however. Not only will many Metal Dogs have the chance to bring their experience to bear, but those who have been in the same position for some time will find that what arises can give them new challenges and incentive.

There will, though, be some Metal Dogs who decide to move elsewhere. For these Metal Dogs, and those seeking work, there may be interesting developments in store. By widening the scope of their search, they may gain a useful foothold in a different line of work during the course of the year. Here again the Metal Dog will need to remain adaptable, particularly as he may need to learn new skills, but by making the most of his situation he will find his new role giving him the challenge he may have been lacking in recent times. April, late May to early August and October could see interesting work developments, but throughout the year all Metal Dogs need to look to move their career forward.

Many Metal Dogs will increase their income over the year and some will also benefit from an additional payment. However, this will be an expensive time, particularly as many Metal Dogs will have ambitious plans for their home. Property matters are prominent in Goat years. Also, initial plans can alter and the Metal Dog could find himself benefiting from an unexpected turn of events. If moving, he may perhaps find an ideal new home by chance, or he may be fortunate in locating and securing specific household items he has been wanting.

Although the Metal Dog will have many expenses this year, he should also try to make provision for a holiday. With a busy lifestyle, he does need a respite, and a carefully chosen destination – and some *rest* – will do him good.

In addition, he should allow time for his personal interests. For Metal Dogs who enjoy creative activities, this can be a particularly inspiring year. As well as developing his own talents, he may delight in some of the many events being held. Metal Dogs who have let their interests lapse recently would do well to give some thought to new ones they might enjoy. They could find activities started this year bringing balance to their lifestyle.

Socially, the Metal Dog will welcome the opportunities that come his way. Some could arise with little warning – it could be that a friend or relation holds a surprise party or the Metal Dog receives an invitation to a prestigious occasion at short notice. Whatever takes place, the Goat year will contain some pleasing times, and March to early May, August and December could be particularly interesting months. Throughout the year the Metal Dog will also value his contact with long-standing friends. Some will seek his views on certain (sometimes delicate) situations and he too will be glad of their opinions when he has concerns of his own.

For the unattached, Goat years can have interesting romantic possibilities. Even though some Metal Dogs may not be seeking romance, a special person could now enter their life.

The Metal Dog's home life will also be eventful this year. In fact he could be bewildered by rapidly changing plans and circumstances. The Metal Dog likes order and organization, but both he and family members could face uncertainties over work choices, and to add to the pressure, he may be involved in some ambitious home projects too, including possibly moving. With so much happening, there will need to be good co-operation as well as willingness to adapt. Amid all the activity, it is also important that more pleasurable activities do not get sidelined. By setting time aside to share with his loved ones, the Metal Dog can not only enjoy some special occasions but also help everyone to strike a good lifestyle balance. Also, busy and possibly difficult though parts of the year will be, when the rewards of his efforts come through, the Metal Dog can look back with pride at the great amount he has accomplished this year.

Overall, the Year of the Goat will be a demanding one for the Metal Dog, especially as he may be affected by changes that are not under his control. However, important benefits can result. Work-wise, developments will allow the Metal Dog to extend his skills, while in his home life he can realize some important goals. He may be fortunate with certain acquisitions too. Throughout the year, effort and flexibility will be needed, but the Metal Dog is tenacious, and his skills, determination and character will ensure he carries through many of his plans and reaps considerable benefits.

Tip for the Year
Balance out your activities and allow time for recreation as well as to share with your loved ones. A lot is set to happen this year, and with support, you can achieve more. Be flexible but determined.

The Water Dog

As the Goat year starts the Water Dog will have certain plans he would like to get underway. However, the Goat year can be one of surprises. It will require flexibility, but is nevertheless a time of good opportunity.

In the Water Dog's work this will be an eventful year. In recent times he will have proved himself in various capacities and built up useful experience. Now he will have the chance to advance his career. If working in a large organization, he could be tempted by a position in another department or sector. During the year, many Water Dogs will be keen to take their career to a new level and will benefit from promotion opportunities or internal vacancies in their place of work. Throughout the year the Water Dog will also be helped by the good working relations he enjoys with those around him and he should continue to seize any chances to raise his profile. With Water as his element, he is an effective communicator, and his talents and ideas will impress many this year.

For Water Dogs who feel their prospects could be improved by moving elsewhere, as well as those seeking work, the Goat year can again open up interesting possibilities. By keeping informed about the employment situation in their area and considering other ways in which they could use their skills, many could succeed in securing an interesting new position. For some, this could be a considerable change, but nevertheless be a valuable entry into a new company or type of work. April, June to early August and October could be significant months, but throughout the year the Water Dog needs to be quick to act when he sees an opening that interests him.

With this being a year which encourages creativity, the Water Dog will also derive considerable pleasure from his personal interests. Water Dogs whose pursuits give them the chance to express themselves in some way could find their talents leading to the production of some fine pieces or performances. In this year of encouraging developments, some Water Dogs may also be inspired to try out a new activity and in the process discover a hidden talent. In so many ways, the Goat year can set significant wheels in motion.

In most of what the Water Dog undertakes this year he will be well supported, with family and friends providing useful input. Some of his interests can also have a good social element. Joint pursuits are favourably aspected, and attending events and sharing activities can make this an enjoyable and often enlightening time. March, April, August and December could see the most social activity, and for the unattached, a chance meeting could become more significant as the year develops.

The Water Dog's home life will also see a lot happen. With accommodation matters prominent in Goat years, quite a few Water Dogs will consider moving or set about ambitious home projects. Such activities can be disruptive and time-consuming, and this year they may also proceed in unexpected ways. It could be that Water Dogs who move decide on a different location from the one they first considered, or a different style of home. Similarly, where practical projects are concerned, initial plans could alter or a project become far more extensive than anticipated. In the Goat year the Water Dog will need to be flexible and make the best of what occurs.

Although much time will be devoted to practical matters, the year can also contain some personal and family highlights. Some Water Dogs may see an addition to their family and those who are already parents will do much to support their children as they adjust to new schools, master new skills and carry out their various pursuits. The Water Dog can play a pivotal role in the lives of his loved ones this year and his empathy and personal qualities will be greatly valued. Amid the activity of the year, there will be many special moments to share, and a holiday, which could be arranged at short notice, can be appreciated by all.

With spending on the home and, for some, moving costs, this will, however, be an expensive year for the Water Dog. Consequently, he will need to keep a close watch on spending and if entering into an agreement, thoroughly check the terms and conditions. Finance requires care. The Water Dog should also keep his paperwork in good order, including making sure insurance policies cover his requirements and guarantees, receipts and important documents are kept safely. Extra vigilance now can prevent problems later on.

Throughout the year the Water Dog will be kept busy and will need to adapt when necessary and make the most of the situations in which he finds himself. With willingness and persistence, however, much can be achieved, and new work positions, ideas and interests all have the potential of developing into something much more significant in following years. On a personal level, this will be a rewarding time, and some significant home plans may go ahead too. Keen and determined, the Water Dog likes to give his best and the Goat year can reward him well.

Tip for the Year

Remain aware of developments around you and adapt as required. You can achieve a great deal this year, often with far-reaching consequences, but it is a case of making the most of your time and opportunities. Also, value the support of those around you. Loved ones can be important and there will be many special times to enjoy this year.

The Wood Dog

This will be a rewarding year for the Wood Dog, with what he learns during it having an important bearing on his future. In addition it can open up new possibilities, and by keeping an open mind and remaining aware, the Wood Dog will find that much can follow on.

For Wood Dogs in education this will be an important year. Although many will often have a bewildering amount to study and may feel overwhelmed, by focusing on what needs to be done they can make major strides towards the qualifications they want. Parts of the year will be pressured, but it is by being challenged that the Wood Dog will gain the knowledge and experience he can build on.

Another important feature of the Goat year will be the opportunities that can suddenly open up. These may include the chance for the Wood Dog to take his studying in a different direction or to choose a subject for more specialist study. The decisions he takes now can have a bearing on his future, including sometimes his choice of vocation.

The arts and culture are favourably aspected in Goat years and for Wood Dogs who are interested in these areas, this can be an exciting time. By making the most of the resources available to them, they will find their knowledge and skills can be considerably advanced over the year.

The Wood Dog will also be well supported in most of what he does and will particularly enjoy the camaraderie that can be generated by activities he can share. In addition, his interests can provide excellent chances to meet new people and many Wood Dogs will widen their social circle as the year progresses. March to early May, August and December could be particularly full and lively months socially, but throughout the year the Wood Dog will have parties and other social gatherings to attend. The Goat year has a capacity for generating fun, too, and for quite a few Wood Dogs, romance can play an exciting part as well. Some who start the year unattached will meet someone who is destined to become significant.

For Wood Dogs in work or seeking work, the Goat year can again have important developments in store. Wood Dogs who are already established in a position will often receive extra training which can lead to them doing more. Developments at work can have a knock-on effect and an offer of additional duties is capable of turning into something much more substantial as the year goes on. By taking advantage of what arises, many Wood Dogs can make important progress.

Wood Dogs who are unfulfilled in what they currently do, as well as those seeking work, will find that by keeping in regular contact with employment agencies and contacting large employers in their area, they may secure an interesting position which has scope for the future. For some Wood Dogs, the year can mark their entry into a type of work they will remain with for a great many years. April, June, July and October could see encouraging developments.

With an often busy social life, personal interests and accommodation outgoings, the Wood Dog will need to be careful in money matters this year. He should aim to keep a close watch on his spending and budget ahead whenever possible. He may well have the chance to travel this year, and early provision for this can be helpful and enable him to do more while away. And, as with much else this year, should he have financial problems or uncertainties, he should seek assistance. More senior relations will be keen to advise.

Overall, the Year of the Goat can be a demanding one for the Wood Dog. For Wood Dogs in education, there will be pressures and a heavy workload, while for those in work or seeking it, there will be duties to learn. However, the Wood Dog is redoubtable and by putting in the effort he will have the chance both to impress *and* to make good headway. Importantly, what he does now can open up other possibilities in the future. Indeed, a lot that the Wood Dog starts in this busy and varied year can have long-term significance.

Tip for the Year
Be open to opportunity. Much can follow on from what you do this year. Also, look to build on your ideas and talents and enjoy the support of those around you. This can be a personally pleasing year for you.

The Fire Dog

A lot is set to happen for the Fire Dog this year, with some interesting opportunities arising.

The Fire Dog likes to look ahead and have plans lined up. With accommodation matters prominent in the Goat year, he may well be keen to go ahead with ambitious projects on his home, including smartening certain areas and updating equipment. With much to consider, it is important that he draws on the help of others and, if undertaking anything strenuous, follows the correct procedures or seeks additional assistance. He may be willing, but a strain or over-exertion could cause him some discomfort. Fire Dogs, do take note and care.

Also, once plans and activities are started, new ideas or possibilities can arise. This is a changeable year and to benefit the Fire Dog should be willing to consider new options rather than remain wedded to his original thoughts. Goat years can be times of positive change, but some flexibility is advised.

Over the year some Fire Dogs will consider moving to accommodation that better suits their requirements. Those contemplating a move will find that once they set the process in motion, sudden developments could surprise them. Some could discover an ideal new home almost by chance or, if looking to sell, could have an unexpected expression of interest in their home. For the Fire Dogs who do move, the year will contain some eventful weeks.

In addition to the practical activity of the year, the Fire Dog will be very much involved in family life and those close to him will be grateful for his views and assistance. A loved one could have a difficult personal choice to make, and the Fire Dog's empathy and judgement will be of particular value. The year will also have its special moments, with some Fire Dogs celebrating the birth of a great-grandchild. The Fire Dog's family has a special place in his heart and the year will contain some news and occasions which will make him proud.

The Goat year also has a certain spontaneity about it, with opportunities arising suddenly. The Fire Dog may see a tempting travel offer and decide to take it up, or learn of a particular event and choose to attend almost on a whim. By making the most of what arises *and* being flexible with planning, he can enjoy a pleasing mix of entertainment in 2015. Late February to early May, August and December could be particularly active and interesting months.

Although the Fire Dog keeps his social circle relatively small, he will also value the contact he has with his friends over the year. Some with specialist knowledge could be particularly helpful. To benefit, though, the Fire Dog does need to be forthcoming.

The Fire Dog likes to absorb himself in specific interests and these are again likely to develop in an encouraging manner this year. Creative activities can be especially satisfying. Some Fire Dogs will also give support to a cause or charity or help in their community in some way, and will be pleased by how they are able to assist.

In view of the considerable costs likely to be involved with his accommodation plans, the Fire Dog will need to be thorough and vigilant when dealing with financial matters this year. When entering into agreements, he needs to check the terms and conditions and resolve any uncertainties before he proceeds. Extra attention could prevent mistakes or later regrets. Similarly, if anything concerns him with regard to paperwork that requires attention, he should seek advice. This is no year to be lax. However, the Fire Dog will delight in much that he is able to acquire this year, including home appliances and entertainment devices. He should also aim to set money aside for travel as well as to enjoy some of the more unexpected treats the Goat year is famed for.

Overall, this will be a busy and eventful year and at the end of it the Fire Dog will be able to look back with delight at the many plans he has carried out and the benefits he has gained. It will require effort, and the Fire Dog may feel the pressure during some months (notably around the middle of the year), but this is essentially a time for action. Support and sometimes unexpected opportunities will enable a lot to happen and the Fire Dog's home life and personal interests can bring him considerable pleasure and add a richness to this full and significant year.

Tip for the Year

Value the support of those around you. The better you co-operate this year, the better your results. Also, allow time to enjoy your personal interests and follow up your ideas. Sometimes unexpected benefits can follow on.

The Earth Dog

The Earth Dog is a careful planner and dislikes uncertainty and sudden change. To his dismay, the Goat year will contain both, although it can also bring important opportunities. What occurs during it can have far-reaching consequences.

As with all Dogs, accommodation matters will feature prominently for the Earth Dog, and some will decide to move. These Earth Dogs will find that once they start to make enquiries and view possible homes, an important sequence of events can be set in motion and quite a few will successfully make the change they may have been contemplating for some time.

Earth Dogs who remain where they are will also focus a lot of time and attention on their accommodation, possibly redecorating, attending to a maintenance issue or going ahead with modifications and acquisitions. By allowing time and considering possibilities with care, they will be satisfied with the improvements made.

In addition to the practical activity, a lot will happen in the Earth Dog's home life. A close relation could have exciting news to share and some Earth Dogs will be celebrating the birth of a grandchild or the academic or career achievement of another family member. Some events will bring the Earth Dog's family closer together and the Earth Dog himself will take a fond interest in developments and dispense timely advice. Once more he will play a full and appreciated part in family life.

He will also have particular interests he enjoys, including some that take him out of doors. The sports enthusiast or Earth Dog who enjoys outdoor life will find the Goat year can give rise to some particularly fine occasions.

If possible, all Earth Dogs should also give themselves the chance of a holiday or break over the year. A change of scene can do them good.

Goat years encourage trying out the new and some Earth Dogs could become intrigued by a different pursuit this year. By following this up, they can find it developing in an interesting and potentially beneficial way. All Earth Dogs do need to be receptive to the possibilities the Goat year opens up. Also, those who are sedentary for much of the day or feel that more exercise or a change of diet might help should seek medical advice on what measures it is appropriate for them to take. Positive lifestyle changes can make a noticeable difference.

Although the Earth Dog will be kept busy over the year, it is also important that he does not neglect his social life. Some Earth Dogs have a tendency to keep themselves to themselves, but Goat years encourage socializing and can bring brightness and fun. March, April, August and December could see the most social activity.

Such is the nature of the year that some Earth Dogs who start the year unattached could find romance and enjoy quite a transformation in their situation.

At work, the Earth Dog will also feel the effects of change. Goat years can be volatile and changes may be introduced suddenly or workplaces altered. Some weeks will be challenging, but there can be unexpected benefits. Earth Dogs who have become set in a particular work pattern will find that new responsibilities can bring fresh challenges – and incentives. Some may also have more opportunity to draw on their area of expertise. By making the most of what arises, the Earth Dog will find that the Goat year can open up interesting possibilities.

There will, though, be some Earth Dogs who have thoughts about moving on and furthering their experience in other ways. These Earth Dogs, and those seeking work, should keep alert for vacancies and also widen the scope of what they are considering. In quite a few instances, an application where they consider their chances slim will get taken up and lead to an offer of work. Other Earth Dogs may receive an offer in the wake of rejection. However it happens, the Goat year can bring change and opportunity for many Earth Dogs. April, June, July and October could see important developments.

In view of the considerable outlay likely on the Earth Dog's home, however, this will be an expensive year. Many Earth Dogs will face additional family expenses and will also be keen to update some personal possessions. In view of this, the Earth Dog does need to keep a close watch on everyday spending and budget in advance for more expensive items. In some instances he could save himself unnecessary expense by waiting to take advantage of attractive purchasing opportunities. He also needs to be thorough when attending to paperwork and seek further guidance if necessary.

In general, this is a year of encouraging and sometimes surprising developments. Changes the Earth Dog may not have envisaged can open up new possibilities at work, reinvigorating his career in the process. Many Earth Dogs will carry out projects on their home and some will move. If the Earth Dog values the support of others and makes the most of his opportunities, he can reap the benefits of his actions both now and in following years.

Tip for the Year
Make the most of what arises. Amid all the changes there are opportunities for you. Don't be restrictive in outlook, but show willing. Know that what you do now will pay off in the future. Also, keep your lifestyle in balance – value your loved ones and develop your personal interests.

Famous Dogs

Brigitte Bardot, Gary Barlow, Candice Bergen, Justin Bieber, Andrea Bocelli, David Bowie, George W. Bush, Kate Bush, the Duke of Cambridge, Naomi Campbell, Peter Capaldi, Mariah Carey, King Carl XVI Gustaf of Sweden, José Carreras, Paul Cézanne, Cher, Sir Winston Churchill, Bill Clinton, Leonard Cohen, Matt Damon, Charles Dance, Claude Debussy, Dame Judi Dench, Kirsten Dunst, Dakota Fanning, Joseph Fiennes, Robert Frost, Ava Gardner, Judy Garland, George Gershwin, Anne Hathaway, O. Henry, Victor Hugo, Barry Humphries, Holly Hunter, Michael Jackson, Al Jolson, Jennifer Lopez, Sophia Loren,

Andie MacDowell, Shirley MacLaine, Melissa McCarthy, Madonna, Norman Mailer, Barry Manilow, Freddie Mercury, Nicki Minaj, Liza Minnelli, Simon Pegg, Elvis Presley, Tim Robbins, Andy Roddick, Susan Sarandon, Claudia Schiffer, Dr Albert Schweitzer, Sylvester Stallone, Robert Louis Stevenson, Sharon Stone, Donald Sutherland, Mother Teresa, Uma Thurman, Donald Trump, Voltaire, Lil Wayne, Shelley Winters.

16 February 1923 to 4 February 1924 — *Water Pig*

4 February 1935 to 23 January 1936 — *Wood Pig*

22 January 1947 to 9 February 1948 — *Fire Pig*

8 February 1959 to 27 January 1960 — *Earth Pig*

27 January 1971 to 14 February 1972 — *Metal Pig*

13 February 1983 to 1 February 1984 — *Water Pig*

31 January 1995 to 18 February 1996 — *Wood Pig*

18 February 2007 to 6 February 2008 — *Fire Pig*

The Pig

The Personality of the Pig

It's the doing,
the giving,
the playing the part,
that makes life what it is.
And what it can be.

The Pig is born under the sign of honesty. He has a kind and understanding nature and is well known for his abilities as a peacemaker. He hates any sort of discord or unpleasantness and will do everything in his power to sort out differences of opinion or bring opposing factions together.

He is also an excellent conversationalist and speaks truthfully and to the point. He dislikes any form of falsehood or hypocrisy and is a firm believer in justice and the maintenance of law and order. In spite of these beliefs, however, he is reasonably tolerant and often prepared to forgive others for their wrongdoings. He rarely harbours grudges and is never vindictive.

The Pig is usually very popular. He enjoys other people's company and likes to be involved in joint or group activities. He will be a loyal member of any club or society and can be relied upon to lend a helping hand at functions. He is also an excellent fundraiser for charities and is often a great supporter of humanitarian causes.

The Pig is a hard and conscientious worker and is particularly respected for his reliability and integrity. In his early years he will try his hand at several different jobs, but he is usually happiest where he feels that he is being of service to others. He will unselfishly give up his time for the common good and is highly valued by his colleagues and employers.

The Pig has a good sense of humour and invariably has a smile, joke or some whimsical remark at the ready. He loves to entertain and to please others, and there are many Pigs who have been attracted to careers in show business or who enjoy following the careers of famous stars and personalities.

There are, unfortunately, some who take advantage of the Pig's good nature and impose upon his generosity. The Pig has great difficulty in saying 'no', and although he may dislike being firm, it would be in his own interests to say occasionally, 'Enough is enough.' He can also be rather naïve and gullible; however, if at any stage in his life he feels that he has been badly let down, he will try to become self-reliant. There are many Pigs who have become entrepreneurs or forged a successful career on their own after some early disappointment in life. Although the Pig tends to spend his money quite freely, he is usually very astute in financial matters and there are many Pigs who have become wealthy.

Another characteristic of the Pig is his ability to recover from setbacks reasonably quickly. His faith and his strength of character keep him going. If he thinks that there is a job he can do or there is something that he wants to achieve, he will pursue it with dogged determination. He can also be stubborn and no matter how many may plead with him, once he has made his mind up he will rarely change his views.

Although the Pig may work hard, he also knows how to enjoy himself. He is a great pleasure-seeker and will quite happily spend his hard-earned money on a lavish holiday or an expensive meal – for the Pig is a connoisseur of good food and wine – or a variety of recreational activities. He also enjoys small social gatherings and if he is in company he likes he can very easily become the life and soul of the party. He does, however, tend to become rather withdrawn at larger functions or when among strangers.

The Pig is a creature of comfort and his home will usually be fitted with the latest in luxury appliances. Where possible, he will prefer to live in the country rather than the town and will opt to have a big garden, for the Pig is usually a keen and successful gardener.

The Pig is very popular with others and will often have numerous romances before he settles down. Once settled, however, he will be loyal to his partner and he will find that he is especially well suited to those born under the signs of the Goat, Rabbit, Dog and Tiger and also to another Pig. Due to his affable and easy-going nature he can also establish a satisfactory relationship with all the remaining signs of the Chinese zodiac, with the exception of the Snake. The Snake tends to be wily, secretive and very guarded, and this can be intensely irritating to the honest and open-hearted Pig.

The female Pig will devote all her energies to the needs of her children and her partner. She will try to ensure that they want for nothing and their pleasure is very much her pleasure. She can be a caring and conscientious parent and has very good taste in clothes. Her home will either be very clean and orderly or hopelessly untidy. Strangely, there seems to be no in-between with Pigs – they either love housework or detest it! The female Pig does, however, have considerable talents as an organizer and this, combined with her friendly and open manner, enables her to secure many of her objectives.

The Pig is usually lucky in life and will rarely want for anything. Provided he does not let others take advantage of his good nature and is not afraid of asserting himself, he will go through life making friends, helping others and winning the admiration of many.

The Five Different Types of Pig

In addition to the 12 signs of the Chinese zodiac there are five elements and these have a strengthening or moderating influence on the signs. The effects of the five elements on the Pig are described below, together with the years in which they were exercising their influence. Therefore Pigs born in 1971 are Metal Pigs, Pigs born in 1923 and 1983 are Water Pigs, and so on.

Metal Pig: 1971

The Metal Pig is more ambitious and determined than some of the other types of Pig. He is strong, energetic and likes to be involved in a wide variety of different activities. He is very open and forthright in his views, although he can be a little too trusting at times and has a tendency to accept things at face value. He has a good sense of humour and loves to attend parties and other social gatherings. He has a warm, outgoing nature and usually has a large circle of friends.

Water Pig: 1923, 1983

The Water Pig has a heart of gold. He is generous and loyal and tries to remain on good terms with everyone. He will do his utmost to help others, but sadly there are some who will take advantage of his kind nature and he should, in his own interests, be a little more discriminating and be prepared to stand firm against anything that he does not like. Although he prefers the quieter things in life, he has a wide range of interests. He particularly enjoys outdoor pursuits and attending parties and social occasions. He is a hard and conscientious worker and invariably does well in his chosen profession. He is also gifted in the art of communication.

Wood Pig: 1935, 1995

This Pig has a friendly, persuasive manner and is easily able to gain the confidence of others. He likes to be involved in all that is going on around him but can sometimes take on more responsibility than he can properly handle. He is loyal to his family and friends and derives much pleasure from helping those less fortunate than himself. He is usually an optimist and leads a very full, enjoyable and satisfying life. He also has a good sense of humour.

Fire Pig: 1947, 2007

The Fire Pig is both energetic and adventurous and sets about everything he does in a confident and resolute manner. He is very forthright in his views and does not mind taking risks in order to achieve his objectives. He can, however, get carried away by the excitement of the moment and ought to exercise more caution in some of the enterprises in which he gets involved. He is usually lucky in money matters and is well known for his generosity. He is also very caring towards the members of his family.

Earth Pig: 1959

This Pig has a kindly nature. He is sensible and realistic and will go to great lengths in order to please his employers and to secure his aims and ambitions. He is an excellent organizer and is particularly astute in business and financial matters. He has a good sense of humour and a wide circle of friends. He also likes to lead an active social life, although he does sometimes have a tendency to eat and drink more than is good for him.

Prospects for the Pig in 2015

In the Horse year (31 January 2014–18 February 2015) events proceed at a fast pace and the Pig will have led a full and busy lifestyle. As the Horse year draws to a close, he will continue to have a lot to do and will see an increase in activity in his domestic and social life. Domestically, there could be important decisions to take, plans to finalize and purchases to make and the Pig will need to allow time to consider his options. The more discussion and less rush, the better.

The Pig will enjoy the social opportunities that arise at the year's end and will appreciate sharing some lively and interesting times with friends, especially in December and early January.

At work, he could face additional pressures and his skills and patience will sometimes be tested. However, in view of the increased activity, there will be the chance for the Pig to use his initiative and improve his reputation. October could see particularly interesting developments, but given the active nature of the Horse year, Pigs seeking work or looking to advance their career could find opportunities arising at almost any time. When the Pig sees an opening, he will need to act swiftly. A few Pigs may also benefit from temporary positions towards the end of the year.

In general, the Horse year will have kept the Pig busy, but he enjoys activity and can enjoy some encouraging results.

*   *   *

The Pig relies a lot on instinct and as the Goat year begins, if not shortly before, he will sense this is a time offering pleasing prospects. And his instinct will be right. The Goat year, which begins on 19 February, is an encouraging one for the Pig and, particularly in his personal life, special times await.

The Pig attaches great importance to his relations with others and has a talent for getting on well with most people. He empathizes with others and converses well, but he also listens and takes note, and this is what many appreciate. Essentially, the Pig is a people person and throughout the Goat year he will find himself in demand.

His home life is particularly well aspected. He will carry out a wide range of activities, helping others as well as enjoying times with his loved ones. They will often seek his advice, which he will be glad to give, and there could be some notable personal and family achievements to mark too. Goat years can contain some particularly joyous occasions as well as see some ambitious plans carried out on the home.

A further feature of Goat years is the many special events that are held during it and the Pig will often be keen to attend. By looking to do things with his family, he will not only enjoy himself but also find his activities helping to strengthen bonds. Domestically, this can be a rewarding year.

The aspects are similarly encouraging for the Pig's social life. For the keen partygoer and socializer, there will be many occasions to look forward to, with May, June, August and September particularly busy months.

For the unattached, the Goat year will bring good romantic opportunities. Many Pigs will enjoy newfound love, while those in the early stages of a relationship could find this strengthening over the year and some will settle down together or marry. For personal relationships, the Goat year can be an exciting time and any Pigs who start the year dispirited will find that it can herald a brightening in their situation.

Although the Pig likes to enjoy himself, he also works hard and can often be ambitious. And, as he recognizes, the key to realizing his potential is personal development. During the year, he should use any chances (and some of his free time) to add to his skills and knowledge. This is an excellent year for personal growth.

The Pig's personal interests can also bring him considerable pleasure, and new knowledge and equipment can enable him to do more. Some interest-related projects will become more absorbing as he gets more fully involved.

In his work this will be a year of steady if sometimes slow progress. Sometimes his work could be affected by issues outside his control. However, while this may exasperate him, often in the wake of problems there can be opportunities for the Pig to demonstrate his resourcefulness, put forward ideas and sometimes use his skills in new ways. Also, with career development favourably aspected, he should take full advantage of any training that is available and make the most of networking opportunities. Knowledge, experience and skills acquired now can be taken much further in following years.

For Pigs who are keen to advance their career or seeking a position, April, May, September and October could see some potentially important openings.

The Pig could enjoy a modest rise in income this year, although he will need to watch his spending. When out shopping or socializing, control over the purse-strings would be wise. Too many impulse buys or indulgences could mount up and lead to possible economies later. Pigs, take note and in some instances exercise restraint.

In general, however, the Goat year is a pleasing and potentially important one for the Pig. His relations with others are splendidly aspected and it is also an excellent time for self-development. At work, progress may be modest, but if the Pig seizes any opportunities to further his skills and knowledge, he can enhance his future prospects. This will be a personally satisfying year in many ways, but best of all will be the good relations the Pig enjoys with those around him, which, to the Pig, mean so much.

The Metal Pig

The Metal Pig sets about his activities with considerable energy, style and resolve, and over the year he can look forward to accomplishing a lot.

At work, many Metal Pigs will have experienced change in recent years and there will have been much to learn. This Goat year will allow most of these Metal Pigs to immerse themselves in their duties and become better established in their role. And while it will have its inevitable challenges (including some matters that cause delay), the Metal Pig will feel more fulfilled by what he does.

Another benefit of the year will be the way the Metal Pig can build on his skills. Whether this comes through training or the duties he carries out, by taking advantage of the chances available to him, he can do his prospects great good. Indeed, some Metal Pigs may find that following training a new opportunity arises or they are alerted to possibilities to consider for the future. Career development is especially well indicated this year.

The majority of Metal Pigs will remain with their current employer, but for those who feel their prospects could be improved by moving elsewhere, the Goat year can open up some interesting opportunities. To benefit, these Metal Pigs, as well as those already looking for a position, would do well to widen their search. With willingness to adapt, not only will there be more possibilities to pursue but also the chance to develop in new ways. Many Metal Pigs will welcome this. If eligible, some may find retraining or refresher courses helpful. An important aspect of the Metal Pig's personality is that he thrives on challenge and many Metal Pigs can secure what can be an important foothold this year. April to early June, September and October could see significant developments.

With the year encouraging new knowledge, the Metal Pig will also enjoy the way he can develop certain interests. Frequently inspired, he will revel in the opportunities the year opens up.

Another favourably aspected area is his relations with others, and he should make the most of chances to talk, liaise and network. As has often been found, the more people you know, the more opportunities come your way.

As a consequence of the Metal Pigs many activities, the year will contain many social opportunities, and the Metal Pig's social circle become more extensive. Any Metal Pig who has had recent personal upset to deal with, is feeling lonely or moves to a new location will find the Goat year can also mark the dawning of a new day and offer the chance to try new activities and build a new social circle. To help bring about this upturn, these Metal Pigs will need to go out and make the effort, but their actions will often lead to a welcome improvement in their situation. May, June, August and September could see the most social activity.

For the unattached, affairs of the heart are splendidly aspected and many Metal Pigs will enjoy what can be a significant new romance.

Family life is very important to the Metal Pig, and this year can see some extensive home improvements, which will benefit from his taste and eye for detail. With some family members likely to be under pressure, especially if currently studying, facing job changes or having an important personal decision to make, his rapport with others and ability to listen and express an opinion will be especially valued, as will any assistance he may give more senior relations. May and August could see pleasing occasions in many a Metal Pig home, and a holiday or break will be particularly appreciated.

The Metal Pig may benefit from a modest rise in income this year, but with an active lifestyle and the various acquisitions he will want to make, he will need to keep a close watch on his outgoings. By being vigilant he can go ahead with many of his plans, but should he proceed on a more ad hoc basis, economies may be needed. The Goat year, with its many temptations, calls for good financial management.

Overall, this will be an interesting year for the Metal Pig. His relations with others are especially well aspected and his home life can be a source of particular pleasure. His social life and personal interests can also be gratifying. Unattached Metal Pigs and those who have had personal misfortune of late will find this year may allow them to turn the corner.

Although progress at work may be modest, there will be opportunities for the Metal Pig to further his skills. By making the most of what arises, he can see important possibilities opening up both now and in succeeding years. A satisfying year with far-reaching effects.

Tip for the Year

Value your relationships and seize any chances to meet new people. You have wonderful personal talents and can gain a lot from the support and encouragement of those around you. Also, look to extend your knowledge and skills. Much good can follow on.

The Water Pig

This can be a special year for the Water Pig and his relations with others are particularly well aspected. Having Water as his element strengthens his communication abilities and when this is combined with the Pig's ability to empathize it results in a powerful communicator who can really relate to others. During the year the Water Pig will find himself in demand, enjoying good times with others and benefiting from the support and goodwill of many.

In the Water Pig's home life this can be a time of special developments. Some Water Pigs will become parents or see an addition to their family and those who are already parents will have much joy in following their children's progress. The Water Pig will also be keen to make improvements to his home. Whether purchasing new equipment or smartening certain areas, he can make a noticeable difference. He takes great pride in his home and the work he undertakes on it this year will be gratifying to him.

Throughout the year there will also be decisions for the Water Pig to take. Some of these will be practical in nature or involve home purchases, but some could concern work activities. In all cases it is important that options are discussed and thoughts shared. By being open, the Water Pig will find that decisions can be made much more easily. This is a year for sharing, and the better the communication, the more rewarding home life can be.

Although the Water Pig will need to keep careful control of his budget, if possible he should make provision for a holiday. Even if not travelling too far, he will appreciate a change of scene. There could also be special events held in his area or recreational facilities he and family members could use. By taking advantage of them, he could enjoy some pleasing times.

The Water Pig's social life can also be full of interest this year. In addition to meeting his friends, he will find that quite a few of his activities have a good social element. Some Water Pigs will derive particular pleasure from a local activity group, while for those who enjoy live entertainment, there could be quite a few special occasions this year.

Water Pigs who are alone, including those who have moved to a new location or have experienced personal difficulty of late, should consider involving themselves in local activities. By making an effort and being a part of their community, they will soon get to meet like-minded people and could meet someone who is destined to become significant. New friendships, romance or just meeting others are all strongly aspected this year. Late April to the end of June, August and September are likely to be particularly active months.

Although the Water Pig will have much to occupy his time, to keep on good form he should also give some consideration to his own well-being. This includes paying attention to the quality of his diet and taking regular exercise. Any positive changes he can introduce can make a real difference.

In addition, he could find it helpful to give some thought to his future. If he feels a new skill or qualification could help his prospects, he should investigate courses he could take, including those that are available online. Goat years are excellent for personal development.

Work-wise, the year can see far-reaching developments. The Water Pig will be encouraged to extend his duties and skills, often in preparation for a greater role in the future. By taking full advantage and showing commitment, he can successfully build on his position, and as with so much this year, his positive relations with those around him will help his situation. By networking and, if appropriate, joining a professional organization, he could further establish himself in his role.

Many Water Pigs will make steady progress with their present employer this year, but for those keen to move elsewhere, as well as those seeking work, the Goat year can hold important possibilities. Employment advisers, friends and contacts could all advise the Water Pig of positions that are or are about to become available and offer suggestions about other ways in which they could employ their skills. By taking heed and actively pursuing openings, many of these Water Pigs can not only secure a new position but also have the chance to establish themselves in a new organization. A key value of the year will be the experience it will enable many Water Pigs to obtain. More substantial growth will follow on. April, May and September to early November could see important developments.

In view of his commitments and the substantial purchases he may make this year, the Water Pig will, however, need to keep a close watch on spending. With care, he can do a great deal, including travelling, but it will require discipline and not succumbing to too many impulse purchases or indulgences. Water Pigs, take note, and also be thorough when attending to financial paperwork.

With his talents and desire to make more of his situation, the Water Pig can do well this year. There will be excellent opportunity for him to add to his skills and developing his personal interests can also be beneficial. However, it is the Water Pig's relations with others which will make this year special. Domestically and socially, he can look forward to some meaningful times.

Tip for the Year
You do so much for others – this year, let others reciprocate. Run thoughts past them, seek their support and share what you do. Also seize any opportunities to add to your knowledge. What you accomplish now can be built on in the future. Don't underestimate the value of this encouraging year.

The Wood Pig

As the Goat year starts, many Wood Pigs will sense that it is going to be special. Not only does it mark the start of a new decade in the Wood Pig's life, but his zest and enthusiasm will ensure an eventful time. A great deal is indeed set to happen.

The sociable Wood Pig attaches great importance to his relations with others and during the year he will be much in demand. Whether spending time with his friends, partying (and this year will certainly bring a lot of lively socializing), sharing interests or getting to meet new people, he is likely to find his social diary fairly full. For the many Wood Pigs who move this year or find themselves in a new environment, there will be excellent opportunities to get to know a new group of people and make some important friends and connections. Some months will be a whirl of activity. May to early July, August and September could be particularly lively months.

For quite a few Wood Pigs, the excitement of romance will add to this favourable year. Sometimes this may not run entirely smoothly, but Wood Pigs who find a relationship faltering (and this will certainly not be all) need not lose heart, as a new romantic interest could quickly follow.

A particular strength of the Wood Pig is his ability to relate to others and during the year he can make an important impression on those around him, including tutors, employers, advisers and those with similar interests. He can look forward to the support of many, and if at any time he has uncertainties or pressures or would welcome guidance, all he need do is ask.

While the majority of Wood Pigs are outgoing, for those who keep themselves to themselves (and there are some) and may at times feel lonely, this is also an encouraging time. Events that take place over the year can help the shyer Wood Pig to become more confident in company. A new friendship could be especially helpful in this respect.

For the many Wood Pigs in education, there will be exams to prepare for and coursework to submit. These Wood Pigs will need to be disciplined and prioritize their work – which may not always be easy with an active social life and other interests to pursue. For some, their life will be akin to a juggling act, but by using their time effectively, many can make excellent progress, and the skills, knowledge and qualifications they gain will be an investment in their future.

For Wood Pigs in work or seeking work, the Goat year can open up interesting possibilities. Those already in a position could find unexpected opportunities becoming available. It could be that a position similar to what they are doing but with better prospects (and remuneration) falls vacant elsewhere or that training is arranged for the Wood Pig or that he has the chance to be involved in different aspects of his work. The emphasis this year is definitely on furthering knowledge and skills.

Wood Pigs seeking work will find it helpful to draw on advice given by employment advisers as well as actively pursue openings. Often their enthusiasm will impress potential employers and once on the employment ladder they will be able to make further progress. April, May and September to early November could see encouraging developments.

The Wood Pig's personal interests can also bring him considerable pleasure and be a good outlet for his ideas and talents. Wood Pigs who have hopes of taking a certain skill or interest further will find that guidance from experts can open up interesting possibilities. This is an excellent time for the Wood Pig to build on what he enjoys.

With a lively social life, together with the purchases he will be keen to make, he will, however, need to be disciplined in money matters and set funds aside for specific requirements, including travel. He should also avoid too many impulse buys. If he is to do all he wants, strict control over spending will be required.

There will certainly be a lot happening this year, but a key occasion for many Wood Pigs will be celebrating their twentieth birthday. Some loved ones could have a surprise in store and tokens of affection which will mean a great deal to the Wood Pig. Throughout the year, the support of family members can be significant. While there may be times when opinions differ, by being willing to share his thoughts and assist in the home, the Wood Pig can benefit from the assistance and advice of family members. Those who know him well are keen to see him make the most of his potential.

In general, the Year of the Goat can be a significant one for the Wood Pig. Whether gaining knowledge, acquiring skills or pursuing interests and a varied social life, by embracing his opportunities and making the most of his support, he can do well and, importantly, prepare himself for future success.

Tip for the Year

Have fun and enjoy your year, but also commit yourself to what you want to see happen in the future. By furthering your knowledge and skills you will be providing yourself with the means of future growth. Seize your opportunities, for your future is rich in potential and possibility.

The Fire Pig

With his active nature and many interests, the Fire Pig uses his time well and this can be a pleasing and constructive year for him. However, while he likes to plan ahead, the Goat year can be one of change. He will need to take note of emerging situations and adapt accordingly.

In his home life this will be a busy year. During it, he will often find himself helping family members, including some who have significant decisions to take. Here his years of experience and ability to understand the situation of others can count for a great deal. He will also enjoy spending time with younger family members, and special bonds will often be forged between them. Family life is important to the Fire Pig.

In addition to the help the Fire Pig gives others, there will also be many activities he will be keen to share with them. In his own home, he will be keen to make some substantial purchases, including updating equipment, and will value the thoughts and recommendations of those around him. When carrying through projects, he will find that if he tackles them with others, both the process and outcome can be appreciated all the more. However, in some practical activities the Goat year can take a curious course. New options can arise or snags occur which will involve rethinking what is being carried out. As many Fire Pigs will find, plans can very easily change this year and flexibility will be needed, not only with ideas but also with timescales.

The Goat year can, however, bring a variety of special occasions for the Fire Pig to attend. It could be that he receives an unexpected invitation, has the chance to go away (often at short notice) or learns of a particular event which appeals to him. By taking advantage of what arises, he can enjoy a lot of what he does. May, June, August and September could be particularly interesting months.

The Fire Pig will also be glad to meet up with his friends. With some of these likely to be facing problems and the Fire Pig himself possibly uncertain about some choices he has to make, all concerned will value their chances to seek advice and sometimes reassurance. A long-standing friend with specific expertise could be particularly helpful to the Fire Pig.

In addition, the Goat year can give rise to some pleasing social occasions. Often these can be related to the Fire Pig's interests. If he is involved in a group, or joins one, he will often delight in the chances to go out and do something different. Any Fire Pig who is feeling lonely or changes location should consider joining a local or community group.

The Fire Pig has widespread interests and during the year he may begin a new activity, start a course or undertake a project he has often thought about. This is a constructive time for him and will often see him absorbed in his own pursuits. Family and friends can be encouraging, and the way his interests develop over the year can bring great pleasure to the Fire Pig.

His outgoings, however, may be considerable and he will need to watch his level of spending. This is no time to be lax. Forms and financial correspondence also need prompt attention. Delays or mistakes could cause problems. Fire Pigs, take note, and do be thorough with your paperwork and manage your finances carefully.

Overall, this will be a full and interesting year for the Fire Pig. Home and family life can be rewarding and the encouragement of his loved ones inspiring. Developing his interests can bring him especial pleasure, as can travel. This will be a constructive if sometimes surprising time which will absorb, inspire and frequently delight the genial and caring Fire Pig.

Tip for the Year

You have an enquiring mind. Follow up what interests you and be receptive to the new. Interesting developments can often follow on. Also, be flexible in planning and enjoy your special relations with those around you.

The Earth Pig

The element of Earth reinforces a sign's practical qualities and the Earth Pig sets about a lot of what he does in a careful and considered way. However, the Goat year can bring volatility and the Earth Pig may be uneasy with the sudden changes facing him. However, amid the uncertainty there will also be opportunity.

At work many Earth Pigs will experience change. New directives, practices and methods could be introduced and changes of personnel could also impact on the workplace. Some weeks could bring considerable pressure for the Earth Pig, but in the wake of developments, opportunities can follow on, and there will be the chance for many of these Earth Pigs to take their career forward. For those who have been in the same position for some time, the changes that take place this year can bring them the very chance they need to advance their career.

A further feature of this Goat year is the way it will allow many Earth Pigs to further their skills. It may be that new duties they take on involve a steep learning curve, but by applying themselves (including taking advantage of any training that is available and keeping themselves informed about developments in their industry), these Earth Pigs will not only be helping their present position but also their prospects for the following years.

The majority of Earth Pigs will remain with their present employer and successfully build on their position where they are, but for those who decide to move on, as well as those seeking work, the Goat year can open up some interesting possibilities. By considering other ways in which they could use their skills, many of these Earth Pigs could find a position in a different capacity with scope for the future. Late March to early June, September and October could see important developments, but throughout the year the Earth Pig needs to seize his opportunities quickly, before the moment is lost.

With the year's accent on personal development, he can also derive much satisfaction from his own interests and the benefits that will often follow on. Whether these involve giving him the chance to get out more, take additional exercise, attend events or enjoy social occasions, this is a year of considerable scope and possibility. Any Earth Pigs who have let their personal interests fall away of late, due to other pressures, should resolve to set time aside for themselves this year. This can help them achieve a better lifestyle balance.

Domestically, this will be a busy year and with the Earth Pig and his loved ones often facing important decisions, developments, options and problems all need to be fully discussed. If the Earth Pig is open and forthcoming, however, he will be helped by the thoughts that emerge, the decisions that are taken and the support that is offered. Goat years favour a coming together, and dialogue and co-operation will help many a situation. This need to join together also applies to practical projects and home purchases. Here the Earth Pig will be grateful for the expert knowledge of some family members. There will be a lot of practical activity in many an Earth Pig household this year. There will also be personal successes to enjoy and the Earth Pig will appreciate just spending time at home with his loved ones.

Travel, too, can bring considerable pleasure and if possible the Earth Pig should try to take a holiday or break with family members. Visits to certain attractions may be among the year's highlights.

The Earth Pig's social life can also see an increase in activity, with him welcoming chances to meet friends and attend various events. By making the most of what arises, he will enjoy himself and possibly find himself benefiting in other ways too, perhaps from ideas that follow on from a particular conversation, the chance to make new acquaintances or just from the pleasure of allowing himself to relax and unwind. He will have opportunities to go out at most times of the year, but May, June, August and September could be particularly active and interesting months.

Earth Pigs who are feeling lonely, and especially any who start the Goat year despondent, will find that if they immerse themselves in their activities and attend events in their area, their prospects will start to become much brighter. For some, the year can have romantic possibilities. In many different ways, Goat years are personally encouraging.

With all the activity, the year can, though, also be an expensive one. In view of possible spending on his home, together with his personal needs, the Earth Pig could be involved in considerable outlay and will need to proceed with care. The more discipline he exercises, the better. He also needs to be thorough and prompt when dealing with financial correspondence. Mistakes or delays could be to his disadvantage. Earth Pigs, take note.

A lot is set to happen this year and the Earth Pig will be kept busy. He will have to adapt and work round some of the changes that occur, but although some of the developments may concern him, the Goat year offers considerable possibility. It favours growth and self-development, and in both his work and personal interests, the Earth Pig will have the chance to further his knowledge and put his ideas and skills to satisfying use. He will also value the support of those close to him and his home life will be busy but with much to appreciate. The Goat year may have its challenging aspects, but it can be a personally rewarding one for the Earth Pig and bring him significant opportunities.

Tip for the Year

Seize any chances to add to your knowledge and skills. This can benefit you now *and* increase your scope for the future. Also, keep your lifestyle in balance and set aside time for your own pursuits and to enjoy with those who are special to you. This can be an active year and your efforts during it can reward you well.

Famous Pigs

Bryan Adams, Woody Allen, Julie Andrews, Marie Antoinette, Fred Astaire, Pam Ayres, Emily Blunt, Humphrey Bogart, James Cagney, Maria Callas, Samantha Cameron, Hillary Rodham Clinton, Glenn Close, Sacha Baron Cohen, Cheryl Cole, Alice Cooper, the Duchess of

Cornwall, Noël Coward, Simon Cowell, Oliver Cromwell, Billy Crystal, the Dalai Lama, Ted Danson, Dido, Richard Dreyfuss, Ben Elton, Ralph Waldo Emerson, Mo Farah, Henry Ford, Jonathan Franzen, Stephen Harper, Emmylou Harris, Ernest Hemingway, Chris Hemsworth, Henry VIII, Conrad Hilton, Alfred Hitchcock, Roy Hodgson, Sir Elton John, Tommy Lee Jones, Carl Gustav Jung, Stephen King, Kevin Kline, Miranda Lambert, Hugh Laurie, David Letterman, Jerry Lee Lewis, Meat Loaf, Ewan McGregor, Ricky Martin, Johnny Mathis, Queen Máxima of the Netherlands, Pippa Middleton, Dannii Minogue, Morrissey, Wolfgang Amadeus Mozart, George Osborne, Sir Michael Parkinson, James Patterson, Maurice Ravel, Ronald Reagan, Ginger Rogers, Winona Ryder, Françoise Sagan, Carlos Santana, Arnold Schwarzenegger, Steven Spielberg, Lord Sugar, David Tennant, Emma Thompson, Herman Van Rompuy, Jules Verne, David Walliams, Michael Winner, the Duchess of York.

Appendix

The relationships between the 12 animal signs, both on a personal level and business level, are an important aspect of Chinese horoscopes and in this appendix the compatibility between the signs is shown in the two tables that follow.

Also included are the names of the signs ruling the hours of the day and from this it is possible to find your ascendant and discover yet another aspect of your personality.

Finally, to supplement the earlier chapters on the personality and horoscope of the signs, I have included a guide on how you can get the best out of your sign and the year.

Relationships between the Signs

Personal Relationships

Key

1.   Excellent. Great rapport.
2.   A successful relationship. Many interests in common.
3.   Mutual respect and understanding. A good relationship.
4.   Fair. Needs care and some willingness to compromise in order for the relationship to work.
5.   Awkward. Possible difficulties in communication and few interests in common.
6.   A clash of personalities. Very difficult.

	Rat	Ox	Tiger	Rabbit	Dragon	Snake	Horse	Goat	Monkey	Rooster	Dog	Pig
Rat	1											
Ox	1	3										
Tiger	4	6	5									
Rabbit	5	2	3	2								
Dragon	1	5	4	3	2							
Snake	3	1	6	2	1	5						
Horse	6	5	1	5	3	4	2					
Goat	5	5	3	1	4	3	2	2				
Monkey	1	3	6	3	1	3	5	3	1			
Rooster	5	1	5	6	2	1	2	5	5	5		
Dog	3	4	1	2	6	3	1	5	3	5	2	
Pig	2	3	2	2	2	6	3	2	2	3	1	2

Business Relationships

Key

1. Excellent. Marvellous understanding and rapport.
2. Very good. Complement each other well.
3. A good working relationship and understanding can be developed.
4. Fair, but compromise and a common objective are often needed to make this relationship work.
5. Awkward. Unlikely to work, either through lack of trust or understanding or the competitiveness of the signs.
6. Mistrust. Difficult. To be avoided.

	Rat	Ox	Tiger	Rabbit	Dragon	Snake	Horse	Goat	Monkey	Rooster	Dog	Pig
Rat	2											
Ox	1	3										
Tiger	3	6	5									
Rabbit	4	3	3	3								
Dragon	1	4	3	3	3							
Snake	3	2	6	4	1	5						
Horse	6	5	1	5	3	4	4					
Goat	5	5	3	1	4	3	3	2				
Monkey	2	3	4	5	1	5	4	4	3			
Rooster	5	1	5	5	2	1	2	5	5	6		
Dog	4	5	2	3	6	4	2	5	3	5	4	
Pig	3	3	3	2	3	5	4	2	3	4	3	1

Your Ascendant

The ascendant has a very strong influence on your personality and will help you gain an even greater insight into your true personality according to Chinese horoscopes.

The hours of the day are named after the 12 animal signs and the sign governing the time you were born is your ascendant. To find your ascendant, look up the time of your birth in the table below, bearing in mind any local time differences in the place you were born.

11 p.m.	to	1 a.m.	The hours of the Rat
1 a.m.	to	3 a.m.	The hours of the Ox
3 a.m.	to	5 a.m.	The hours of the Tiger
5 a.m.	to	7 a.m.	The hours of the Rabbit
7 a.m.	to	9 a.m.	The hours of the Dragon
9 a.m.	to	11 a.m.	The hours of the Snake
11 a.m.	to	1 p.m.	The hours of the Horse
1 p.m.	to	3 p.m.	The hours of the Goat
3 p.m.	to	5 p.m.	The hours of the Monkey
5 p.m.	to	7 p.m.	The hours of the Rooster
7 p.m.	to	9 p.m.	The hours of the Dog
9 p.m.	to	11 p.m.	The hours of the Pig

Rat

The Rat ascendant is likely to make the sign more outgoing, sociable and careful with money. A particularly beneficial influence for those born under the signs of the Rabbit, Horse, Monkey and Pig.

Ox

The Ox ascendant has a restraining, cautionary and steadying influence that many signs will benefit from. This ascendant also promotes self-confidence and willpower and is especially good for those born under the signs of the Tiger, Rabbit and Goat.

Tiger

The Tiger ascendant is a dynamic and stirring influence that makes the sign more outgoing, action-orientated and impulsive. A generally favourable ascendant for the Ox, Tiger, Snake and Horse.

Rabbit

The Rabbit ascendant has a moderating influence, making the sign more reflective, serene and discreet. A particularly beneficial influence for the Rat, Dragon, Monkey and Rooster.

Dragon

The Dragon ascendant gives strength, determination and ambition to the sign. A favourable influence for those born under the signs of the Rabbit, Goat, Monkey and Dog.

Snake

The Snake ascendant can make the sign more reflective, intuitive and self-reliant. A good influence for the Tiger, Goat and Pig.

Horse

The Horse ascendant will make the sign more adventurous, daring and on some occasions fickle. Generally a beneficial influence for the Rabbit, Snake, Dog and Pig.

Goat

The Goat ascendant will make the sign more tolerant, easy-going and receptive. It could also impart some creative and artistic qualities. An especially good influence for the Ox, Dragon, Snake and Rooster.

Monkey

The Monkey ascendant is likely to impart a delicious sense of humour and fun to the sign. It will make the sign more enterprising and outgoing – a particularly good influence for the Rat, Ox, Snake and Goat.

Rooster

The Rooster ascendant helps to give the sign a lively, outgoing and very methodical manner. Its influence will increase efficiency and is good for the Ox, Tiger, Rabbit and Horse.

Dog

The Dog ascendant makes the sign more reasonable and fair-minded and gives an added sense of loyalty. A very good ascendant for the Tiger, Dragon and Goat.

Pig

The Pig ascendant can make the sign more sociable and self-indulgent. It is also a caring influence and one that can make the sign want to help others. A good ascendant for the Dragon and Monkey.

How to Get the Best from your Chinese Sign and the Year

Each of the 12 Chinese signs possesses its own unique strengths and by identifying them you can use them to your advantage. Similarly, by becoming aware of possible weaknesses you can do much to rectify them and in this respect I hope the following sections will be useful. Also included are some tips on how you can get the best from the Year of the Goat.

The Rat

The Rat is blessed with many fine talents, but his undoubted strength lies in his ability to get on with people. He is sociable, charming and a good judge of character. He also possesses a shrewd mind and is good at spotting opportunities.

However, to make the most of his abilities, he does need to impose some discipline upon himself. He should resist the (sometimes very great) temptation of getting involved in too many activities all at the same time and should decide upon his priorities and objectives. By concentrating his energies on specific matters he will fare much better. Also, given his personable manner, he should seek out positions where he can use his personal relations skills to good effect. For a career, sales and marketing could prove ideal.

The Rat is astute in dealing with finance, but while often thrifty, he can sometimes give way to moments of indulgence. Although he deserves to enjoy the money he has so carefully earned, it would sometimes be in his interests to exercise restraint when tempted to satisfy too many expensive whims!

The Rat's family and friends are important to him and while he is loyal and protective towards them, he does tend to keep his worries and concerns to himself and would be helped if he were more willing to discuss his anxieties. Others think highly of him and are prepared to do a lot to help him, but for them to do so the Rat does need to be less guarded.

With his sharp mind, keen imagination and sociable manner, he does, however, have much in his favour. When he has commitment, he can be irrepressible and, given his considerable charm, often irresistible as well! Provided he channels his energies wisely, he can make much of his life.

ADVICE FOR THE RAT'S YEAR AHEAD

General Prospects
The Rat likes to be busy and involved and the Goat year will suit him well. This is a time to build, seize opportunities and try out the new. For the active and enterprising Rat, a lot may become possible.

Career Prospects
A year of good opportunities which will see the Rat encouraged to take his skills further. Whether by taking on greater responsibilities, securing promotion or moving to somewhere offering a fresh challenge, he should seek out chances to progress. Important headway can be made and the Rat's efforts and creativity well rewarded.

Finance
An improved year. However, finances do need managing well. If the Rat takes his time and considers his options, he can conduct some important transactions and make purchases on favourable terms.

Relations with Others
The Rat will be on great form this year and enjoying an active domestic and social life. There are excellent romantic possibilities, and personal interests can bring social opportunities as well as help the Rat keep his lifestyle in balance.

The Ox

Strong-willed and resolute, the Ox certainly has a mind of his own! He is persistent and sets about achieving his objectives with dogged determination. In addition he is reliable and tenacious and is often a source of inspiration to others. He is an achiever, and he often achieves a great deal. However, to really excel, he would do well to try and correct some of his weaknesses.

Being so resolute and having such a strong sense of purpose, the Ox can be inflexible and narrow-minded. He can be resistant to change and prefers to set about his activities in his own way rather than be dependent on others. His dislike of change can sometimes be to his detriment and if he were prepared to be more adaptable and adventurous he would find his progress easier.

The Ox would also be helped if he were to broaden his range of interests and become more relaxed in his approach. At times he can be so preoccupied with his own activities that he is not always as mindful of others as he should be, and his demeanour can sometimes be studious and serious. There are times when he would benefit from a lighter touch.

However, the Ox is true to his word and loyal to his family and friends. He is admired and respected by others and his tremendous will-power usually enables him to achieve a great deal in life.

Advice for the Ox's Year Ahead

General Prospects
A tricky year, as the orderly Ox will not be comfortable with the sudden changes the Goat year can bring. He will need to keep alert and adapt to the situations in which he finds himself, but he can benefit from the opportunities that emerge and gain new experience.

Career Prospects
Situations can alter quickly this year and the Ox will be able to put his skills to good use. This may not be an easy time for him, but by making the most of what occurs, he can make progress. Positions taken on now will often have scope for later development.

Finance
Great care is needed. This is not a year for risks or hurried decisions. Where major transactions are concerned, the Ox should seek professional advice and be aware of the terms and conditions.

Relations with Others
The Ox sets great store by his home life and in this mixed year it can be a source of much contentment. However, with so many decisions being taken, he does need to be forthcoming and open-minded. Joint projects can be especially satisfying and friends and contacts helpful. For the unattached, a romantic encounter has the potential to become significant.

The Tiger

Lively, innovative and enterprising, the Tiger enjoys an active lifestyle. He has a wide range of interests, an alert mind and a genuine liking of other people. He loves to live life to the full. However, despite his enthusiastic and well-meaning ways, he does not always make the most of his considerable potential.

Being so versatile, the Tiger does have a tendency to jump from one activity to another or dissipate his energies by trying to do too much at the same time. To make the most of himself he should try to exercise a certain amount of self-discipline. Ideally, he should decide how best he can use his abilities, give himself some objectives and then stick to them. If he can overcome his restless tendencies, he will find he will accomplish far more.

Also, in spite of his sociable manner, the Tiger likes to retain a certain independence in his actions, and while few begrudge him this, he would sometimes find life easier if he were more prepared to work in conjunction with others. His reliance on his own judgement does sometimes mean that he excludes the views and advice of those around him, and this can be to his detriment. He may possess an independent spirit, but he must not let it go too far!

The Tiger does, however, have much in his favour. He is bold, original and quick-witted. If he can keep his restless nature in check, he can enjoy considerable success. In addition, with his engaging personality, he is well liked and much admired.

ADVICE FOR THE TIGER'S YEAR AHEAD

General Prospects
Situations can change quickly this year and opportunities arise suddenly. By being open-minded and aware and acting smartly, the Tiger can benefit. This is a time when his talents and resourcefulness can reward him well.

Career Prospects
With the year being characterized by change, there will be scope for the Tiger to make good headway. By looking to build on his skills and make the most of the openings that arise (even if they require adjustment), he stands to benefit. His creative talents can also reward him well and should be promoted.

Finance
A year for increased vigilance. Spending needs to be closely monitored and budgets adhered to throughout the year. Important correspondence needs attention and valuables should be looked after with care.

Relations with Others
In this active year the Tiger does need to consult others *and listen to them*. Preoccupation or distraction could cause problems. There will be good opportunities to meet new people, however, and quality time with family and friends will be appreciated.

The Rabbit

The Rabbit is certainly one who appreciates the finer things in life. With his good taste, companionable nature and wide range of interests, he knows how to live well – and usually does!

However, for all his finesse and style, the Rabbit does possess traits he would do well to watch. His desire for a settled lifestyle makes him err on the side of caution. He dislikes change and as a consequence can miss out on opportunities. Also, there are many Rabbits who will go to great lengths to avoid difficult and fraught situations, and again, while few may relish these, sometimes in life it is necessary to take risks or stand your ground. At times it would certainly be in the Rabbit's interests to be bolder and more assertive in going after what he desires.

The Rabbit also attaches great importance to his relations with others and while he has a happy knack of getting on with most people, he can be sensitive to criticism. Difficult though it may be, he should really try to develop a thicker skin and recognize that criticism can provide valuable learning opportunities, as can some of the problems he strives so hard to avoid.

However, with his agreeable manner, keen intellect and shrewd judgement, the Rabbit does have a lot in his favour and invariably makes much of his life – and enjoys it too!

ADVICE FOR THE RABBIT'S YEAR AHEAD

General Prospects

A year of many encouraging developments. The Rabbit should look to improve on his situation – this is a time to build on strengths and seize the moment. He should also liaise well with others – the support he is given can be instrumental to his success.

Career Prospects

With opportunities arising suddenly and situations undergoing change, there will be good chances for the Rabbit to prove himself in new ways. New duties can often open up further possibilities. A year to move forward, but chances do need to be seized before the moment is lost.

Finance

Although usually careful in financial matters, the Rabbit must not relax his vigilance. Important transactions and correspondence require careful attention and spending levels need to be watched.

Relations with Others

The Rabbit enjoys company and those around him will often help to make his year more successful. New friends and contacts can be helpful and this is an excellent time for networking and also romance. Some Rabbits could make some significant personal decisions and all Rabbits will often find themselves in demand.

The Dragon

Enthusiastic, enterprising and honourable, the Dragon possesses many admirable qualities and his life is often full and varied. He always gives his best and even though not all his endeavours meet with success, he is nonetheless resilient and hardy, and is much admired and respected.

However, for all his qualities, the Dragon can be blunt and forthright and, through sheer strength of character, sometimes domineering. It would certainly be in his interests to listen more closely to others rather than be so self-reliant. Also, his enthusiasm can sometimes get the better of him and he can be impulsive. To make the most of his abilities, he should give himself priorities and set about his activities in a disciplined and systematic way. More tact and diplomacy might not come amiss either!

However, with his lively and outgoing manner, the Dragon is popular and well liked. With good fortune on his side (and the Dragon is often lucky), his life is almost certain to be eventful and fulfilling. He has many talents, and if he uses them wisely he will enjoy much success.

ADVICE FOR THE DRAGON'S YEAR AHEAD

General Prospects

Dragons may need to temper their ambitions this year and concentrate on what they can do now. This includes setting time aside for personal development and striving for a better lifestyle balance. A good year to take stock.

Career Prospects

An excellent year for both using and adding to key strengths. By being involved in what is happening, including putting forward ideas, the Dragon can enhance his reputation and may have the opportunity to switch to a different type of work. What is accomplished this year can prove significant, especially as prospects will be greatly improved next year.

Finance

The Dragon may be born under the sign of luck, but this is a year for care and caution. Risks should be avoided and spending levels monitored.

Relations with Others

The Dragon will revel in the domestic and social activity the year offers and can look forward to some gratifying times. If he involves others in his activities, not only will more be accomplished but he will also benefit from some useful suggestions.

The Snake

The Snake is blessed with a keen intellect. He has wide interests, an enquiring mind and good judgement. He tends to be quiet and thoughtful and plan his activities with considerable care. With his fine abilities he often does well in life, but he does possess traits which can undermine his progress.

The Snake is often guarded in his actions and sometimes loses out to those who are more action-oriented and assertive. He also likes to retain a certain independence in his actions and this too can hamper his progress. It would be in his interests to be more forthcoming and involve others more readily in his plans. The Snake has many talents and possesses a warm and rich personality, but there is a danger that this can remain concealed behind his often quiet and reserved manner. He would fare better if he were more outgoing and showed others his true worth.

However, the Snake is very much his own master. He invariably knows what he wants in life and is often prepared to journey long and hard to achieve his objectives. He does, though, have it in his power to make that journey easier. Lose some of that reticence, Snake, be more open and assertive, and do not be afraid of the occasional risk!

ADVICE FOR THE SNAKE'S YEAR AHEAD

General Prospects
A satisfying year, but, in view of quickly changing situations and emerging opportunities, the Snake needs to keep alert and act swiftly when necessary. Time is of the essence.

Career Prospects
Some good opportunities can emerge and the Snake's skills and reputation will ensure he is well placed to benefit. However, he does need to seize the initiative, act quickly and adapt if need be. An excellent year for promoting ideas and making the most of creative talents.

Finance
A fortunate year. Early planning and good management will allow the Snake to go ahead with his plans. Expensive purchases should not be hurried, however, and time should be allowed to assess suitability.

Relations with Others
The Snake should overcome his independent tendencies and join in more readily with others. With involvement, his year can be made so much richer and more rewarding. His home life can bring some special

times and his social life can do him great good. Situations that arise over the year will bring out his strengths.

The Horse

Versatile, hardworking and sociable, the Horse makes his mark wherever he goes. He has an eloquent and engaging manner and makes friends with ease. He is quick-witted, has an alert mind and is certainly not averse to taking risks or experimenting with new ideas.

He possesses a strong and likeable personality, but he does also have his weaknesses. With his wide interests he does not always finish everything he starts and he would do well to be more persevering. He has it within him to achieve considerable success, but to make the most of his talents he does need to overcome his restless tendencies. When he has made plans, he should stick with them.

The Horse loves company and values both his family and friends. However, there will have been many a time when he will have lost his temper or spoken in haste and regretted his words later. Throughout his life he needs to keep his temper in check and be diplomatic in tense situations, otherwise he could jeopardize the respect and good relations he so values.

However, the Horse has a multitude of talents and a lively and outgoing personality. If he can overcome his restless and volatile nature, he can lead a rich and highly fulfilling life.

ADVICE FOR THE HORSE'S YEAR AHEAD

General Prospects
An encouraging year offering the chance for the Horse to put his strengths to effective use. This is a time to be determined to move forward. With purpose, a great deal can now open up for the Horse.

Career Prospects

There will be a good chance for the Horse to make more of his specialist talents and he should look to advance. By taking advantage of training and networking opportunities, he can do his prospects a lot of good. The year rewards commitment and enterprise.

Finance

While many Horses will increase their income, this will be an expensive year, with accommodation costs likely. The Horse will need to keep careful control over his finances and thoroughly check the terms of any new commitments he takes on.

Relations with Others

Sociable and outgoing, the Horse will be much in demand. Involvement in joint activities can lead to helpful developments and more support. Many a Horse will be on impressive form this year.

The Goat

The Goat has a warm, friendly and understanding manner and gets on well with most people. He is generally easy-going, has a fond appreciation of the finer things in life and possesses a rich imagination. He is often artistic and enjoys the creative arts and outdoor activities.

However, despite his engaging manner, there lurks beneath his skin a sometimes tense and pessimistic nature. The Goat can be a worrier and without the support and encouragement of others can feel insecure and be hesitant in his actions.

To make the most of himself he should aim to become more assertive and decisive as well as more at ease with himself. He has much in his favour, but he really does need to promote himself more and be bolder. He would also be helped if he were to sort out his priorities and set about his activities in an organized and disciplined manner. There are some Goats who tend to be haphazard in the way they go about things and this can hamper their progress.

Although the Goat will always value the support of others, it would also be in his interest to become more independent and not be so reticent about striking out on his own. He does, after all, possess many talents, as well as a sincere and likeable personality, and by giving his best he can make his life rich, rewarding and enjoyable.

ADVICE FOR THE GOAT'S YEAR AHEAD

General Prospects
The Goat will be keen to make his own year special. And it can be, but the Goat does need to put in the effort and work steadily towards his goals. This is no time for rush or speedy results. Much can be achieved, but results will need to be worked for.

Career Prospects
Good progress can be made and there will be the chance for the Goat to put his skills to more effective use. His ideas and talents can reward him well this year. He should also make the most of any networking opportunities and be active (and visible) in his workplace. He has much to offer.

Finance
While income may increase, spending needs to be watched. Important financial decisions and paperwork should also be addressed with care. This is not a year for rush but for consideration and, where applicable, consultation.

Relations with Others
The Goat enjoys company and with support, advice and the synergy shared actions can bring, many of his activities can proceed well. He should make the most of his relations with others and seize any opportunities to meet new people. His personal skills can reward him well this year.

The Monkey

Lively, enterprising and innovative, the Monkey certainly knows how to impress. He has wide interests, a good sense of fun and relates well to others. He also possesses a shrewd mind and often has a happy knack of turning events to his advantage.

However, despite his versatility and considerable gifts, he does have his weaknesses. He often lacks persistence, can get distracted easily and also places tremendous reliance upon his own judgement. While his belief in himself is a commendable asset, it would certainly be in his interests to be more mindful of the views of others. Also, while he likes to keep tabs on all that is going on around him, he can be evasive and secretive with regard to his own feelings and activities, and again a more forthcoming attitude would be to his advantage.

In his desire to succeed, the Monkey can also be tempted to cut corners or be crafty and he should recognize that such actions can rebound on him!

However, he is resourceful and his sheer strength of character will ensure that he has an interesting and varied life. If he can channel his considerable energies wisely and overcome his sometimes restless tendencies, his life can be crowned with success. And with his amiable personality, he will have many friends.

ADVICE FOR THE MONKEY'S YEAR AHEAD

General Prospects

The Monkey needs to keep his wits about him and proceed with care. He may well find himself in volatile and testing situations. However, by adapting as required and being mindful of others, he can steer his way through many of the year's challenges and emerge with achievements he can build on, especially in the following Year of the Monkey.

Career Prospects

Many Monkeys will be able to advance their career this year. Sometimes this may be in a different capacity from what the Monkey expected, but it will allow him to add to his skills and, importantly, broaden his scope for later. A year to keep alert for opportunity.

Finance

While income can improve, the Monkey will face many expenses this year and should keep careful control of his budget.

Relations with Others

A disagreement with a friend or someone letting the Monkey down could cause upset and if he detects difficulties arising, he needs to act quickly. Extra care and attentiveness can make an important difference.

The Rooster

With his considerable bearing and incisive and resolute manner, the Rooster cuts an impressive figure. He has a sharp mind, is well informed on many matters and expresses himself clearly and convincingly. He is meticulous and efficient in his undertakings and commands a great deal of respect. He also has a genuine and caring interest in others.

The Rooster has much in his favour, but there are some aspects of his character that can tell against him. He can be candid in his views and over-zealous in his actions, and sometimes he can say or do things he later regrets. His high standards also make him fussy, even pedantic, and he can get diverted into relatively minor matters when in truth he could be occupying his time more profitably. This is something all Roosters would do well to watch. Also, while the Rooster is a great planner, he can sometimes be unrealistic in his expectations. In making plans – indeed, in most of his activities – he would do well to consult others. He would benefit greatly from their input.

The Rooster has many talents as well as commendable drive and commitment, but to make the most of himself he does need to channel his energies wisely and watch his candid and sometimes volatile nature. With care, however, he can make a success of his life, and with his wide interests and outgoing personality, he will enjoy the friendship and respect of many.

ADVICE FOR THE ROOSTER'S YEAR AHEAD

General Prospects
The Rooster may like to plan and organize, but should allow himself some slack. Sudden developments, emerging opportunities and new ideas can all bring change and the Rooster needs to adapt to situations *as they are*. Some extra 'me time' can also do him great good.

Career Prospects
The Rooster will have more chance to use his strengths to good effect and may well find greater fulfilment in what he does. If dissatisfied, he needs to explore other options. By making the effort and seizing his opportunities, he can make important progress.

Finance
With all that the Rooster will want to do, he will need to manage his finances carefully. When making larger purchases, time spent considering options will lead to better decisions.

Relations with Others
The Rooster can be greatly helped by the support of others, but to benefit fully he does need to be forthcoming *and listen*. This is no time to be single-minded or rigid in his thinking. Shared activities and interests can bring particular delight and this is an excellent year for the Rooster to network and extend his social circle.

The Dog

Loyal, dependable and with a good understanding of human nature, the Dog is well placed to win respect and admiration. He is a no-nonsense sort of person and hates any sort of hypocrisy and falsehood. With the Dog you know where you stand and, given his direct manner, where he stands on any issue. He also has a strong humanitarian nature and often champions good causes.

The Dog has many fine attributes, although there are certain traits that can prevent him from either enjoying or making the most of his life. He is a great worrier and can get anxious over all manner of things. Although it may not always be easy, he should try to rid himself of the 'worry habit'. Whenever he is tense or concerned, he should be prepared to speak to others rather than shoulder his worries all by himself. In some cases, they could even be of his own making! Also, he has a tendency to look on the pessimistic side and he would certainly be helped if he were to view his undertakings more optimistically. He does, after all, possess many skills and should have faith in his abilities. Another weakness is his tendency to be stubborn over certain issues. If he is not careful, at times this could undermine his position.

If the Dog can reduce the pessimistic side of his nature, he will not only enjoy life more but also find he is achieving more. He possesses a truly admirable character and his loyalty, reliability and sincerity are appreciated by all he meets. In his life he will do much good and befriend many people – and he owes it to himself to enjoy life too. Sometimes it might help him to recall the words of another Dog, Sir Winston Churchill: 'When I look back on all these worries, I remember the story of the old man who said on his deathbed that he had had a lot of trouble in his life, most of which never happened.'

Advice for the Dog's Year Ahead

General Prospects
The Dog likes order and consistency, but the Goat year is a time of change and volatility. Although the Dog may feel uneasy about certain developments, very often opportunities will follow in their wake. The Dog needs to adapt and make the most of what is before him.

Career Prospects
The winds of change will affect many a workplace but also bring opportunities for the Dog to develop his skills and prove himself. Again, a year to adapt and move forward.

Finance
Accommodation matters will figure prominently, with many Dogs carrying out costly projects or moving home. Vigilance and care are needed, and professional advice should be sought if necessary. A year for discipline and good financial management.

Relations with Others
With this being a busy year, the Dog will need to be forthcoming. He will be grateful for the support of those around him and the more that can be undertaken jointly, the better. Family, friends and, for the unattached, affairs of the heart can all be significant and special.

The Pig

Genial, sincere and trusting, the Pig gets on well with most people. He has a kind and caring nature, a dislike of discord and often a good sense of humour. In addition, he has a fondness for socializing and enjoying the good life!

The Pig possesses a shrewd mind, is particularly adept at dealing with business and financial matters and has a robust and resilient nature. Although not all his plans may work out as he would like, he is tenacious and will often rise up and succeed after experiencing setbacks and difficulties. In his often active and varied life he can accomplish a great deal, although there are certain aspects of his character that can tell against him. If he can modify these or keep them in check then his life will certainly be easier and possibly even more successful.

In his activities the Pig can sometimes over-commit himself and while he does not want to disappoint, he would certainly be helped if he were to set about his activities in an organized and systematic manner and give himself priorities at busy times. He should also not allow others to take advantage of his good nature and it would be in his interests to be more discerning. There will have been times when he has been gullible and naïve; fortunately, though, he quickly learns from his mistakes. However, he possesses a stubborn streak and if new situations do not fit in with his line of thinking, he can be inflexible. Such an attitude may not always be to his advantage.

The Pig is a great pleasure-seeker and while he should enjoy the fruits of his labours, he can sometimes be self-indulgent and extravagant. This is also something he would do well to watch.

However, though the Pig may possess some faults, those who come into contact with him are invariably impressed by his integrity, amiable manner and intelligence. If he uses his talents wisely, his life can be crowned with considerable achievement and he will also be loved and respected by many.

Advice for the Pig's Year Ahead

General Prospects
By making the most of his opportunities, the Pig can benefit now as well as help his future prospects. His personal life will be especially pleasing and this is an excellent year for meeting others, networking and enjoying the many social occasions the year will bring.

Career Prospects
Progress may be slow and some situations (and delays) challenging, but there will be excellent chances for many Pigs to take on different duties

and widen their options for the future. It will be a case of adapting as required and seizing opportunities when they arise.

Finance
With some expensive purchases and a busy lifestyle likely, spending will need to be controlled. A year for discipline and good budgeting.

Relations with Others
With a lot happening and so much to share with others, the genial Pig will be in his element. Shared activities can lead to a powerful synergy being created and many plans being advanced. Romantic prospects are excellent and personal celebrations likely.

A Closing Thought

I hope that having read *Your Chinese Horoscope 2015* you have found it of value and interest.

The Goat year is a time of great possibility, both on the world stage and for the individual. It is very much a time to aim for a better lifestyle balance and to appreciate your loved ones and what you have around you. Believe in yourself and your capabilities and work towards what *you* want. Your positive actions *can* make a difference.

Within you are the riches of your tomorrow.

I wish you well and all good fortune.

Neil Somerville